+ + + + + + + + + + + + + + + + + + + + + + + + +

*The Clergy Sexual Abuse Crisis*

THE

# Clergy Sexual Abuse Crisis

REFORM AND

RENEWAL

IN THE

CATHOLIC

COMMUNITY

## Paul R. Dokecki

Georgetown University Press

WASHINGTON, D.C.

Georgetown University Press, Washington, D.C.
© 2004 by Georgetown University Press. All rights reserved.
Printed in the United States of America

10 9 8 7 6 5 4 3 2 1    2004

This book is printed on acid-free paper meeting
the requirements of the American National Standard
for Permanence in Paper for Printed Library Materials.

Material for chapter 3 is adapted from the author's book
*The Tragicomic Professional: Basic Considerations for Ethical Reflective-Generative Practice*
(Pittsburgh: Duquesne University Press, 1996), used by permission.

Design and composition by Wilsted & Taylor Publishing Services

Library of Congress Cataloging-in-Publication Data

Dokecki, Paul R.
The clergy sexual abuse crisis : reform and renewal in the Catholic
community / Paul R. Dokecki.
p. cm.
Includes bibliographical references and index.
ISBN 1-58901-006-X (pbk. : alk. paper)
1. Child sexual abuse by clergy. 2. Catholic Church—Clergy—Sexual behavior.
3. Church renewal—Catholic Church. 4. Catholic Church—Discipline. I. Title.
BX1912.9.D65 2004
261.8'3272'088282—dc22

2003019464

+++++++++++++++++++++++++++++++++++++++++++++++++

FOR KATHERINE

*Wife, mother, grandmother,*

*and limitless source*

*of love and support*

++++++++++++++++++++++++++++++++++++++++++++++++++

# Contents

+ + + + + + + + + + + + + + + + + + + + + + + + + + + + + + + + + + + + + + + + + + + + + + + + +

# Acknowledgments

I thank several people who read and commented on aspects of the manuscript or provided helpful consultation. Dianne Schwartz consulted on legal issues. Faculty colleagues J. R. Newbrough, Isaac Prilleltensky, and Paul Speer, and doctoral student Diana Jones in the Peabody/Vanderbilt Department of Human and Organizational Development and its doctoral program in Community Research and Action helped me think through the human science aspects of my analysis of clergy sexual abuse. Other helpful Vanderbilt colleagues included Edward Farley, Denis O'Day, and Don Welch. Two people who served as ongoing sources of counsel and support over the several years of researching and writing the book were Robert O'Gorman of Loyola University Chicago and James Mallett, pastor of Christ the King parish. Don Boehm of Christ the King also provided thoughtful comments on a draft of the manuscript. I am grateful to Peabody College and Vanderbilt University for granting me sabbatical leave in the fall of 2002 to complete my research and writing. Finally, I thank Richard Brown of Georgetown University Press, whose advice and guidance helped turn an unruly manuscript about an ever-changing topic into a focused story with a beginning, middle, and end.

For permission to quote extensively from her 1998 dissertation, I thank Barbara Balboni of Bridgewater State College. I thank Duquesne University Press for permission to use edited portions of my 1996 book *The Tragicomic Professional: Basic Considerations for Ethical Reflective-Generative Practice*, and I thank the *Journal of Community Psychology* for permission to quote extensively from my 2001 article "Toward a Community-Oriented Action Research Framework for Spirituality," coauthored with R. T. O'Gorman and J. R. Newbrough.

+ + + + + + + + + + + + + + + + + + + + + + + + + + + + + + + + + + + + + + + + + + + + + + + + + + + + + +

# Introduction

**M**Y AIM IN THIS BOOK is to develop a multilevel analysis of clergy sexual abuse, a crisis facing the Catholic Church in the United States and throughout the world. Clergy sexual abuse is a complex personal, relational, and social system in which part relates to part, and the whole is greater than the sum of its parts. Beyond matters of personal responsibility, concupiscence, and criminal or civil liability, the particular encounter between an abusing priest and his child victim takes place in an overlapping set of historically influenced contexts and social structures and processes involving a host of actors inside and outside the church. The clergy sexual abuse system frustrates the public's penchant for simple chains of cause and effect and focused solutions.

In a particularly notorious instance of this morally corrosive problem, the year 2002 saw the latest stages of a clergy abuse scandal that has been plaguing the Archdiocese of Boston since the 1990s and other dioceses throughout the United States since the mid-1980s, although certain aspects of the problem seem to have long been part of church life (Jordan 2000). The New England newspapers, the *New York Times* and *Los Angeles Times*, and most papers in between, along with the major network television news programs, exposed the (formerly) mostly secret sexual abuse of scores of Massachusetts Catholic children by scores of their trusted priests. The management of this phase of the clergy sexual abuse problem by church officials took the public's typical outrage at the harm done to the abused children and their families to new and unprecedented levels. Associated Press readers selected the clergy sexual abuse scandal as the third most important story of 2002.

The Boston story was nationally and internationally important because many of these acts of abuse and the church's problematic response took place on the watch of Cardinal Bernard F. Law, for years the dean of the American

1

short, it has all the elements of a truly epic news story, the sort of thing that comes along once or twice in a generation and winds up changing society in fundamental ways. (*The Atlantic*, 23 April 2002)

The Catholic Church's use of power and secrecy over the years had set the stage for a crisis in confidence and widespread calls for reform from the media and the general public, and especially from the Catholic laity, conservative and progressive alike.

The maelstrom occasioned by the Archdiocese of Boston scandal is important, and I will have more to say about it later. Yet it provides only the immediate context for this book: my purpose is to look at the larger picture. Many factors can distort our understanding of the fundamental meaning of the clergy sexual abuse crisis. The glare of the media spotlight, the search for sound bites and instant solutions, and frenzied, sometimes hysterical, public reactions can obscure its deeper aspects, its fundamental causes, possible routes to its amelioration and prevention, and necessary church and societal reforms. What is needed is a way to penetrate the confused and confusing social reality of this vexing societal problem. Toward that end, I will present (in chapter 1) the detailed story of an earlier case of clergy sexual abuse in the Catholic Diocese of Nashville, Tennessee, as the initial vehicle for launching my analysis of the clergy sexual abuse system.

I focus on the Nashville case for several reasons. First, it is an interesting, compelling, and all too human story portraying the maze-like complexity of the clergy sexual abuse system. Second, although it has been covered in some detail by the Nashville media for several years, the case has virtually escaped the distorting influence of national media coverage. Third, it permits detailed telling ("thick description") of a story that has spanned more than forty years, enabling detection of underlying processes that take time to unfold. And finally, it manifests patterns and processes seen in virtually all cases of clergy sexual abuse, providing a microcosmic view of the larger clergy sexual abuse system and helping identify needed policies and reforms. The case, therefore, provides a unique opportunity to anchor initial attempts to understand the clergy sexual abuse system in one in-depth narrative.

The Nashville case, the legal aspects of which continue to drag on as of this writing in fall 2003, involves formerly active Catholic priest Edward J. McKeown, a man in his late fifties, who is in a Tennessee prison for sexually molesting a teenage boy. The boy surreptitiously captured McKeown's admission of guilt on tape. The sexual abuse had begun several years earlier when the boy was twelve and McKeown, then a politically active employee of Metropolitan Nashville Davidson County Government, was the boy's neighbor. He had known the boy for several years, and, in a bizarre development, Juvenile Court officials at one point had even named him the boy's guardian.

In February 1999, Nashville prosecutors indicted McKeown on multiple felony counts. He pleaded guilty to one count of rape and two counts of sexual battery and received a twenty-five-year sentence. Significantly, beyond the specific criminal acts with the boy in question, all of which happened several years *after* the Diocese of Nashville had dismissed him from the active priesthood, McKeown reportedly also admitted molesting more than twenty boys since the early 1970s. Most of these instances of sexual abuse occurred during his tenure as an ordained and functioning priest.

One consequence of these headline-making events was that the family of the boy in the criminal case, and the family of another boy allegedly molested by McKeown beginning in 1994, sued a variety of persons and institutions, claiming they had contributed to the harm caused to their children by McKeown's sexual abuse. In January 2000, they sued the Diocese of Nashville for $70 million, alleging a pattern of damaging diocesan actions during the 1980s, several years *before* the children in question had their sexual encounters with the by-then inactive priest.

In the world beyond Nashville, the decade of the 1980s saw the initial rise of intense media coverage of clergy sexual abuse in the Catholic Church. Serious questions continue to exist about what the church and its bishops knew and didn't know about clergy sexual abuse at that time and what moral, ethical, and legal obligations it had in dealing with (1) abusing priests, (2) victims and their families, (3) the laity, (4) the media, the police, and other societal institutions, and (5) the public at large. The so far unsuccessful attempt in the McKeown case to hold the church liable for acts committed by its officials several years *before* subsequent acts of sexual abuse by a formerly active priest, however, was a first. This had the potential of setting a far-reaching legal precedent, affecting churches throughout the United States by greatly expanding the number of eligible litigants. Moreover, a particular legal strategy adopted by Nashville diocesan lawyers (a strategy that was used later in Boston and elsewhere) caused a major controversy in the Nashville community. To mitigate financial damages for which the church might be found liable, the lawyers claimed that the victims of McKeown's sexual abuse and their families bore comparative fault, or co-responsibility, for their failure to report the many instances of his sexual abuse over the years. The desire to protect the diocese, an organization with "deep pockets," from what were viewed as unjust or overblown claims undoubtedly motivated this legal maneuver. Nonetheless, it resulted in the *Tennessean* charging the church with "blaming the victim." Many people in the Nashville community, Catholics and non-Catholics alike, believed that the church, through its lawyers, was setting a dangerous legal precedent, shooting itself in the foot by creating a public relations disaster, and betraying basic tenets of Catholic ethics and morality. To many, it seemed the church was experiencing a tension between its moral call to be compassionate and truthful and its need to protect its power and fiscal resources. This tension has shown itself in the church's handling of most instances of child abuse throughout the country over the years.

The story of McKeown's career as a sexual abuser and the lawsuit it spawned allow us to track the workings of a diocese—from its initial contacts with a young man, himself abused by a priest as a child, as he enters training for the priesthood; to the pathways it follows in attempting to deal with this troubled and troubling priest; to its ways of relating to his victims and their families, the laity, professionals, government agencies, and the criminal and civil legal systems; to the effects its decisions have on people in the community, both Catholics and non-Catholics.

## VALUE ANALYTIC PERSPECTIVE

The clergy child sexual abuse crisis in the Catholic Church is an emotionally charged topic impervious to neutral or value-free analysis. In recent years, analysts across the ideological spectrum, from radical and liberal/progressive to conservative/reactionary, have offered ideologically drenched theories and recipes for helping prevent or ameliorate the problem. Liberal Catholics have tended to blame factors such as the hierarchy's abuse of power and overinsistence on secrecy, celibacy and the church's inadequate theology of human sexuality, the lack of women priests, and inadequate representation of the laity in church decision making. Conservatives have tended to blame factors such as the weakening of authority, orthodoxy, and discipline—in effect, the diminishment of the church's power—brought on by Vatican II, tolerance of homosexuality in the clergy, and the weakening of the sense of sin. Since I am not neutral on the topic and do not claim that my analysis is value-free, I feel obliged to state my value perspective to enable the reader to "consider the source" in evaluating the validity of my observations, analyses, and recommendations.

I was born and raised a Catholic, attended Catholic schools from first grade through college, sent my three daughters to Catholic elementary and high schools, have been active in church affairs at the parish, diocesan, and national levels, and have focused many of my scholarly efforts on church-related topics. Throughout, one of my central understandings of the church has entailed the traditional concept *ecclesia semper reformanda est*—in effect, the church must always be open to reform and development. Reform involves an is-ought discrepancy, wherein we judge an existing state of affairs (the *is*) to be problematic according to certain value standards relative to needed change or reform (the *ought*). The purpose of reform, then, is to work toward removing or lessening the discrepancy. I intend my analysis of clergy sexual abuse to contribute to the ongoing conversation about needed reform of the church. Although I will develop my reform-oriented value/ethical perspective in detail in chapter 3, a brief overview here will help the reader place the material of the initial chapters in context.

Over the years as I have taught professional ethics to Vanderbilt University graduate and undergraduate students and have written about value/ethical issues in public policy affecting families and children, I have developed a perspective that argues for human development and community as interrelated ethical first principles (Dokecki 1996). My position is that professional practice and organizational action and policy ought (1) to enhance the human development of persons (their growth and wellness) and (2) to promote community and thereby the common good—two sides of the same value/ethical coin. Being ethical entails using professional power to change current problematic social conditions (the *is*) in pursuit of a more caring and competent community (the *ought*). Actions that lessen the discrepancy include caring, telling the truth, treating persons as persons not things and respecting their autonomy, doing no harm, doing good, and being just.

The dynamics of power suffuse these matters, since much of ethics entails understanding the abuses and uses of power. People may abuse power to coerce and manipulate others, in what amounts to a power struggle with winners and losers, or they may use power cooperatively and generatively, in service of others, where the human development of all is the goal. Relatedly, I argue that we ought to work toward political, economic, and social arrangements characterized by: (1) community members who experience well-being and are empowered and self-efficacious; (2) communication that is free and uncoerced, devoid of secrecy and the abuse of power; and (3) just governance geared to the empowerment of persons through deeply democratic and participatory political processes (Bandura 1989; Dokecki 1996; Green 1999; Habermas 1984; Prilleltensky 2001).

Addressing the church as a societal institution, I argue that, although institutional hierarchy and power are to some degree necessary, those in the hierarchy ought to be servants of the people and not their hierarchical power-wielding masters. The church, moreover, ought to be understood fundamentally as the People of God working and living in community and using their powers in pursuit of their common good (Dulles 1974/1987; Maritain 1947). People in the church should be helped to lead meaningful and spiritual lives, feel empowered, and have a psychological sense of community. This sense of community entails: (1) a sense of membership and belonging; (2) an experience of shared values and emotional connection with others; (3) an experience of their helping meet each others needs for social support, meaning, and spiritual growth; and, especially, (4) the experience of mutual influence—influencing and being influenced by others in using their power to affect what happens in the church (Dokecki, Newbrough, and O'Gorman 2001). An ethical societal institution, therefore, is one that promotes human development, well-being, and community. It does this by functioning openly and transparently as a just and democratic community, thereby empowering its members and enhancing their experience of community.

I am a practitioner of human science (Dokecki, Newbrough, and O'Gorman 2001; Polkinghorne 1983), a well-established approach to inquiry in which "traditional narrow and limited positivist methods are complemented with a wide variety of methods, chosen to be adequate to particular phenomena to be studied at this or that time in varying contexts" (Dokecki 1986, 5). In human science, the inquirer's task is do methodological justice to the total world of the person, through investigating "all of the experiences, activities, constructs, and artifacts that would not ever have existed, if human beings had not existed" (Polkinghorne 1983, 289). At the heart of this methodological approach is the assertion that all inquiry is value-laden, and this is one of the major reasons I have outlined my value perspective as it relates to clergy sexual abuse.

Given my method in this book, however, it is even more important that I be clear about my value stance. I have based my coverage of the McKeown case, and other instances of clergy sexual abuse, on a vast amount of material in the public record—for example, court documents, books, journals, monographs, newspaper articles from all over the country and the world, especially articles found on newspaper websites, and Internet material from official organizations and from advocacy groups representing a range of ideological positions. Since a variety of narratives can be told about any given event, the reader must be continually aware that, as the writer, I am socially constructing the McKeown story and the many other instances of clergy sexual abuse that I offer as material for analysis. Obviously, I have not reported every detail from every available source; I have had to be quite selective. I am not, however, a relativist, and I am not building fanciful castles in the sky and asking the reader to move into them. I have tried to make my selections and constructions bear reasonable and defensible relationships to the actual events, but I make no claims for their absolute truth. Rather, the reader should hold me to standards of credibility, consistency, clarity, logic, and, especially, fairness in my presentation and interpretation of the events implicated in clergy sexual abuse.

## PLAN OF THE BOOK

In what follows, I analyze the clergy sexual abuse system through the lenses of professional ethics, the human sciences, and ecclesiology, the theology of the church. I develop a nuanced understanding of clergy sexual abuse in the Catholic Church by examining both the actions of the abusing priest and the church's organizational processes, especially regarding the use and abuse of power. I also draw theoretical and practical implications for the conduct of the clergy and other professionals, the functioning of organizations, and the possible reform of the church as an organization serving the community. My analysis starts with the McKeown case and extends to more generalized issues.

I begin with the details and complexities of the McKeown case in order to provide a narrative that places us in the concrete particulars of one case of clergy sexual abuse and provides hints for the analyses presented in subsequent chapters. Chapter 1 presents the personal, relational, and social domains of McKeown's story. In chapter 2, while not ignoring the motivations and attributes of individual priests and members of the hierarchy, I focus on the historical, cultural, and organizational context of the clergy sexual abuse system, especially concerning the abuse of minor male children. I also present an analysis of the developments in the national and universal church, focusing on the situation of Cardinal Law and the Archdiocese of Boston, which gained notoriety in 2002. I address a number of questions: Are the many concerns about clergy sexual abuse expressed by Catholics and non-Catholics alike well founded, or are they manifestations of overblown and irrational public response? What aspects of the overall clergy sexual abuse phenomenon spring from the pathology of a few "rotten apples" among an otherwise healthy, dedicated, and well-functioning clergy? What are the power dynamics in clergy sexual abuse and its handling by authorities? What aspects arise from the "imperfect tree" that is the church, and every other human organization? What role has the laity played in the church's handling of clergy sexual abuse?

In chapter 3, I analyze the behavior of the many actors involved in clergy sexual abuse using a framework called the ethics of human development and community, focusing on church officials' use and abuse of power and the issue of participatory decision making. In chapter 4, I examine clergy sexual abuse using a variety of human science theories in order to lay the foundation for reasonable and feasible reform measures. I address the organizational culture of the Catholic Church and its ideology, the degree to which authoritarianism or authority has characterized the church's use of power, and the idea that clergy sexual abuse can be understood as a form of elite crime.

In chapter 5, I investigate clergy sexual abuse from the perspective of the theology of the church. If the hints about reform concerning clergy sexual abuse developed in earlier chapters are to have any credibility and utility, they must be placed in context, particularly the context of the church's understanding of itself, and this places us in the realm of ecclesiology. My first task in this chapter is to describe the U.S. bishops' highly controversial efforts to reform the clergy sexual abuse system in 2002. I then analyze these efforts in terms of the contrasting ways in which the church has understood itself, viewed in light of the Pope John XXIII–inspired Second Vatican Council. This analysis concerns the interplay of power, participation, and community in the church, and I pose the question: What would Pope John have done? In chapter 6, I conclude by developing recommendations for church reform. I focus on issues such as developing more transparent, open, and participatory governance in the church, enhancing collegiality and the role of the laity, and paying more attention to cultural and national diversity and the principle of subsidiarity—as all these factors relate to the clergy sexual abuse system.

+ + + + + + + + + + + + + + + + + + + + + + + + + + + + + + + + + + + + + + + + + + + + + + + + +

CHAPTER ONE

# *One Clergy Sexual Abuser's Story*

*It's an abomination. . . . It's inexcusable. . . . It's rotten to the core. . . .*

*[It has] pretty much destroyed any credibility I may have, had or built up*

*in my 41 years [as a priest]. . . . I realize this may have been the tip of an*

*iceberg. . . . I hope your [addressed to victims] misplaced pride will not*

*overwhelm good sense and you will not remain silent. . . . I will go to any*

*length to ease your pain. . . . [It] really puts a crimp in the way I operate.*

*I am now fearful of saying appropriate things, like "I love you."*

—A Nashville priest (quoted in the *Tennessean*, 5 July 1999)

S INCE 1999, the *Tennessean* and other Nashville news media have extensively covered the story of Edward J. McKeown, a formerly active Catholic priest and convicted child sexual abuser.[1] Now in his late fifties, McKeown
is serving a twenty-five-year prison term that will keep him from society and potential child victims until he is an old man. What follows is my attempt to sift
through the public record to tell the McKeown story as accurately as possible
across the personal, relational, and social domains of the clergy sexual abuse
system.[2] This story sets the stage for a discussion of the more general phenomenon of clergy sexual abuse in the Catholic Church in chapter 2 and introduces
themes to be pursued in a series of ethical, human science, and theological
analyses in subsequent chapters.

## THE DIOCESAN SETTING

The McKeown story took place in many locations across the state of Tennessee, with its notorious legal drama set in Nashville. Although the state participates in southern culture, it is not part of the deep south. The three stars on the Tennessee flag stand for the three grand regions of the state: western Tennessee, in the Gulf Coastal Plain, bordered by the Mississippi River—encompassing Memphis and its surrounds; middle Tennessee, in the rolling hills of the Central Basin—centered on Nashville; and east Tennessee, in the eastern highlands at the base of the Appalachian Mountains—including Knoxville, Chattanooga, and, further north, the tri-cities of Bristol, Johnson City, and Kingsport.

Founded in 1837, the Diocese of Nashville is one of the oldest sees in the Catholic Church in the United States. For most of its history, the diocese took in the entire state of Tennessee, with the bishop presiding in Nashville. The Diocese of Memphis became a separate entity in 1971, and the Diocese of Knoxville followed in 1988, reproducing the three grand regions.

Throughout its history, Tennessee's Catholic Church has occupied a decidedly minority status among the many Christian denominations in a state sometimes called "the buckle on the bible belt." As of 2002, only 182,609 of the state's 5.7 million residents were Catholic, a mere 3.2 percent of the population. The Diocese of Memphis's 64,944 Catholics constitute 4.5 percent of its population, and the Diocese of Knoxville's 48,185 Catholics less than 2.5 percent of its population. The Diocese of Nashville's 16,302 square miles contain 69,480 Catholics (3.3 percent of its population). The diocese has fifty-one parishes and sixty-nine active priests (including religious order and extern priests), or about one priest for every 1,007 Catholics (*Official Catholic Directory* 2002). These figures suggest that the diocese spreads its priests thinly across a broad area and a large number of parishes—in an era of rapid growth in the Catholic population, characterized by a large number of recently arriving Hispanic immigrants and a shortage of priests. The current cadre of Nashville priests, moreover, includes many who are more than sixty years old and near retirement. Further, in the most recent year for which data were available, the diocese ordained only one new priest and had only five seminarians in training. The priest shortage in Nashville and throughout the Catholic Church in the United States is an important demographic reality that may have played a role in the way the bishops have managed clergy sexual abuse, since they may have been reluctant to dismiss any of its small and diminishing cadre of priests.

Despite its minority status, the church in Nashville is well known to the public. One of its downtown churches has historic architectural significance, and the Catholic cathedral is a well-known part of the Nashville cityscape. The media avidly cover the often successful play of a diocesan high school's athletic teams. For a time, the editor/publisher of the *Tennessean* came from a prominent local Catholic family. Catholics are represented well beyond their percentage of the population in business and political leadership. An order of Catholic sisters runs one of the city's major hospitals, and the diocese provides more than its share of social services, especially in work with immigrant populations. A scene from Robert Altman's cult classic, *Nashville*, was even shot in a local parish church.

Some degree of anti-Catholic feeling has been historically fairly typical throughout the South. The degree of such feeling in overwhelmingly Protestant Nashville is difficult to estimate, but it has certainly lessened in recent years. An example is the dramatic change in perception and reality of how welcoming Nashville's Vanderbilt University is to Catholics. Until fairly recently, Catholic officials were reluctant to send priests to Vanderbilt's divinity school because of an alleged anti-Catholic bias. Today, the divinity school has many Catholic students and an endowed chair of Catholic studies, and Catholics make up the single largest religious group across the Vanderbilt campus. The university even boasts of having awarded a doctorate to the current president of Notre Dame University.

## THE MCKEOWN STORY BEGINS

Edward McKeown, a native of Nashville, attended local Catholic schools and was ordained a priest in 1970. He was in an early wave of priests educated and ordained during and shortly after Vatican II, the council convened by Pope

John XXIII in the early 1960s. This council had nothing short of revolutionary potential for changing church operation and how Catholics viewed their church.

Vatican II was instantly controversial. As Garry Wills has observed: "Some would say the council ruined the liturgy, undermined church authority, and caused a widespread crisis of faith. Others would say it brought honesty and renewal to their lives" (Wills 2002, 225). Many Catholics approvingly viewed Vatican II as, paradoxically, moving the church forward into the modern world of science and democratic/participatory forms, and also back into the earliest history of the church to reclaim a view of the church as a community, the "People of God." More progressive Catholics initially felt encouraged by the many community-oriented and laity-involving changes that developed during the late 1960s and 1970s. Recently, however, an apparent backsliding to pre–Vatican II's more hierarchical, authoritarian, and laity-excluding style has discouraged them. For their part, more conservative Catholics saw Vatican II's modernizing of the church and consequent weakening of the hierarchical church by communitarian ideas and democratic/participatory principles as dangerous and subversive to the faith. Many have viewed this movement away from the tradition of the papal, hierarchical, even monarchical, church of the premodern era as a recipe for the destruction of the church as they knew it and, as they believe, as Christ had ordained it.

Actually, both during and since Vatican II, there has been a potentially healthy tension between the more communitarian and more hierarchical views of the church. The papacy of John Paul II, however, has seen this tension become contentious, even destructive (Steinfels 2003). The tensions, ambivalences, and ambiguities characterizing the Catholic Church since 1960, especially but not exclusively in the United States, should be kept in mind as the McKeown story unfolds.

McKeown reportedly told one of his victims that a priest had molested him as a child, presumably sometime during the 1950s or 1960s. This admission is telling, since people often erroneously believe clergy sexual abuse is a recent phenomenon that has only emerged since the mid-1980s (Jenkins 1996/2000; Jordan 2000). McKeown's career as a child sexual abuser,[3] moreover, conformed to the conventional wisdom that sexual abusers of children are often themselves victims of abuse as children. Having been victimized by a powerful figure, the victim becomes a victimizer when he assumes a powerful role. McKeown's abuse by a priest as a child is a dramatic example of the harm often caused by such abuse (Dorais 2002), manifesting, in effect, a reverse golden rule—do unto others as others have done unto you—doubly played out here, with a priest abuser contributing to the development of a second-generation abusing priest.

Observers of the priesthood in the United States have suggested that the last decade or two have witnessed marked changes both in the way the church recruits and selects men for the priesthood and in the seminary education process (see, e.g., Cozzens 2000). It has sought older candidates than in the past to avoid the pitfalls of recruiting teenage boys with little life experience and consequent unformed personal identity. Such youngsters often lacked the maturity to make a considered choice of vocation and rarely had the psychological capacity to come to grips with their sexuality, especially important given the demands of priestly celibacy. In part due to the clergy abuse crises of the late 1980s and early 1990s, the church has become more careful in screening seminary candidates, often using in-depth interviews and psychological tests to uncover developmental issues and psychological problems. Moreover, beyond the expected focus on spiritual formation during the years of preparing for ordination, many seminary programs now also attempt to address psychosocial development, sexual orientation, and sex education, although critics claim that such attempts are often inadequate (see, e.g., the remarks of Leslic Lothstein, director of psychology at the Institute of Living, in the *National Catholic Reporter*, 9 [DiGiulo, August 2002]). Yet it is worth noting, as Anson Shupe does, that even though "[s]eminaries can screen candidates more rigorously . . . religious groups need to recognize that potential abuse of congregants is organizationally built into their power structures just as mortar is into their walls. Given the opportunity, it will manifest itself" (Shupe 1995, 31). Although the specifics of McKeown's seminary training are unknown, he clearly was not a product of these recent developments. If he had been, seminary officials might have discovered his history of abuse by a priest and related psychological issues, and might either have screened him out or offered special help to increase his like-lihood of developing into a mature and well-functioning priest.

McKeown was an active priest in the Diocese of Nashville between 1970 and 1989, holding a variety of pastoral, teaching, and administrative positions. Ac-quaintances described him as a pleasant, jovial, and socially outgoing person—a hail-fellow-well-met, quite active in community affairs. In his ministerial ca-reer, he served in several parishes in east and middle Tennessee. He typically managed to be close to children, even serving as director of the Catholic Youth Organization in Chattanooga and Nashville and for fifteen years as a basketball official in the state athletic association. He also taught at his alma mater, a Nashville diocesan high school, where he seems to have begun his career as a child sexual abuser in the early 1970s. McKeown apparently molested one or more boys during his stay there. Remarkably, while serving as a chaplain for a rural police department, McKeown reportedly even served as a volunteer to house runaway youths in his rectory, testimony to this outgoing and trusted man's ability to conceal the dark side of his double life.

Diocesan officials claim to have learned of McKeown's abusing behavior for the first time only in 1986, approximately fifteen years after his activities be-gan—a delay that reflects the shame, guilt, and reluctance to speak about such matters experienced by sexual abuse victims and their families. The mother of one of McKeown's earliest reported victims finally brought the matter to the au-thorities' attention. Her son, then in his middle twenties, was experiencing many personal problems, presumably related to his abuse by McKeown.

The public's knowledge of the vast majority of clergy sexual abuse cases over the past twenty years has come from the often reluctant reports of adults or their family members many years after victimization. Children, especially boys, are extremely reluctant to report their abuse to authorities either during or soon af-ter its occurrence.[4] This makes it difficult to estimate the recent and ongoing extent of clergy sexual abuse. It is impossible, therefore, to evaluate the claim of church defenders (e.g., Steinfels, *New York Times*, 4 May 2002; Steinfels 2003; Weigel 2002) that the church has markedly changed in a positive direction over the last decade, as evidenced by the fact that most cases of reported clergy sex-ual abuse happened prior to 1990, with very few instances reported since then.

Victims since 1990 are likely to remain unknown for many years because they are loath to report their abuse, especially by a trusted priest.

On his arrest in 1999, McKeown reportedly constructed a list from memory of more than twenty children he had victimized since 1971. He undoubtedly molested some, if not most, of these children several times. The police said they found eight or nine additional victims not on his list who came forward during their investigation, many years after their encounters with McKeown. He molested most of his victims during his active ministry, and he also admitted victimizing eight of them between the time the diocese learned of his sexual abuse in 1986 and his arrest in 1999. McKeown admitted committing his abusive acts in every location to which his priestly duties took him in Tennessee (from Nashville to Chattanooga and several points between). Venues included his living quarters, camping sites, and state parks. The abuse involved such acts as fondling and anal and oral sex, often with alcohol and marijuana to lower the children's inhibitions.

McKeown also had a partner-in-crime during at least some of this time. An Associated Press piece (30 July 1999) and several stories in the *Tennessean* reported information obtained from the Nashville police and the Diocese of Nashville regarding McKeown's friend and colleague Franklin T. Richards.[5] Now an employee of Palm Beach County government in Florida, Richards, in his mid-fifties, admitted sexually abusing about twenty-five schoolboys during the 1970s and 1980s. Often, as with McKeown and many other clergy sexual abusers, he enhanced his position of power over his victims by molesting them under the resistance-lessening and memory-impairing influence of alcohol. Like McKeown, Richards was a one-time teacher at a Nashville diocesan high school, and he also served for a time as the principal of Knoxville's diocesan high school and as pastor of several parishes in the diocese. He reportedly joined McKeown on outings with altar boys involving sexual encounters. Several of these instances reportedly took place on a farm owned by Richards's family outside the city of Nashville.

In 1984, parents of three Knoxville high school students confronted Richards about his victimization of their children, and he admitted his guilt. Diocesan officials claimed to have reported his sexual abuse to the Tennessee

Department of Human Services, whose officials, they said, recommended he receive treatment. For claimed administrative reasons, the state destroyed records of the report, the recommendation, and the entire case file in 1991. Richards underwent psychiatric treatment and was part of an out-of-court settlement in which he agreed to pay the three victims' families $10,000, which the diocese reportedly loaned him. On 30 July 1999, the *Naples Daily News* website carried an Associated Press report of an event not mentioned by any of the Nashville media or any other media outlets, and, therefore, one that must be treated with caution. The story said that the Diocese of Nashville agreed to pay the families $30,000 in the settlement, which may be the same money reported to have been paid by Richards looked at from a different perspective. The details are not altogether clear; however, in 2002, in the wake of Cardinal Law's handling of the Archdiocese of Boston situation, the media and the public have often cited this kind of situation as indicative of a cover-up by way of hush money in attempts to keep clergy sexual abuse secret. Virtually every such instance gives rise to claims and counterclaims. On the one hand, secrecy is necessary to avoid giving scandal, to protect innocent victims, and to safeguard the rights of the accused priest. On the other hand, secrecy is necessary to cover up wrongdoing by church officials in order to preserve and protect the church's power and position at any cost (Balboni 1998).

Richards returned from treatment in 1985 and became pastor of a Nashville parish, with the stipulations that he continue in therapy, not associate with children, and always keep his office door open. From this time on, there was no reported evidence that he molested children anew. For unexplained reasons, however, the diocese moved him from this assignment to another parish, where he worked until he left the active priesthood in 1989. Since the diocese had not allowed parishioners and staff members there to participate in dealing with this situation—indeed, they were never informed of Richards's sexual proclivities—they claimed to have trusted and admired him and were shocked to learn of his sexual abuse when the news broke in 1999 as part of the McKeown story.

The Nashville police also claimed not to have known of Richards's crimes until 1999. Since there is an eight-year statute of limitations in such cases in Tennessee, and since there was no evidence at that time of his sexually abusing additional children, the authorities could not prosecute him—unlike Mc-Keown, who continued to molest children well into the 1990s until he was arrested. The events in the Richards situation—the church's failure to notify parishioners and the police, provision of treatment for the clergy sexual abuser, alleged financial settlements paid to victims' families by the priest and/or the diocese, and pastoral reassignment—conform to a pattern seen in many clergy sexual abuse cases over the years (see, e.g., Berry 1992/2000; Bruni and Burkett 1993/2002; Shupe 1995), including cases brought to light in 2002 and 2003.

Ironically, in an unexplained coincidence, both Richards and McKeown left the active priesthood on the same day, 1 March 1989. Richards inexplicably resigned, and the diocese reportedly gave him temporary financial support. Today, he claims to have overcome his desire to abuse children and says he is now involved in adult homosexual relationships. McKeown refused to resign and was forced out by the diocese, also receiving diocesan financial assistance, but he reportedly continued sexually abusing children outside the church context.

Two years after Richards's confrontation with the parents of his Knoxville victims, and one year after his return from psychiatric treatment and his assumption of new pastoral duties, the Diocese of Nashville claims to have become aware of McKeown's sexual abuse for the first time. The mother of one of his first victims came forward in 1986 to report her son's victimization to church officials. She said she had not learned about her son's sexual abuse until, as a young adult, he underwent treatment for alcoholism, presumably related to his abuse, and even then she came forward quite reluctantly. In a 1999 interview reported in the *Tennessean*, her son claimed that at the time of his assault by McKeown he had informed another priest, but to no effect. He also claimed that the church had not done anything to reach out to him since learning of his plight—a disturbing situation, if true, since the church had a stated policy of victim support.

The boy's mother stated that, in her 1986 meeting, the bishop said he was sorry to learn about her son's victimization. He told her he was unaware of McKeown's sexual abuse, and, although the details are fuzzy, he also said he would accede to her request that McKeown not receive further pastoral assignments. After this meeting, the bishop confronted McKeown, who admitted he had sexually abused the young man in question and agreed to go for evaluation at St. Luke Institute, a church-affiliated facility in Maryland. After the evaluation, in the fall of 1986, the facility could not immediately accommodate McKeown's treatment, so the bishop sent him to the Hartford Institute for Living for between six and nine months of treatment.

## THE NATURE OF MCKEOWN'S SEXUAL ABUSE

Although full copies of McKeown's St. Luke Institute and Hartford Institute for Living records have been sealed by the court, selected quotations from them appear in a plaintiffs' appeal document released by the court in May 2002 in the course of the civil suit that would come to be brought against McKeown and the Diocese of Nashville.[6] The reported St. Luke material said that McKeown admitted "his age preference and experience in the past had been exclusively homosexual and for adolescents from the ages of 14–20," and he claimed to have abused thirty victims in the previous fourteen years. "The sexual contact was usually limited to masturbation, but occasionally included oral sex. Father McKeown estimates that he has had sexual contact with minors on the average of 'once or twice a month' for the past 14 years. He cannot recall a sustained period of abstinence that was not motivated by the unavailability of young males." And where did he find his victims? "Most of his contact . . . was made through the parish." One possible motive for a child sexual abuser entering the priesthood is his belief that he will thereby encounter children who trust him because of his honored and powerful role. Alternatively, such a person might choose the priestly life because he believes that the moral tenets of the church concerning sexuality will help him avoid acting out his urges. In either case, when he sexually abuses a young parishioner, he abuses his professional ministerial role.

In a subsequent St. Luke Institute document reportedly sent to the bishop in the late 1980s, the medical director was concerned about McKeown's use of alcohol, because of "its use in association with inappropriate sexual behavior with young people. Not uncommonly he would drink, not to the point of intoxication, but perhaps to the point of lowering inhibitions. In a similar way he would sometimes offer alcohol to young people he was with to facilitate sexual interaction." Admission material from the Hartford Institute for Living, also reported in the plaintiffs' appeal brief, described McKeown's reason for referral as a "longstanding problem with pedophilia," and subsequent case notes said that, since his "activity has been prevalent with young men ages 14 to 20 a diagnosis of regressed pedophilia would be appropriate."

An Institute for Living case history described McKeown as follows:

> Father McKeown indicates that the report to the bishop was just the "tip of the iceberg." Father McKeown admits to well over thirty incidents involving young men in sexual activity over the last fifteen or so years. . . . Over the years he has developed a pattern which remains relatively consistent. Sexual activity involves only mutual masturbation or fellatio. . . . Father McKeown indicates that many of his relationships extended for a year or more and generally involved activity anywhere from once a week to once a month. He had a history of having multiple partners over the same course of time. . . . It was not until . . . 1976 that the frequency of his sexual acting out became more frequent. He states that he would get to know a young man over time and "get the sense that sexual activity was okay for them." He would then invite them into circumstances where it was possible.

Thus, although the bishop initiated McKeown's medical diagnostic and treatment process in 1986 because of one reported instance of his having abused a youngster in the early 1970s, McKeown's activities had been far more extensive. Seemingly unbeknownst to the bishop, other church officials, his fellow priests, and parishioners, he had been amassing a long list of victims over the years, which, it turned out, would grow even longer in subsequent years.[7]

The precise diagnostic label for McKeown's type of sexual abuse seems to be a matter of doubt and contention. His 1986 reported preference for fourteen- to twenty-year-old victims would lead some to call him an ephebophile, not a pedophile as suggested in the above reports, since victims in this age range would not be prepubescent. As we will see later, however, the two children who occasioned the eventual lawsuit in 2000 were twelve when McKeown began his abuse of them in 1995. It is useful at this point to review the best current think-

[The] diocese reported McKeown in 1986, as soon as it learned for the first time of his misdeeds. The diocese immediately confronted McKeown, investigated the matter, had McKeown evaluated, followed the recommendations of the experts, maintained an ongoing treatment regimen, paid him monetary support for the necessities of life and continued his medical insurance coverage even after his dismissal. This support was reviewed periodically, reduced, and finally ended in 1994. (*Tennessee Register*, 8 June 2002)

A church official also claimed that "not only did the diocese respond to what it knew of at the time, it did so in a manner that most consider to be on the cutting edge at that time, in dealing with these issues." Do the events we have reviewed so far really justify this claim?

### MCKEOWN LEAVES THE ACTIVE PRIESTHOOD

The argument can be made that when the church dissociates itself from a known clergy sexual abuser—for example, in a zero-tolerance policy of one strike (a single past or present act of abuse by a priest) and you are out (dismissed from active priestly status by a diocese or laicized by the Vatican)—it is unleashing the abuser on a secular society filled with unsuspecting future victims. This raises the issue of what, if any, ongoing responsibility the church has for an inactive or laicized priest's future behavior and, correlatively, whether or not the church should make every effort to keep an abusing priest within the clerical fold, away from potential victims, rather than removing him from all ministerial functions. That question, in fact, would eventually be raised in civil court by two of McKeown's victims. It was raised on many other fronts as well, as the American church was attempting to craft clergy sexual abuse policies in the wake of the 2002 scandal.

In early 1990, soon after McKeown's departure from the active priesthood in the Diocese of Nashville, he took his first of several jobs in Metropolitan Nashville Davidson County Government. This set him on a path that would lead to his involvement with several governmental agencies and to his eventual arrest, conviction, and imprisonment as a child sexual abuser. Not only was the nature of the church's ongoing responsibility thereby put into question, but the responsibility of governmental agencies in dealing with the church—in the person of a clergy sexual abuser, even one only formerly associated with the church—also became a matter of public debate. Throughout the history of clergy sexual abuse in the United States, the challenge of maintaining constitutionally and societally appropriate church-state relations has been at the center of the problem.

After leaving the active priesthood, McKeown worked in a number of local government agencies until his arrest in 1999. Consistent with the reactions to him by those who knew him during his years as an active priest, those meeting him throughout the 1990s saw him as a personable and altogether trustworthy person. His duties did not seem to entail direct contact with children, but, as with his service in the church, he often managed to position himself in situations that in one way or another involved children. Beyond his official job duties, he was an active and visible volunteer in local political affairs.

McKeown the child sexual abuser began to show himself publicly again in 1995, although, on his own admission, he had been abusing other children the public hadn't known about during the first part of the decade. In 1995 he began the molestation of a boy that eventually led to his arrest and conviction (let us call the boy John Doe 1, to be consistent with the lawsuit that would be filed against the Diocese of Nashville and others). At about the same time, he was also having encounters with another twelve-year-old boy (John Doe 2). On the surface, he had a seemingly healthy relationship with John Doe 2, including taking him to baseball games, Boy Scout events, and political rallies, as well as giving him little errands to run and visiting with the family. The mother characterized McKeown in the *Tennessean* (28 February 1999) as "very protective. . . . He was a very nice man, a very credible individual. He really seemed to go out of his way to serve other people. And it didn't seem to be just a gesture. He would really inconvenience himself. He seemed genuine. If you look at our family pictures, Ed is in them. . . . My son would go to the polls with Ed. He has served barbecue at . . . [the] juvenile court clerk's ranch. All this stuff seemed good for him." John Doe 2, however, eventually told his mother that McKeown had played strip poker with him, provided beer, slept in the same bed with him on overnight visits to McKeown's mobile home in the trailer park in which both lived, and engaged with him in only vaguely remembered unspecified physical activities.

During one earlier period, John Doe 2's mother had left the boy with McKeown for several days while she was out of town for a family member's funeral. The family pediatrician reportedly came to claim that the boy eventually showed behavioral, emotional, and physical signs consistent with sexual abuse, including anal soreness, a strep infection, and a behavior pattern of increasingly poor functioning and adaptation, more than enough evidence, she said, to warrant police intervention. Later court documents contain an allegation that McKeown molested the boy on approximately fifteen different occasions (*Memorandum and Order*, 20 June 2001, 5).

The mother notified the police, and after an experienced and decorated Metro youth service division officer interviewed John Doe 2, she says he suggested that she wear a wire during a confrontation with McKeown, a suggestion allegedly made in the presence of a neighbor. The officer said he consulted with a prosecutor, but the police eventually dropped the investigation sometime in 1996, without any report to the Department of Human Services, which, presumably, would have conducted its own investigation. The neighbor warned the mother that politics might be involved, and she eventually came to see it that way as well. The mother felt strongly that, had McKeown been arrested and tried in 1995 for molesting her son, subsequent incidents of his sexual abuse would have been prevented. She filed a complaint with the police internal affairs division, but no further official action ensued.

## MCKEOWN IS FINALLY ARRESTED

In 1997, authorities filed charges in Metro Juvenile Court accusing a young teenage boy, John Doe 1, of sexually battering a young child. They sent the boy—who may himself have been abused as a very young child and who had frequently been a runaway—for counseling. With the mutual agreement of his divorced mother and the Tennessee Department of Children's Services, the court assigned John Doe 1 for temporary custody to, of all people, formerly active priest Edward McKeown. Two years earlier, in 1995, McKeown had begun molesting this then twelve-year-old at about the same time he was also allegedly molesting twelve-year-old John Doe 2. McKeown and both boys had lived in the same trailer park.

Fast-forwarding to 1999, McKeown and his former court-assigned ward and long-standing abuse victim had a meeting in which the now sixteen-year-old boy tape-recorded their conversation. The tape revealed McKeown apologizing to John Doe 1 for the many times he had sexually molested him and confessing that a priest had molested him as well when he was a child. On 30 January 1999, Metro police officers arrested McKeown, who admitted fondling and having oral sex with the boy, earlier, at the trailer park where both lived and, more recently, in McKeown's house. The boy confirmed these encounters. McKeown said he manipulated the boy, using his adult-child power differential, "by allowing him to do things that he would normally not be allowed to do, such as smoking cigarettes and providing him with beer" (*Tennessean*, 3 June 2001). As we have seen, McKeown was also able to recall more than twenty other children he had molested over a twenty-seven-year period, at least eight of whom he claimed to have molested between 1986 and 1999.

When news of McKeown's arrest and the fact that he had been an active priest in the Diocese of Nashville prior to 1990 reached the media, the bishop — successor to the bishop who had presided over McKeown's dismissal from the active priesthood — released a statement. As reported in the *Tennessean* (2 February 1999), he said: "My immediate concern is for the welfare of the alleged victims. All sexual misconduct is contrary to Christian morals and principles and harms spiritual, physical and emotional welfare."

Metro prosecutors looked into the possibility of filing criminal charges against diocesan officials for possible violation, during the late 1980s, of the child abuse reporting laws in their handling of McKeown's acts of sexual abuse while he was a priest. They had to abandon the matter, however, because the statute of limitations had passed on that pre-1989 situation. Beyond issues of the passage of time and statutes of limitation, Nashville diocesan actions, or failures to act, during the late 1980s were not violations of the then prevailing sexual abuse reporting statutes. One might argue, however, that moral/ethical concerns set a higher standard that the church neither acknowledged nor acted on, remembering that the diocese has maintained it had at least informed the Tennessee Department of Children's Services about McKeown's abuse of children.

It should be noted that much of what has caused trouble for Boston's Cardinal Law and many other bishops, both in the United States and throughout the world, fits the general pattern of these late-1980s Nashville events. By mid-2002, moreover, a number of states were considering lengthening the statute of limitations for clergy sexual abuse, and prosecutors and grand juries were seriously considering lodging criminal charges against Cardinal Law and several of his fellow bishops for allegedly covering up earlier acts of clergy sexual abuse.

On 17 June 1999, after three months of legal wrangling, McKeown pleaded guilty to one count of rape and two counts of sexual battery. He received a twenty-five-year sentence, avoiding a possible sentence of eighty-four years on the original four counts of rape, six of sexual battery, and two of aggravated assault. On 18 June 1999, the *Tennessean* reported this outcome, and McKeown's lawyer said: "He's very sorry. He pleaded guilty because he didn't want to put this young man through any more pain. If that meant he spends more time in prison than he might have received with a trial, he was prepared to do that. . . . He would rather die in prison than put him through a trial." McKeown's reported expression of remorse and social concern for his victim seems to suggest that he may not be a conscienceless sociopath.

In the aftermath of the McKeown verdict, Catholics throughout the Diocese of Nashville had a variety of reactions. The 19 June 1999 issue of the *Tennessean* reported one Catholic as saying, "You can't apply the acts of one man to the whole," while another said, "I would still trust another priest as much as I would trust any other person." In other words, McKeown was a rotten apple who didn't spoil the bunch. A Nashville priest, however, spoke candidly in saying: "It raises the veil of suspicion. It has a general effect on the trust that people place in their priests. . . . You become self-conscious. You ask yourself how everything you do will be interpreted. . . . By our very nature, ministers are caring people. People are attracted to them, and dealing with children is part of my ministry. If I am hugged by a child, do I hug back? If a teen-ager wants to meet with me privately, how do I protect myself? . . . It can make you hesitant to be present for people at certain times in their need. . . . It begins a whole cy-cle where you think of yourself first. That is not what ministry is about." This priest's reaction speaks to the relational and community corrosiveness caused by cases like McKeown's besetting the church since the 1980s. Trust and caring are essential aspects of any well-functioning community, and one expects, rather demands, them to characterize relations in the church as a community. As we will see in chapter 2, clergy sexual abuse causes harm that goes well be-yond its effects on the personal realm of victims and their families and the so-cial realm of the church as an organization. More generally, in the relational realm, it poisons the well of priest-parishioner interaction and lessens the peo-ple's sense of community.

## THE MCKEOWN CASE ENTERS
## THE BROADER SOCIAL DOMAIN

Clergy sexual abuse, once exposed, so quickly spills over into societal institu-tions beyond the church that the way these institutions respond is an important aspect of such cases. After it became public in 1999 that McKeown had been employed by Metro government throughout the 1990s, and had been granted temporary custody of John Doe 1 in 1998, even after the police had conducted their 1995 aborted investigation of the John Doe 2 case, the *Tennessean* reported a public blame game involving a number of public officials. McKeown con-fessed that he had abused at least six children from the time he took his local government positions until his arrest in 1999. At stake was who might have con-tributed to these acts of sexual abuse by failing to act in a way that might have kept McKeown away from his victims.

In mid-1999, the presiding Metro Juvenile Court judge appointed a blue-ribbon commission, which included a Catholic deacon, to look into the McKeown case. Although the December 1999 commission report did not officially affix blame, it did say the court and the diocese could have done more: "The commission cannot escape the conclusion that McKeown left the priest-hood because of inappropriate sexual misconduct with young males, which was known to others and which should have been reported to proper authorities at the time. . . . The failure to conduct a more thorough investigation into the report of McKeown's prior misconduct was unfortunate and led to disastrous results" (*Tennessean*, 29 December 1999). Yet what of the trail of victims left in the wake of McKeown's sexual abuse?

The actions of two victims and their families set in motion a chain of events that moved the case beyond the personal and relational domains of the clergy sexual abuse system and plunged it into the broader social domain. From what we have seen so far concerning the personal and relational domains, it should come as no surprise that the new millennium brought civil litigation regarding the McKeown case. The December 1999 Metro commission findings, coupled with the extensive reporting on McKeown in the *Tennessean* since early 1999, were the stuff of lawsuits. The press coverage often contained instances of reporters, and those reported on, making implicit and explicit charges against the church and Metro government officials of cover-up or lack of effective action to protect victims.

If any of McKeown's victims' families were primed by the extensive media coverage to pursue legal action against the Diocese of Nashville, one would expect such a move by families of victims abused *during* his tenure as an active priest. This did not happen. Rather, parents filed a $70 million action against the church (and others) on behalf of John Doe 1 and John Doe 2, children whose involvement with McKeown began six years *after* he had left the active priesthood. This attempt to hold the church liable for acts committed by its officials years before acts of sexual abuse committed by a formerly active priest was a legal first. It had the potential of setting a far-reaching legal precedent affecting churches throughout the United States, greatly expanding the number of potential litigants.

### VICTIMS' PARENTS FILE
### MULTIMILLION-DOLLAR LAWSUITS

So, late January 2000 saw the initiation of legal action on behalf of John Doe 1 and John Doe 2 in two related lawsuits filed in Davidson County Circuit Court. Each suit sought $35 million for the victims and their mothers—$8 million and

$2 million in compensatory damages for each boy and each mother, respectively, and $25 million for each family in punitive damages—for a total of $70 million. The plaintiffs named the Diocese of Nashville, the Diocese of Knoxville (once part of the Nashville diocese but separated from it several years earlier), Metropolitan Nashville Davidson County Government, Edward McKeown, and Franklin Richards as defendants. The lawyer for John Doe 1 said: "If any of these people had followed through, what happened to this little boy would not have happened. This ruined a whole lot of kids" (*Tennessean*, 20 January 2000).

Plaintiffs said their concern to protect children in the future motivated them, using the mechanism of steep monetary penalties to compensate for alleged moral and civilly liable lapses by the defendants in dealing with McKeown. Over the years, many victims who have brought suit against the church have claimed this kind of unselfish motivation. Vatican officials and many officials in the American church, however, have claimed that their motivation was greed in their unjust attempts to gouge money from the church, an organization with "deep pockets."

## BLAMING THE VICTIM?

The plaintiffs' attorneys sought court and police records from Metro government, which subsequently tried to hold confidential its information on investigations involving John Doe 1 and John Doe 2. Plaintiffs described the conduct of the diocese as "outrageous," claiming: "The diocese knew young males were at risk if they were in the presence of Eddie McKeown. . . . They knew after they pushed him out the door, protecting children in their own church, that he went to work at Juvenile Court, and that he fraternized with young males. Would any person, hearing that information, not say that was outrageous?" (*Tennessean*, 21 January 2000). In addition, in trying to establish that the church's behavior showed a pattern—"Failure to report one pedophile might be negligent. Repeated failure would be reckless"—they also sought the following from the diocese: names of all employees who might have sexually abused children; a number-coded list of all known victims, with names only made known to attorneys;

and a description of what the church did after learning of abuse allegations. "We're asking what they knew, when they knew it and what they did about it," said one of the plaintiffs' attorneys. One can imagine that church officials, ordinarily circumspect about the church's inner workings, felt beleaguered by what must have seemed like a combination fishing expedition and witch hunt.

On 9 June 2000, diocesan lawyers filed what turned out to be an extremely controversial document titled *Answer of the Defendant, Catholic Diocese of Nashville, to the Plaintiffs' Second Amended Complaint*. Beyond responding to the plaintiffs' charges and requests for information, the diocese claimed to be in no way at fault for any harm caused by McKeown to the defendants, who had been molested by him many years after he left the active priesthood, and they referred to "individuals and their *comparative fault* to any injuries and damages sustained by the plaintiffs, or their acts or omissions that were the cause in fact for the injuries sustained by the plaintiffs" (14, emphasis added). Thus, they invoked the legal principle of comparative fault, arguing that there was a certain kind of person who "had actual knowledge of the illness and condition suffered by Edward McKeown, and failed to report McKeown to the Department of Children's Services so as to protect John Doe 1 and Jane Doe 1 [John Doe 1's mother] from McKeown, and is thus, *at fault for injuries and damages sustained by these plaintiffs*. This individual's fault must be compared to the fault of all other persons or parties, or in the alternative should be considered the cause in fact of plaintiffs' injuries and damages" (16, emphasis added).

Who would qualify as instances of this kind of person under the doctrine of comparative fault? Physicians who, at the request of the diocese, had treated McKeown for his sexual abuse in the late 1980s qualified—and the plaintiffs promptly added them to their list of defendants because the diocese identified them here. The Tennessee state official to whom diocesan officials said they had reported McKeown's abuse also qualified, as did the Metro court officials discussed earlier, and members of a Sexaholics Anonymous support group McKeown had attended. Finally and most controversially, *McKeown's sexual abuse victims during his priesthood qualified*. In addition, diocesan lawyers claimed that John Doe 1's mother was "guilty of negligence in allowing her minor child to consort with people about whom she did not have adequate information to assure their [*sic*] well-being and safety, such as Edward McKeown, and such action constitutes negligence and fault on her behalf" (12).

Diocesan lawyers were claiming that any financial damages for which the church *might* be found liable—although they strongly denied *any* church liability—should be mitigated by comparative fault or co-responsibility borne by the very victims of McKeown's sexual abuse themselves (and others) for their failure to report his abuse of them in the past. To put the best possible face on this legal maneuver, one could argue that they were attempting to use a *reductio ad absurdum* legal strategy—branding the plaintiffs' theory that the church was responsible for harm done to McKeown's unknown *future* victims, based on church actions many years in the *past*, as so far-fetched that they might just as well have blamed his past victims. The church was not seeking money from these individuals but was attempting both to argue against this theory and to reduce its percentage of liability in order to reduce any money damages the court might award. One problem with such a legal strategy is that it can be seen as re-victimization of the victims, in effect, rubbing salt in their already painful wounds.

On learning of the diocese's use of the comparative fault argument, the *Tennessean* put the worst possible face on it, and used this headline for its 16 August 2000 story: "Diocese: Victims should share blame." Some people engaged in unconfirmed but plausible speculation that, because of the potentially explosive negative effect on public opinion that certain interpretations of the diocese's use of the comparative fault argument might have, the plaintiffs' attorneys had brought the presumably nonpublic legal filing containing the comparative fault argument to the attention of the media.

Reactions from Catholics came quickly. The headline for a 17 August 2000 story in the *Tennessean* read: "Catholics debate church responsibility." One priest agreed with the comparative fault legal argument, saying: "Anyone that knows bears some responsibility." But a Catholic professor of religious education said: "There seems to be a greater concern for the stewardship of the material resources of the diocese than for the stewardship of the diocese's image and good name. I think the image is incredibly tarnished by this." On the other hand, a diocesan official said: "The Diocese of Nashville is deeply sympathetic and compassionate to the victims of sexual abuse. Yet at the same time we have to defend ourselves against a lawsuit based on legal theories that we believe don't hold up. If you follow their (the plaintiffs' attorneys') theories on out, it would seem like there are many, many people who would have been covered by that same reporting statute." For his part, the bishop said: "[T]he plaintiffs assert that any person who suspected or had knowledge of any abuse is equally responsible to the plaintiffs for any failure to report." He also said that "our diocese strongly rejects this reasoning." He did not, however, give any reasons why he rejected this reasoning or why the diocesan lawyers' claim of victim comparative fault was not, in fact, an instance of faulting or blaming the victim, as the *Tennessean* and others had charged. Even a cursory reading of the diocesan legal filing quoted earlier supports the claim of victim blaming. In that regard, one of the plaintiffs' lawyers, in clarifying their role in the diocese's use of the comparative fault doctrine, said: "We have never said that any of those persons that were named in the answer (to the lawsuit) by the diocese were negligent. . . . It was the diocese that first maintained that all of these other persons, including the victims, were negligent. I don't understand how the bishop can blame the plaintiffs for bringing all of these other persons in. We have never raised that issue" (*Tennessean*, 17 August 2000).

Whatever the nature of the legal subtleties involved, the making of the comparative fault argument in the Nashville case created conditions for a surefire public relations disaster when reported by the media. Diocesan lawyers may not have anticipated that their strategy would be made public; however, today, when lawyers often try high-profile cases in the media, their failure to anticipate the resulting media debacle was at the very least a strategic error. In addition, critics might wonder if the church's defensiveness and failure to explain these matters clearly also had caused scandal, as in the case of Cardinal Law in 2002.

## FURTHER LEGAL MANEUVERING

Issues of secrecy, both within and beyond the legal system, have permeated the phenomenon of clergy sexual abuse, and the months of September and October 2000 saw heated legal wrangling in Nashville over what court-related materials should be kept secret. The *Tennessean* reported, on October 28, that lawyers for the Diocese of Nashville had argued for placing under seal its further responses to inquiries made by the plaintiffs, perhaps attempting to avoid any further public relations difficulties like those occasioned by the comparative fault matter. They were making this request for concealment, they said, to protect the privacy of persons beyond those specifically contending the lawsuit, and to help prevent contamination of potential jurors. The diocese also said that the First Amendment protects information about church matters, including its mode of handling people like McKeown and others requiring church discipline. Diocesan lawyers argued further that keeping matters under seal was important so lawyers for both sides could "develop and test their respective theories free from the scrutiny of persons who have limited understanding of those theories." A plaintiff's attorney responded that "the church wants to test its legal theories without wanting to test (them) in a public forum." The presiding judge rejected the First Amendment argument, saying it did not apply to court proceedings, and having read the church's written responses, he ruled that "there is nothing embarrassing to any individual in there sufficient to support a protective order." By November 2000, then, all legal matters to date were officially open to public scrutiny and media coverage. Justified or not, many people believed the diocese had been trying to hide possibly incriminating or embarrassing material, information that would weaken its moral standing, power, and influence in the Nashville community.

The next legal development concerned the two physicians who had treated McKeown for his sexual abuse in the late 1980s. These people had been working at the request of the diocese and had been added to the lawsuit by the plaintiffs because they were among those named by the diocese in advancing the comparative fault defense. Their lawyers filed a motion to dismiss them from the suit, and their arguments are important in shedding light on the situation of professionals who work with clergy sexual abusers at the church's request. First, these medical professionals claimed not to have been aware of the specific identity of any of McKeown's victims, having only treated him generally for his sexual abuse. Since the reporting statute requires only that the identity of specific children suspected of having been abused be reported to appropriate authorities, the lawyers argued, these physicians had no duty to report

McKeown. Second, state laws concerning mental health professionals, they argued, required reporting of individuals who have threatened harm to specific people, and such laws do not cover the situation of *"unknown future victims of sexual abuse,"* such as John Doe 1 and John Doe 2, who were involved with McKeown only several years after the physicians treated him (*Tennessean*, 14 November 2000, emphasis added). On 28 November 2000, the judge removed the two medical professionals from the lawsuit.

Importantly, lawyers for the diocese also made this "future victims" argument, claiming that the boys' lawyers had "come up with some theories that really stretch the applicability" of the Tennessee reporting law. In that regard, as with the physicians, the judge disallowed the future-victims legal theory for holding the diocese liable. Rejecting the plaintiffs' "broad interpretation" of the reporting law and the attendant claim of "negligence per se," one of the three grounds on which plaintiffs were suing, he ruled that the situations of John Doe 1 and John Doe 2 "are simply too far removed in time and place from the alleged nonreporting of abuse to have an action for negligence per se under the Tennessee abuse reporting statutes" (*Memorandum and Order*, 28 November 2000, 10). The judge concluded that the time elapsed between McKeown's departure from the priesthood and the molestation of the plaintiffs, together with the fact that the duty to report sexual abuse does not apply to future victims, provided grounds for dismissing the negligence claim.

Plaintiffs subsequently dropped claims against the Diocese of Knoxville and Metro Nashville government, as well as all claims against remaining defendants based on "negligent infliction of emotional distress." All that remained in their suit, therefore, were claims based on the legal theory of "outrageous conduct" — "the heart of our case," said one of the plaintiff's lawyers.

The plaintiffs' lawyers filed their fourth amended complaint in mid-December 2000, based, in part, they claimed, on information from McKeown's medical records and several other documents they said they had recently obtained. As reported by the *Tennessean* on 16 December 2000, they emphasized that the diocese didn't do enough on learning about McKeown's long-standing pattern of abusing children to protect present and future victims. A diocesan official said these charges were "really just a rehash of a lot of old information . . .

filled with half-truths, innuendos, and outright misinformation. . . . I think this fourth amended complaint is an attempt to breathe life into a lawsuit that's just hanging by a thread." The official, however, did not comment on any of the specific allegations, possibly on advice of counsel.

Six months later, on 15 June 2001, diocesan lawyers asked the judge to dismiss the case entirely, saying that the plaintiffs' lawyers were making "inference upon inference upon inference" and failing to support the claim of "outrageous conduct" in their futile attempt to blame the church for harm caused by McKeown's sexual abuse of their clients. Importantly, a lawyer for the plaintiffs admitted that he was unable to provide any legal precedent for his legal theory of the case, but "the fact that it hasn't happened before doesn't mean that it shouldn't happen now. The fact that they didn't care who they hurt (by sending McKeown into the community without warning) shouldn't be an excuse for avoiding liability" (*Tennessean*, 16 June 2001).

Less than a week later, on 21 June 2001, the *Tennessean* carried a story with the headline "Sex abuse suit dismissed against Nashville Diocese," and the headline of the next day's edition of the *Tennessee Register* read: "Court dismisses lawsuits against Nashville Diocese." While allowing claims of liability against the imprisoned McKeown to continue to stand, the judge dismissed claims against ex-priest Franklin Richards and also dismissed the "outrageous conduct" claim against the diocese, the final ground for the lawsuit. We should, however, pay careful attention to the judge's opinion, which read, in part: "The Court declines to enter into a detailed discussion and analysis of all the facts related to the conduct of the Diocese. That kind of discussion is simply unnecessary for the resolution of the motions before the Court. *However one might judge the conduct of the diocese*, the plaintiffs' case is fatally flawed because there is simply not the appropriate link between the alleged conduct and the sexual assaults on the plaintiffs" (*Memorandum and Order*, 20 June 2001, 7, 10–11, emphasis added)

Obviously pleased, a church official said: "The thorough discovery process, that reviewed volumes of records and testimony, clearly showed that the diocese followed the law and the best medical advice of the time in addressing the situation. The judge's ruling of June 20 affirms what we have been saying all along. . . . Edward McKeown was solely and completely responsible for his actions against the plaintiffs in this lawsuit" (*Tennessee Register*, 22 June 2001). The judge's decision, however, did *not* exactly do what this church official claimed it did. The judge neither agreed nor disagreed "that the diocese followed the law." He neither approved nor disapproved of the church's actions in handling the McKeown situation. Rather, the judge did not view the diocese's actions during the last half of the 1980s to be relevant to the lawsuit. The earlier actions of the diocese, whatever they might have been or however they might be judged, were beside the point. Moreover, saying that the judge's ruling "affirms what we have been saying all along. . . . Edward McKeown was solely and completely responsible for his actions against the plaintiffs" ignores the controversy over the diocese's use of the comparative fault defense. The official's statement seemed more attuned to the court of public opinion than to the Davidson County Circuit Court.

### THE BOSTON SCANDAL ENTERS PUBLIC CONSCIOUSNESS

From September 2001 until Cardinal Law's actions in Boston came under such intense media scrutiny in early 2002, the Nashville media reported very little on the McKeown situation. Through late winter 2002, the *Tennessean*'s website fairly regularly carried newswire stories on the emerging national clergy sexual abuse situation, but its own coverage of McKeown-related material was mostly in the context of the Boston situation and the widening scandal throughout the United States and beyond. On 30 March, Tim Chavez, a columnist for the *Tennessean* and himself a Catholic, called for the church to abandon mandatory celibacy and, in the 24 April issue, went on to create controversy by calling for a laity "watchdog" group to oversee the diocese's handling of clergy sexual abuse. In the 26 April edition, a diocesan spokesperson strongly disagreed, saying that while "we agree wholeheartedly that a watchdog to help detect, prevent and apprehend anyone who abuses our children should be in place . . . I disagree . . . that yet another bureaucracy, committee or layer of inspection needs to be implemented. There is already a watchdog. In fact, there are several." He urged the *Tennessean* not to complicate matters further by calling for the "creation of some 'laity watchdog' to receive complaints of child abuse."

At that very time in the spring of 2002, many voices in the nationwide Catholic community were contending that meaningful involvement of the laity was the only hope the church had to restore its image and moral credibility so tarnished by the sexual abuse scandal. In that regard, a widely representative group of lay Catholics in the Archdiocese of Boston formed Voice of the Faithful, an organization promoting meaningful participation of the laity in dealing with clergy sexual abuse and, more broadly, in the church's decision-making processes. The Diocese of Nashville, however, appeared to be publicly repudiating any expansion of laity involvement in its handling of clergy sexual abuse, seemingly reverting to a policy of keeping its dealings with the problem secret, even from its own laity. What would it take to get the diocese to be more transparent and responsive to the issue of laity involvement, so much on the church's agenda nationally at this time?

Regarding this stance of secrecy, on 18 May 2002, the *Tennessean's* Chavez bitterly complained that he had been denied interviews with the bishop and other church officials—interviews he had sought for the purpose of clarifying the diocese's view of the spreading national clergy sexual abuse scandal. About a month later, he used the bully pulpit of his column to invite Nashville Catholics to a meeting he was organizing to encourage laity involvement in the diocese's handling of clergy sexual abuse. The upshot was the establishment of a group that would eventually affiliate with Boston's Voice of the Faithful. The organization chose to focus on "structure and leadership, protecting priests of integrity, protecting children, healing victims, promoting a spiritual response and policy and practice" (*Tennessean*, 6 July 2002). Chavez led the group, reported on its workings, and served as a very visible advocate for meaningful involvement of the laity in the church.

As with the *Boston Globe's* reporting of the Cardinal Law story, the *Tennessean's* reporting of the McKeown case had turned the newspaper into an active player rather than a passive reporter. In that regard, the 6 July 2002 issue of the *Nashville Scene* carried the headline "The Diocese of Nashville says the *Tennessean* is unfair." After reviewing the back and forth between the paper and the diocese since 19 May, the article concluded that the *Tennessean* reporter at the center of its recent controversial stories "while avoiding the appearance of overt bias, . . . managed through innuendo, omission and what appears to be minor carelessness to convict the church of complicity in McKeown's crimes." Mitigating somewhat the reporter's blame, the article said that the *Tennessean's* attempts to seek clarification on its allegations, except in one instance, were rebuffed by the diocese "citing a judicial gag order." Regarding the substance of the *Tennessean's* coverage, however, the article concluded that the church, for its part, was not blameless: "Even as described by the church's lawyers, the facts indicate that church officials could have done a better job supervising McKeown after learning of his pedophilia. But, as the trial court ruled, that doesn't make the diocese legally responsible for two boys McKeown molested years after he left the priesthood. In all likelihood, the Court of Appeals will agree." One interpretation of this statement is that, although Nashville diocesan officials may have done problematic things in the past, which foreshadowed what we would come to learn about the Archdiocese of Boston and other dioceses during the 2002 phase of the clergy sexual abuse scandal, the lawsuit that arose from McKeown's abuse as an inactive priest may likely result in a finding, even on appeal, that holds the diocese legally blameless.

The original judge's ruling to dismiss the lawsuit was made in 2001, a time of national media inattention to clergy sexual abuse in the Catholic Church. The Court of Appeals, however, heard oral arguments on 5 August 2002, in the midst of the media blitz occasioned by the Boston scandal, with a ruling expected some time after. The purpose of the appeal was to overturn the original judge's finding that the case did not have enough legal merit to be brought before a jury. On 6 August 2002, the *Tennessean* reported the legal interchange. Lawyers for both sides agreed that the case was now in uncharted legal waters because of the plaintiffs' novel theory attempting to link the church's prior behavior in regard to McKeown-the-priest to the plight of future victims abused by McKeown-the-former-priest. The church argued that such a theory would open "Pandora's box" and allow liability claims to be brought against organizations that have acted responsibly in the past in their dismissal of a troublesome and dangerous employee if that employee injures someone in the future. "We want the right . . . to allow a jury to decide whether this conduct is what we expect from leaders of our community, let alone a church in our community," countered a lawyer for the plaintiffs. The diocesan paper, for its part, concluded: "The attorneys representing the diocese felt as though the questions asked of both sides by the panel of three appeals court justices indicate that they understand the legal arguments before them, and that they have reviewed the voluminous written filings in this appeal" (*Tennessee Register*, 16 August 2002).

On the heels of the oral arguments concerning the McKeown lawsuit appeal, the bishop met with the Nashville chapter of Voice of the Faithful on 17 August in a local Catholic parish. He gave an update on the latest national and diocesan church response to the scandal, and told the audience that not only would the diocesan clergy sexual abuse review panel membership be updated to bring it in line with the U.S. bishops' call for independent laity review groups, but the diocese was also in the process of establishing a lay pastoral council to facilitate ongoing participation by the laity in diocesan affairs. The group appreciatively acknowledged that it was rare for bishops to meet with Voice of the Faithful groups, but, understandably, because of the prevailing upset over the national clergy sexual abuse scandal, reactions to the meeting were mixed. They ranged from, "He's telling us that there are no priests in the Diocese of Nashville that have a credible allegation of sexual abuse against them.... That sounds straightforward, and I believe him," to "I wasn't very impressed at all with the bishop's answers.... I thought he was being evasive" (*Tennessean*, 18 August 2002).

The Nashville bishop's willingness to meet with Voice of the Faithful and listen to its viewpoints and concerns was important, potentially a watershed event for the diocese. This willingness may have been motivated by a renewed appreciation for Vatican II's call for increased lay participation in church affairs, spurred now by the laity's horror at the way the church hierarchy has been handling the clergy sexual abuse scandal. It may have been motivated by the pressure brought by the *Tennessean's* coverage of the McKeown case and related matters. Whatever the reason, the diocese's willingness to communicate more freely and openly with its people may signal a promising change of course. One can only hope that this apparent shift in the direction of meaningful laity involvement—unfortunately still uncommon in most dioceses across the U.S., especially in Cardinal Law's Boston—will be followed with additional good-faith efforts.[11] After facing the many challenges and vagaries of the McKeown case, the Diocese of Nashville had the opportunity to serve as a model—a model characterized by willingness to face the truth that the Nashville church may have been exercising coercive power by discouraging participatory decision making, with consequent threat to people's sense of community; a model that uses human development and community-enhancing power to liberate the church to function as the People of God.

Taking a long view of the McKeown legal proceedings, the plaintiffs' lawyers' attempt to make the "outrageous conduct" argument regarding the church's responsibility toward those victimized by McKeown after he left the formal priesthood was novel, even exotic, controversial, and virtually certain to have had problems in the courts. A legal precedent that might have applied to the Catholic Church throughout the United States for sexual abuse committed by formerly active priests has so far not been set. Putting aside the validity of that argument, questions remain about clergy sexual abuse and the church community in the social domain of the clergy sexual abuse system, both in Nashville and throughout the church.

Before identifying some of the generalizable questions arising from the McKeown case, fairness requires that I put the actions of the Diocese of Nashville in perspective. As reported in the preceding narrative, the diocese has apparently been home to very few clergy sexual abusers over the years, and there is no credible evidence that any currently active priest has abused children. McKeown and Richards were moved from assignment to assignment during the 1970s and 1980s; however, church officials only learned of their abuse in the mid-1980s. Subsequently, although there were several problematic aspects of church officials' handling of these priests, these problems pale in comparison to what we have been learning about the Archdiocese of Boston and many other dioceses throughout the country and the world. Moreover, the diocese seems to have been among the early adopters of a systematic clergy sexual abuse policy. Although it has been the target of a large, potentially precedent-setting civil suit and the subject of numerous critical media stories since 1999, it has fared better than most other dioceses. Trust in the Nashville church has eroded somewhat, but not nearly as much as in Boston. Secrecy and lack of transparency, blaming-the-victim legal tactics, and inadequate involvement of the laity are the major negative features of the diocese's clergy sexual abuse legacy. The bishop's recent willingness to meet with the Voice of the Faithful and to increase participatory decision making, however, bode well for the future. Victims are still angry and frustrated, and some parents are still fearful, but church officials are becoming more open rather than retreating behind the walls of legalism and the arrogant exercise of power. Finally, it should be noted that on September 22, 2003, the Tennessee Court of Appeals upheld the original 2002 ruling that exonerated the Diocese of Nashville, although plaintiffs may attempt to advance the case to the Tennessee Supreme Court.

## QUESTIONS AND ISSUES ATTENDANT TO
## THE MCKEOWN CASE

A story appeared in the 22 May 2002 issue of the *Tennessean* with this headline: "Minister has record as sex offender." The piece focused on the pastor of a middle Tennessee Protestant congregation, alleged to have sexually abused a number of children. What is striking about this story is that it was one of the newspaper's few reports over the years of non-Catholic clergy sexual abuse of children. Undoubtedly, some people in Nashville were surprised to learn the problem occurs in other than Catholic religious settings. Others probably thought it was about time other denominations were placed in the public spotlight, feeling that much of the coverage, both locally and nationally, has unjustly focused on Catholic cases to the exclusion of other denominations. Then we have the issue, touched on briefly at the end of the McKeown saga, of whether or not anti-Catholic bias has motivated the media coverage. Two questions worth posing, then, are: (1) Is clergy sexual abuse of children mostly a phenomenon within the Catholic context?[12] and (2) What is the evidence for media bias in reporting the phenomenon?

McKeown's history of being molested by a priest as a child, presumably helping cause his own sexual dysfunction, suggests two further questions: (1) How far back in history can we document the existence of clergy sexual abuse in the Catholic Church, and, relatedly, is the spate of cases since 1985 indicative of the emergence of a new social problem or merely the result of increased pub-

lic awareness, possibly brought on by an explosion of media coverage and related factors? (2) Could the church have done more in detecting the likelihood
of future sexual abusers in those entering the seminary and in screening such
persons out of training for the priesthood?

The similarity of McKeown's career in the church as a child sexual abuser
to that of his friend and fellow ex-priest, Franklin Richards, as well as to a number of other clergy sexual abusers, leads to these questions: (1) Are these men
similar psychologically, or do the ways the church has typically called on priests
to conduct their ministry across a variety of settings provide a supportive context for acting out their sexual impulses with children? (These two possibilities,
of course, are not mutually exclusive.) Relatedly, (2) is there something inherent in the way the Catholic Church operates, in its exercise of power, its "corporate culture" (for example, its hierarchical/paternalistic, even monarchical,
structure; the nature of its ideology) that leads its officials to handle clergy sexual abuse in what many people believe to be an overly secretive, nontranspar-
ent, defensive, and imperious manner? (3) What has been the motivation of
church officials in handling these kinds of cases, in light of the fact that many
observers, Catholic and non-Catholic alike, have criticized the church for being more concerned with preserving and protecting the church as an institution than with safeguarding the welfare of its members?

Clergy sexual abuse is the stuff of lawsuits, especially where the Catholic
Church is concerned. Although the McKeown case is unique in focusing on
the actions of church officials several years before a formerly active priest molested his victims, the church's approach to the lawsuit was unsettling to many
observers. One might pose these questions: (1) What is it about the Catholic
Church that makes it such a ready target of litigation over the harm claimed to
result from clergy sexual abuse? (2) Is the media's handling of these invariably
high-profile court cases accurate and fair, or do the media play a role in encouraging potential plaintiffs to go to court for redress, in the first place, and
then provide a forum for their lawyers to try the case in public, easily tapping
into the public's fears of large institutions, religious and otherwise? (3) Is the
church ethically justified in using any available legal defense—for example,
blaming the victim—to protect itself from claims made for fiscal damages attendant on clergy sexual abuse, damages that are often thought to be exorbitant

and unjust? Or should the Christian ethic of love and compassion limit the maneuvers the church allows its attorneys to use in its name?

The use and abuse of power is central to the whole of the clergy sexual abuse system—from the general climate of power and control permeating the church hierarchy's relationships to both the laity and priests; to the abuse of power at the heart of the abusing priest's molestation of children; to the power tactics used by the Vatican, the bishops, and other church officials in dealing with abuse once discovered. Key questions, then, include: (1) Is manipulative and coercive power a necessary feature of the way the Catholic Church operates, or are alternative views of the church available? (2) Can the clergy sexual abuse crisis become an occasion for redistributing power in the Catholic Church, such that more transparent, open, and participatory governance that enhances collegiality and the role of the laity and pays more attention to cultural and national diversity and the principle of subsidiarity becomes the norm?

All these questions regarding the clergy sexual abuse system are interrelated, and they do not admit of simple answers. Moreover, a thorough examination of the clergy sexual abuse phenomenon should acknowledge and address the various theories that have been proposed to account for it. Fran Ferder and John Heagle, in the *National Catholic Reporter* (10 May 2002), have succinctly described several of the more salient and controversial theories sparked by Cardinal Law's plight in Boston:

> *The ancient history theory*: Most of these are old cases. They happened 20 or 30 years ago. Implied in this response is the assumption that fewer more recently ordained men have abused minors or are likely to do so.
>
> *The rotten fruit theory*: Every organization has a few "bad apples" in the bushel. The vast majority of priests (usually cited close to 98 percent) are dedicated individuals who would never abuse a child.
>
> *The ontological sameness theory*: Priests are only human. They can be expected to have the same weaknesses and dysfunctions that characterize other males in our culture.
>
> *The Vatican theory*: This is primarily a problem of materialistic, self-indulgent industrialized cultures such as the United States, Canada, and Europe.
>
> *The "gays did it" theory*: Since most victims of clergy sexual abuse are boys, homosexual priests must be responsible.

*The lax morals theory*: Priests who sexually abuse minors represent a logical outcome of a permissive attitude toward sexual morals fostered by liberal theologians.

*The media conspiracy theory*: The press is out to get Catholics. When Protestant ministers, teachers, scout leaders, and athletic coaches molest minors, it doesn't attract the same national attention. (It might, if 2,000 of them were reported for doing it.)

*The celibacy theory*: Some priests are driven to molest minors because of the frustrations caused by imposing a lifetime of sexual abstinence on them.

Except for the celibacy theory, the others listed by Ferder and Heagle have typically been advanced to defend the basic soundness of the church as an institution. No single theory, regardless of ideological orientation, is adequate without careful consideration of the others and of many additional ethical, human science, and ecclesiological factors. I begin to address some of the foregoing questions and theories in chapter 2, where I attempt to place the McKeown story in the context of other cases of clergy sexual abuse of children over the years in the Catholic Church and beyond, in order to expand our understanding of the clergy sexual abuse system.

++++++++++++++++++++++++++++++++++++++++++++++++++++

# CHAPTER TWO

# Clergy Sexual Abuse in the World

*The tale of widespread sexual abuse of children by Roman Catholic*
*priests riveted people's attention not just because it demonstrated that abusers*
*in general could appear in benign guises, but because it contradicted every*
*expectation that people had about Catholic priests in particular.*

—Frank Bruni and Elinor Burkett, *A Gospel of Shame*

JOKES TOLD BY late-night comedians often concern social phenomena of broad public concern—ironically, fit issues for serious public discourse. Interestingly, it took David Letterman several months after the events of September 11 to begin telling Osama bin Laden jokes, which then turned up almost nightly in his opening monologues. Similarly, after the story of the clergy sexual abuse situation in the Archdiocese of Boston broke in early 2002, it took Letterman some time before he very gingerly introduced the topic, only gradually increasing the frequency and intensity of his comedic focus. Although both terrorism and clergy sexual abuse got rapidly expanding media coverage immediately after the public first learned about them—as for example did President Clinton's sexual escapades with Monica Lewinsky and the Enron scandal— unlike Monicagate and Enrongate, these topics apparently were too shocking and sensitive to become the immediate butt of jokes. That terrorism and clergy sexual abuse took time to become topics of irreverent comedic attention suggests public sensitivity and depth of feeling; that they finally arrived on the

53

comedy scene with staying power suggests the breadth of public awareness and interest. Despite certain claims of media hype and exaggeration, it is fair to say that the acts of terrorists and of abusing priests, and those who cover up for them, have significantly, perhaps permanently, changed social reality.

My purpose in this chapter is to build upon the analysis of the McKeown story that I have presented and to extend that analysis of the clergy sexual abuse system beyond Nashville to the many places the scandal is developing in the church. Later in the chapter, I specifically compare the situations of the Diocese of Nashville and the Archdiocese of Boston.

## MORAL CRISIS OR MORAL PANIC?

For those wanting to place a particular social phenomenon at the top of the public agenda, likening it to the events of September 11 is among the currently favorite rhetorical devices. As the clergy sexual abuse story grew in the first half of 2002, certain critics and observers attempted to shape its social reality by claiming it had September 11–like implications for the Catholic Church, claims already on the verge of becoming clichéd and trite. A lingering question, however, has infiltrated public consciousness: Is the Catholic Church's clergy sexual abuse scandal indeed a moral crisis, or is it merely a moral panic? Following Philip Jenkins's (1998) use of these terms, if clergy sexual abuse is a *moral crisis*, the attendant extensive media coverage would be justified because of the breadth and depth of the problem and the harm done to innocent persons, to the church, and to society at large. We must go to the root of such a moral crisis and search for meaningful structural reform. Alternatively, the Catholic Church may be the victim of a misconceived *moral panic*. The media, both Catholic and non-Catholic, have perhaps mistakenly and unfairly exaggerated both the gravity and the extent of clergy sexual abuse. Using this issue as the rationale for structural church reform, therefore, would be wrongheaded and ideologically motivated. A moral crisis calls for intervention and organizational reform; a moral panic calls for debunking and reform of mistaken understandings.

Jenkins, a source frequently cited by church defenders, is probably the leading advocate of the moral panic interpretation of clergy sexual abuse in his books *Pedophiles and Priests* (1996/2000), *Moral Panic* (1998), and *The New Anti-Catholicism* (2003). In his 24 March 2002 article in the *Sunday Visitor*, Jenkins said the "scandal is nothing as sinister as it has been painted—or, at least, it should not be used to launch blanket accusations against the Catholic Church as a whole." He didn't urge that we ignore the problem. His "concern over the 'pedophile priest' issue is not to defend evil clergy, or a sinful Church (I cannot be called a Catholic apologist, since I am not Catholic)." Rather, he worried that "justified anger over a few awful cases might be turned into ill-focused attacks against innocent clergy. The story of clerical misconduct is bad enough without turning it into an unjustifiable outbreak of religious bigotry against the Catholic Church." Fair and reasonable people can certainly join Jenkins in wishing to avoid blaming the vast majority of priests who have never been sexual abusers and in not wanting to exacerbate bigotry against the church or to contribute to anti-Catholic sentiment. Yet the changes in social reality wrought by the recent clergy sexual abuse scandal in the Catholic Church are so broad and deep that the church and its members, and society more generally, might profitably look for root causes and entertain the possibility that an agenda for organizational change may need to be developed.

Interest in clergy sexual abuse in the U.S. Catholic Church has waxed and waned since the mid-1980s, with particularly notorious cases periodically serving as the focus of media attention and public concern. Among the cast of characters, there was Gilbert Gauthé in Louisiana in the late 1980s; James Porter in Massachusetts and Rudy Kos in Dallas in the 1990s; Chicago's Cardinal Joseph Bernardin, the victim of widely heralded and eventually discredited sexual abuse charges in the mid-1990s; and, most recently, Fathers John Geoghan and Paul Shanley, among others, in Boston and beyond in 2002. Each time, the reported harm done to innocent victims shocks and overwhelms the public anew, and there are calls for reform of both the church and societal institutions implicated in the problem. Reformers propose changes, and some are even implemented, but the furor eventually subsides, the status quo eventually returns, and the more things seem to have changed, the more they seem to have remained the same.

But the *Boston Globe*'s coverage of the Geoghan and Shanley stories that began in earnest on 31 January 2002—focusing especially on Cardinal Law's unsuccessful attempts to manage and cover up their abuse in order to avoid scandal and protect the church—moved the clergy sexual abuse phenomenon to new and unprecedented levels of public awareness and concern. There was talk of sea changes and paradigm shifts, stimulated by the very newspaper on which Cardinal Law had called down the wrath of God because of its coverage of the Porter case in the early 1990s.

One immediate product of the *Globe*'s coverage was the publication of *Betrayal: The Crisis in the Catholic Church*, a muckraking book and winner of a 2003 Pulitzer Prize, written by the *Globe*'s investigative staff. The book became available in June 2002—scarcely five months after the eruption of the worldwide media attention the paper had sparked by its 31 January 2002 watershed story and by its lawsuit that succeeded in making public thousands of pages of formerly secret documents embarrassing to the Archdiocese of Boston.

Defenders of the Catholic Church, especially in the Vatican, have often called the clergy sexual abuse story peculiarly American and, à la Jenkins, one of extremely limited scope—in effect, a very small tempest in a very large teapot: a moral panic. But, as reported in *Betrayal*: "Across the country, and across the Catholic world, priests implicated in abuse were pulled from assignments—176 in the United States alone in the first four months of 2002" (7). Further: "There were stories about clergy sexual abuse in virtually every state in the Union. The scandal reached Ireland, Mexico, Austria, France, Chile, Australia, and Poland, the homeland of the Pope" (99). Since January 2002 alone, the authors might also have included Argentina, Brazil, Canada, Costa Rica, Germany, Guatemala, Hong Kong, Italy, Malta, New Zealand, the Philippines, Puerto Rico, Scotland, South Africa, Switzerland, and the United Kingdom. New countries seem to enter the list regularly.

In a 12 June 2002 story, moreover, the *Dallas Morning News* reported the results of an extensive survey conducted by newspaper staff members alleging that "at least 111 of the nation's 178 mainstream, or Roman rite, Catholic dioceses are headed by men who have protected accused priests or other church figures."[1] Adding this recent cluster of incidents to the prior periods of notorious clergy sexual abuse scandals, it seems as if clergy sexual abuse may have touched every place the Catholic Church operates, entailing a yet to be determined number of abusing priests and a yet to be determined, but far greater, number of victims.

Throughout the world in 2002, the U.S. Catholic Church has generated the lion's share of media coverage of what have typically been "old" clergy sexual abuse cases, ones that occurred before 1990; however, the claim that what we have is a passé, mostly American, phenomenon is open to serious challenge (Steinfels, *New York Times*, 4 May 2002; Steinfels 2003; Weigel 2002). In navigating the clergy sexual abuse waters, we should keep in mind (a) that although the majority of reported clergy sexual abusers were active before 1990, we know virtually nothing about the extent of possible or likely recent and ongoing cases; (b) that the ways of the American media make public reporting more likely than in many other countries, which may have comparable rates of clergy sexual abuse; and (c) that the ways of the American legal system make it likely both that cases will be reported and that they will get protracted and controversial attention because of lawsuits brought against the church.

Numbers alone, moreover, should not settle the question of whether clergy sexual abuse in the Catholic Church is a moral panic or a moral crisis. Large public organizations or private corporations often behave defensively when one or several employees or officials are exposed as perpetrators of outrageous acts. In defense, they claim that only a very small percentage of the organization's members are involved—witness the rationalizations that filled the air in early 2002 about Enron and related business scandals. In effect, so the argument goes, a few isolated apples have gone rotten—their acts are regrettable, albeit not preventable, and to be expected in any large organization. The organization, therefore, should not be subject to blanket indictment. This is a moral panic argument that attempts to rationalize and contain the destructive effects of public relations disasters. Sometimes ingenuously, such organizations may add that even these few cases are too many because of the seriousness of the acts—hinting, but stopping well short of acknowledging, that there may be something deeper than an overblown moral panic.

Defensive explanations of this sort have been offered by church officials and defenders over the years concerning clergy sexual abuse. But what about cases, even if there is only a relatively small number, where Catholic priests have abused their power by sexually molesting parishioners, especially minor children, and where, in the interests of avoiding scandal and protecting the church's power, authority, and reputation as a "sinless" institution, bishops have moved these priests from place to place, allowing them to molest even more unsuspecting innocent victims in the future? Even a few cases of this nature in an organization like the Catholic Church, which publicly proclaims its moral authority and sinlessness, especially in the realm of human sexuality, might indeed be too many and might signal the possibility that a moral crisis affects the larger organization. Why might this be so?

Any given instance of clergy sexual abuse has personal, relational, and social implications. From the standpoint of professional ethics, a priest is a professional, a parishioner is a client, and mutual trust between them is required for a meaningful ministerial relationship to operate, one that benefits the parishioner and the larger church community (Lebacqz 1985). We should keep in mind, however, that this professional perspective, while important and useful, is only a secular and surface understanding of the ministry of Catholic priests. While priests are professionals we can view through the lens of professional ethics, in the mind of Catholics their sacred and sacramental office goes well beyond that of a secular professional, as do their moral/ethical obligations to those to whom they minister. In the face-to-face relationship between a priest and a child, the typical power discrepancy between a professional and a client, as, for example, between a therapist and a client, is greatly magnified (Dokecki 1996, chap. 3). This is so partly because the professional is a priest, partly because the client is a child, and partly because the relationship is in the context of the church.

Catholic children are socialized from their earliest years to see the church ("mother church") and the priest ("father") as trusted means to achieving their most important ends—the salvation of their immortal soul, the avoidance of eternal punishment in hell, and the achievement of the perfect end to a good life, the beatific vision—living happily with God in heaven for eternity. Catholic schools and religious education teach children very early *the* answers to life's most fundamental questions:

Who made me? God made me. Why did God make me? God made me to know, love, and serve Him in this world and be happy with Him in the next. We should love God with our whole being and love our neighbor as our self.

These rote slogans eventually become taken-for-granted, comforting, and demanding truths, reinforced in the classroom, in other Catholic settings, and at home.

So Catholic children grow up influenced by teachers, family members, peers, and church community members, most of whom believe what they believe and reinforce each other in their beliefs. It is within this context that we must attempt to understand the meaning of the breach of trust between minor children and priests who abuse their power and sacramental mystique by abusing and harming them. Abuse by priests violates the social covenant that is the church—the abuse violates the children; the abuse violates the relationship between children and priests (believed to be God's surrogates); the abuse violates the church.

Although sexual abuse by teachers, scout masters, coaches, or professional persons may violate children, such abuse pales by comparison to their abuse by priests, because the life of children in the Catholic Church entails their total immersion in the church's powerful and tightly woven webs of beliefs and social relationships. Frank Bruni and Elinor Burkett (1993/2002, 138) quoted a therapist who worked with clergy sexual abuse victims as saying: "I've seen kids abused by a YMCA leader. I've seen kids abused by Boy Scout leaders. This is different. These victims were much more vulnerable and much more traumatized. They didn't respect their own parents. They didn't respect their own Church. They didn't respect anyone. They were completely empty. I saw bodies, empty bodies. That's something I had not seen before in my work."

Similarly, although there are clergy sexual abusers in other religious denominations, possibly even in proportionally equal or greater numbers than in the Catholic Church (although there are no reliable data on which to base such estimates), it is likely that their victims' experience of violation is not as fundamental as that of Catholic children, again because of Catholic children's degree of enmeshment in pervasive Catholic social reality. Bruni and Burkett quoted a Protestant minister who works with congregations bruised by clergy sexual abuse as saying: "If a Methodist is abused by a minister, he can simply become a Presbyterian. Catholics don't have that choice. They've been taught that theirs is the only true Church" (139).

Altar boys are among the typical targets of clergy child sexual abusers.[2] Imagine the situation of an altar boy molested by a priest early one morning in the church sacristy as they both don their vestments for mass. The boy's family encouraged and prodded him to undertake the preparation necessary to be an altar boy, stressing the honor it would bring the family for him to serve at mass. That morning, he proudly and nervously anticipates serving mass in front of the congregation, probably including his parents, at the single most important public event in his parish church, the holy sacrifice of the mass. He feels honored to help the priest minister to his friends and family by mediating between them and God in the recreation of Christ's sacrifice on the cross, making possible the congregation's receipt of the body and blood of Christ in holy communion. What must it feel like in this context when, in the solemnity and privacy of mass preparation time, his priest touches him sexually and forces him to do the same to him, or masturbates him and forces him to reciprocate, or forces him to commit fellatio or have anal intercourse? To add insult to this injury, when the morning's nightmare is over, the priest tells him that what they did is perfectly normal, despite what he has learned in his religious education; that God thinks it is OK, for after all, a priest represents God; that he must not tell anyone because no one will believe him; that if he should tell, he will burn in hell, or his family will be harmed. And the boy suspects, rather is certain, that the priest will abuse him again, and again. In fact, an unknown number of clergy sexual abusers repeatedly molest a given child, as well as many others, in living out the life of a serial sexual predator.

It should come as no surprise that such victims typically initially experience shock, fear, confusion, and physical, psychological, and spiritual pain. The abuse shatters their basic sense of trust and personal well-being. They are terrified to tell anyone what was done to them, including, perhaps especially, their parents, siblings, friends, and those in authority. In the long run, often the very long run, many victims experience anxiety, depression, alienation, and fear of relationships and intimacy. They often manifest antisocial behavior, alcohol or drug abuse, and problems coping with the demands of everyday life. As in the case of McKeown, they may act out the reverse golden rule—do unto others as others have done unto you—by becoming sexual abusers themselves. In other words, at the personal level, the immediate and long-term consequences of clergy sexual abuse for victims are disruptive, harmful, and pose threats to their human development. The accounts and histories of many victims/survivors clearly show that they have been fundamentally and unalterably damaged. This explains, in part, the position of victim/survivor advocacy groups that even a single act of clergy sexual abuse should be regarded as a cataclysmic event, and that the offending priest should be totally and permanently removed from the priesthood.[3]

Disruptive and harmful consequences do not stop with the person of the abused child. Clergy sexual abuse also seriously affects the relational realm, especially the church's ability to be a caring and nurturing community that fosters spiritual growth and development, provides social support during many of life's crises, and fosters a psychological sense of community among the faithful. Caring and nurturing occur in face-to-face relationships grounded in trust. Clergy sexual abuse destroys many victims' ability to trust priests, as well as other people in the church and people in general. Once clergy sexual abuse becomes known, victims' parents, fellow parishioners, and Catholics more generally also experience an erosion of trust in the church. They become suspicious of their once respected and trusted priests, and their sense of community is threatened: their sense of membership and belonging to the church may weaken; their sense of shared values and emotional connection with others in the church may diminish; their experience of being with others in the church to help meet each others' needs for social support, meaning, and spiritual growth may erode; and their sense of influencing and being influenced by others in using their power to affect what happens in the church may decline. As we have seen, the vast majority of priests who are not sexual abusers may also become alienated. They wonder what people think of them, often being overly cautious about relating warmly and personally to their parishioners for fear they

Archdiocese of Boston to paint a biased and distorted picture of the clergy sexual abuse situation in the Catholic Church. He maintained, among his many criticisms of the media, that coverage had been one-sided and had tended to ignore two facts: namely, nearly all of the reported cases occurred during the 1970s and 1980s, and many dioceses had made great strides in altering their mode of operation in dealing with clergy sexual abuse since the early 1990s. He also complained bitterly of the tendency to overgeneralize to "the church," "the clergy," and "the bishops" based on a very small number of cases. Statement 2 came from a 13 June 2002 invited address to the historic meeting of the United States Conference of Catholic Bishops in Dallas held to address the clergy sexual abuse scandal. The author? Margaret O'Brien Steinfels, editor of *Commonweal Magazine* and wife of Peter Steinfels. While her husband was wary about calls for reform based on the clergy sexual abuse scandal, Margaret Steinfels took the rare opportunity for a layperson to address the bishops to call for reform, especially regarding the laity's role in church decision-making.

So, is clergy child sexual abuse in the Catholic Church a moral crisis or a moral panic? The answer cannot be "objectively" or definitively given, because precious little reliable information exists on the extent of the problem. This is partly because the church has discouraged the systematic collection of data over the years. In his article in *The Tablet*, Peter Steinfels observed: "The one kind of response that could have received a hearing was hard data: how many dioceses had established lay-run review boards? Screening in their seminaries? Counselling programmes for victims? Exactly how many instances of predatory priests had come to light, over what period of time, and how had they been resolved? Tragically, the national bishops' conference had never been mandated to collect such information." In that regard, it should be noted that in July 2002 the American Catholic bishops finally called for, and pledged to cooperate in, the creation of an accurate database on abusing priests and victims, although a number of bishops resisted or only reluctantly participated in this database effort. And regarding statistics, as I have noted, the number of currently identified abusing priests and victims underestimates to an unknown degree the actual number of past and present cases because of victims' reluctance to report and the church's secrecy in responding to the problem. A 29 September 2002 article in the Louisville *Courier-Journal* reported David Clohessy's argument "that it would be 'absolute folly' to conclude the numbers show that fewer priests are molesting children. [Clohessy] said children victimized now and in recent years aren't likely to come forward until 2010 or 2020—until they undergo some kind of triggering event that makes them realize they were abused and can do something about it." More fundamentally, the moral crisis versus moral panic judgment cannot be made validly by mere identification and cataloguing of particular cases, however accurate and current the count may be, unless we interpret the numbers in the context of the personal, relational, and social webs of meaning and relationship that constitute the Catholic Church.

After considering the details of the McKeown case, and in light of what I have just presented about clergy sexual abuse in the world, one can reasonably conclude that *clergy child sexual abuse is a moral crisis*. My earlier Nashville-based suspicion that this might be the case crystallized and grew in light of all that has come to light since early 2002—in Boston and throughout the United States and the world—in the aftermath of Cardinal Law's handling of clergy sexual abuse. Adding to this an account of the personal meanings and social consequences of clergy sexual abuse for the social reality of all involved—child victims and their families; the laity and ministers; the society at large—confirms how truly significant the clergy sexual abuse crisis really is. Given the importance of what has happened in Boston, I now consider the complexities and implications of this still-developing explosive situation with its local, national, and world consequences.

## THE JOURNALISTIC SHOT HEARD 'ROUND THE WORLD

Cardinal Bernard F. Law was at the center of the clergy sexual abuse maelstrom of 2002. In a review of *Betrayal* in the *New York Times*, Scott Appleby wrote that, as portrayed in the book, Cardinal Law "is a fascinating and tragic figure. Clearly a man of great faith, dedication and loyalty, Bernard Law has upheld the church's noblest traditions of compassion and social justice in his service to the new immigrant communities; in his unswerving commitment to the protection and dignity of human life; in his crusade for civil rights and condemnations of racism, both in the South of his early episcopal career and as cardi-

credibly intense international media scrutiny and drafted a clergy sexual abuse framework and norms; they submitted them to the Vatican, which asked for many revisions. Cardinal Law once again went secretly to Rome to discuss his fate with the pope, but this time his tendered resignation was accepted. The public continued to express its anger, concern, frustration, and disappointment at what were perceived as the church's continually inadequate policies and actions. I deal with this reform-oriented chain of events in chapter 5, placing them in the context of the search for needed church reform.

## A COMPARATIVE LOOK AT THE CLERGY SEXUAL ABUSE SYSTEM IN NASHVILLE AND BOSTON

With the foregoing overview in mind, I begin by exploring the situations of four abusing priests—Nashville's Edward McKeown, in his late fifties and currently in prison, and Franklin Richards, in his mid to late fifties and living in Florida (about whom we know very little); and Boston's infamous John Geoghan, in his mid to late sixties when he was murdered in prison in August 2003, and Paul Shanley, in his early seventies and awaiting criminal trial. Since no empirical studies exist describing and analyzing the common essentials and the range of clergy sexual abuse specifics, the purpose of this comparative analysis is to expand the Nashville narrative and search for patterns that give hints about the most important processes comprising the overall phenomenon. In many respects, each case of clergy sexual abuse, with its own contexts, dynamics, consequences, and human particulars, is unique. Although a universal template may not exist, and I do not pretend to offer one here, I do intend to create a reasonably detailed sketch—useful in subsequent chapters when viewed from the vantage points of professional ethics, human science, and ecclesiology—in pursuit of implications for reform.

## The Contexts

I begin with the demographic aspects of these priests' working environments. As I have noted, the Diocese of Nashville is 16,302 square miles in size and has 69,480 Catholics (3.3 percent of the population), fifty-one parishes, and sixty-nine active priests (including religious order and extern priests), or about one priest for every 1,007 Catholics. In contrast, the Archdiocese of Boston is geographically smaller (2,465 square miles), but Catholics are much more numerous, and Catholicism is the majority religion—2,069,225 Catholics out of a total population of 3,857,751 (54 percent)—with 362 parishes and 1,302 active priests (including religious order and extern priests), about one priest for every 1,589 Catholics, even more thinly spread than in Nashville (*Official Catholic Directory* 2002). We can truly say that Boston is a "Catholic town" and, as in Nashville, priests there are scarce resources, crucial for the church's various ministries, especially saying mass and administering the sacraments. Beyond these demographics and the greater number of ethnic neighborhoods in urban Boston compared to Nashville's typically ethnically mixed "middle American" character, the day-to-day lives of the clergy and the Catholic laity in the two cities seem to be roughly comparable.

Although Nashville's Catholic minority is visible and has become generally accepted without prejudice over the years, Catholics in modern-day Boston are everywhere, often occupying the highest business, government, and media positions. For years, these officials often "looked the other way" or otherwise tolerated scandalous behavior on the part of Boston-area priests and church officials. In 2002, reflecting a major shift in attitude toward the church, Catholics have been the most vocal critics of the church's handling of Boston's clergy sexual abuse scandal—though we should remember that Catholics have also been visible and vocal critics of the church in Nashville.

## The Priests

As young men, Southerners McKeown and Richards and New Englanders Geoghan and Shanley did not accumulate much worldly experience, since they were all ordained as diocesan priests in their mid to late twenties. Seminary reforms, such as they may be, in the area of helping future priests explore the meaning of celibacy and of sexual identity and maturity, were still in the offing, so none of these priests would have received much help to understand and come to grips with the challenges of their psychosexual development. And challenges there were. Significantly, McKeown and Shanley both claim that they themselves were victims of sexual abuse by priests as children, and Shanley claims that he was later abused as a seminarian. Seminary officials said Geoghan was quite immature and questioned his suitability for the priesthood. His monsignor uncle had to intercede to keep him from being expelled from his seminary studies. Richards's developmental history is unknown.

The Nashville priests had their first parish assignments in the early 1970s, just as the effects of Vatican II were beginning to be felt, the Boston priests in the early 1960s, on the cusp of Vatican II. As active priests, McKeown and Richards committed their abuse during the 1970s and 1980s, each admitting to having abused about twenty-five children. Geoghan and Shanley sexually abused children from the 1960s until the early to mid-1990s, the former having abused about 200 children, the latter, about thirty-five. Thus, the Nashvillians got started later and finished somewhat earlier than the Bostonians, with Geoghan by far the most prolific sexual predator. The priests' abusing actions did not arise from years of toiling in the often daunting priestly vineyard, nor were they occasioned by the possibility of long-standing celibacy-induced sexual frustration. They abused children from the earliest days of their priestly careers, apparently undetected (or unreported) during early parish assignments.

Males were the primary victims of all four priests, with Geoghan preferring prepubescent grammar school boys (some victims were as young as four) and the others leaning more, although apparently not exclusively, toward somewhat older pubescent boys. McKeown's victims were as young as ten but mostly in their early to middle teens; Richards's were altar boys and boys in high school; Shanley's were mostly adolescents and young adults (at least one was as young as six).[4] They sometimes lowered their victims' (and their own) sexual inhibitions with such devices as intimate conversation, playing strip poker, and using alcohol and drugs. Although we don't know specifically what Richards did to children, the others engaged in fondling, masturbatory acts, and various forms of oral and anal sex.

Regarding the particulars of abuse, all we know about Richards is that he victimized children from his parishes and during his tenure as principal at a Catholic high school. Beyond his parish assignments, Shanley served as a counselor to troubled youths for some of his career, seeking victims in the course of his highly visible street ministry and in his assigned parishes. Both McKeown and Geoghan often sought child victims who were vulnerable by virtue of coming from large single-parent families without male role models. Parents welcomed the priests into their homes and were grateful for the priestly attention paid to their children. Geoghan even assaulted some of his victims in their own beds, sometimes abusing several children in the same family during a given visit. It seems as if the four priests used virtually any setting for their acts, including churches, schools, counseling rooms, rectories or living quarters, automobiles, and hideaways.

In general, then, these priests took advantage of the status, mystique, and power inherent in their professional priestly role to prey on persons who were weak and vulnerable by virtue of their age and life circumstances. Sex between professionals and their clients is unethical and often criminal no matter what the age, gender, and status of the client, but, when priests-as-professionals have sexual encounters with vulnerable minor children, the potential for harm and the ethical/legal implications are greatly magnified.[5]

## Internal Church Response

When did their bishops first learn about the four priests' clergy sexual abuse? Richards was found out in 1984, McKeown in 1986, and Nashville's bishop sent them for treatment and subsequently reassigned them several times, subject to restrictions involving proximity to children. Nashville church officials claim to have reported the men to state child welfare officials but not to the police. Both men left the active priesthood in 1989. It is a matter of dispute whether the church paid McKeown hush money and paid settlement money to Richards's victims. After leaving the active priesthood, McKeown continued to molest children until 1999, and Richards claimed to have stopped abusing children after adopting an adult gay lifestyle. Subsequent to that time, there have been no known incidents of clergy sexual abuse among currently active Nashville priests.

In Boston, the bishop may have become aware of Geoghan's actions in the early 1960s and of Shanley's in 1967. They too received treatment, but whereas Richards and McKeown each received only one or two reassignments in

Nashville over a period of five or so years, several Boston bishops reassigned both Geoghan and Shanley numerous times over a period of more than thirty years. Boston church officials made many secret and confidential settlements involving the two priests along the way. Geoghan was finally forced to leave the active priesthood in 1998 and was in prison when he was brutally murdered in August 2003; Shanley is currently awaiting trial on multiple counts of indecent assault and battery and child rape but is still officially a priest. In all four cases, bishops kept the reasons for reassignment secret from past, present, and future parishioners, from other priests, and from the public. In addition, there is no evidence that Boston church officials reported the men to either state child welfare authorities or to the police. Whereas McKeown and Richards appear to have been the beginning and end of Nashville's recently trumpeted clergy sexual abuse scandal, the Geoghan and Shanley situations were merely the latest instances of a long-standing problem. The extensive media coverage of the cases unleashed a virtual tidal wave of additional cases, many of them reportedly known to Boston church officials for years, but kept secret until the early part of 2002, almost twenty years into Cardinal Law's tenure as leader of the Archdiocese of Boston.

## External Church Response

So far, we have looked at the two dioceses' reactions to their abusing priests mostly at the level of internal church workings. How did they react externally, beyond the chancery office, regarding the victims and their families, the media, the courts, the general public, and, perhaps most importantly for our purposes, the Catholic laity? While the two dioceses had similar general patterns of response to clergy sexual abuse, Boston church officials outstripped their Nashville counterparts at almost every turn regarding problematic and controversial, often believed to be "wrongheaded," actions that became the focus of critical attention. Nashville diocesan officials came across as secretive, legalistic, and at times uncaring. These tendencies, however, were much more pronounced in Boston, where the phrase "arrogance of power" was commonly heard from media critics and Catholics of all stripes. The contrasting styles of leadership might account for some of this difference—Nashville, mostly quietly defensive; Boston, in-your-face aggressive. The difference in approach may also reflect the Nashville church's minority status as compared to Boston's being a "Catholic town." Nashville's Catholic hierarchy operated in the shadow of the city's many Protestant churches, whereas Cardinal Law and his associates inherited the mantle of Boston Catholic cultural/religious preeminence.

The four priests' victims joined clergy sexual abuse victims across the country and the world in feeling angry and frustrated. They complained about the treatment they received over the years at the hands of church officials, again with wider and greater depth of feeling in Boston. Until recently, they strongly felt that church officials were not listening to them, were not acknowledging and taking responsibility for the harm and ongoing suffering they experienced at the hands of (initially) abusing priests and (subsequently) church officials. "They just don't get it" became the common characterization of the institutional church's response to clergy sexual abuse—"they" ranging from the Nashville and Boston bishops, to the U.S. bishops, and on up the hierarchy to Vatican officials and the pope. Both dioceses did offer victims the opportunity to receive counseling, eventually apologizing and voicing deep concern for their plight. True or not, most victims and many in the laity perceived these responses to be "too little, too late," because they seemed motivated more by intense media pressure and fiscal worries than by basic Christian justice and charity. Especially in Boston, many victims felt the hierarchy and its lawyers had mistreated and revictimized them in attempting to prevent or defend the numerous lawsuits they and their families brought against the church.

Not surprisingly, the institutional church and its defenders, on the one hand, and victims/survivors and many ordinary Catholics, on the other, have interpreted victims' decisions to sue the church quite differently. The former group have often claimed that the suits were products of overly litigious American society, the greed of victims and their lawyers, or ill will toward the church. The latter group viewed them as good-faith efforts initiated by Catholics who love the church but believe it must be helped to reform itself. In addition, the suits were viewed as matters of simple justice, of victims'/survivors' last-ditch desperate efforts to get the church to pay attention to their plight, and of preventing harm to future potential victims.

Over the years, accounts of the media's coverage of Catholic clergy sexual abuse cases have also varied—from assertions that the media often tended not to cover such cases in the past, either because of fear of the church's retribution or because of an overly tolerant and accepting attitude toward the church; to assertions, especially by church defenders, that anti-Catholic feeling was the prime motivation for the media's incessant and allegedly sensationalist coverage. As we have seen, the McKeown case and, collaterally, the Richards case have been covered extensively, and controversially, since 1999 by the Nashville media, especially the *Tennessean*. Since early 2002, the Geoghan and Shanley cases have received even more intense, negative, and controversial coverage than did the Porter case from the early 1990s. The media in New England, especially the *Boston Globe*, were joined by media outlets throughout the world because of Cardinal Law's stature and reputation in the United States church and in the Vatican. Moreover, both the *Tennessean* and the *Boston Globe* not only aggressively covered the scandals but also went to court and successfully argued that legal and church documents should be made public (e.g., appellate briefs in the McKeown case, Cardinal Law's depositions in the Geoghan and Shanley cases, and a variety of other church documents). The papers promptly, and controversially, made these materials available on their websites. These firsthand documents gave people the chance to make up their own minds. The resulting judgments, especially in Boston regarding the charges of church cover-ups, were devastating to the church and raised the clergy sexual abuse scandal to new and unprecedented levels. The *Globe* even went as far as using streaming media on its website to present Cardinal Law's actual testimony, and what came across to many was the picture of a paternalistic, defensive, legalistic, arrogant church leader with a very high frequency of "I can't recall" or "That wasn't my job" responses.

Whatever media motivations might have been, and they will be endlessly debated, the two dioceses were perhaps most similar on the matter of their approach to the media. Cardinal Law had dramatically called down the power of God on the *Boston Globe* for its early 1990s coverage of the Porter case, and he all but did the same in 2002 in his bitter complaints about media unfairness and the scandal it gave to the faithful and the general public. In Nashville, diocesan officials repeatedly cried foul, insisting that the *Tennessean's* coverage was inaccurate, incomplete, and misleading. The media portrayed church officials in both dioceses as saying, in effect: If you in the media only knew what we in our exalted and privileged position in the church know, you would see how misguided you are in your church-bashing muckraking journalism. Much of the public in the two dioceses, including many Catholics, tended to view the church's response as defensive at best and arrogantly stonewalling at worst. Many liberal and conservative Catholics, media people, and members of the public called the institutional church to openness, transparency, and accountability. To characterize the church's interactions with the media as public relations disasters would be to understate the results of these dioceses' failed media relations.

The extensive media coverage of the clergy sexual abuse scandal in both Nashville and Boston seemed to contribute to victims'/survivors' initial willingness to sue the church. The emerging minutely detailed coverage of the resulting court proceedings made the church look worse and worse, and seemed to have encouraged even more suits to be filed in Boston and throughout the country. As church officials gradually did admit liability, arriving at settlements was a tortuous process, with promises made and broken. When Cardinal Law finally committed $30 million to a settlement with many of Geoghan's victims in early 2002, he later went back on this commitment because of claimed disastrous consequences for diocesan finances and the crippling blow it would deal to the church's ability to carry out its various ministries to the poor and others in need. The eventual settlement for a portion of the cases was for $10 million. "I had no choice but to take the settlement. I couldn't take another five years of this. It sort of went on and on and on. I just caved in. I couldn't take it," said one of the plaintiffs (*Boston Globe*, 20 September 2002).

The Boston civil suits occasioned the highly unusual spectacle of an American prince of the church aggressively grilled in several depositions, which, as I have noted, were eventually made public. What did we learn? Recall the Diocese of Nashville's use of the comparative fault argument in the McKeown case: Any fault the church might have for the actions of its priests should be mitigated by comparative fault or co-responsibility borne by the families of the victims for their failure to protect their children or report their abuse in the past. In a videotaped segment of Cardinal Law's 6 June 2002 deposition in the Shanley case, one of the plaintiffs' lawyers asked the cardinal about diocesan lawyers' use of this argument regarding victims as young as six and their parents. The cardinal denied being aware that his lawyers had done so but acknowledged there were problems with the approach.[6] Critics complained that the church was hiding behind its lawyers. In the 31 May 2002 *National Catholic Reporter*, Diana L. Hayes, an associate professor of theology at Georgetown, asked:

> Are we really going to allow these men and women who are already victims to be victimized yet again? To countercharge negligence on the part of parents who entrusted their children to the care of priests and religious of the church is certainly viable legally but just as certainly not morally. It inflicts further harm, clouds the issues even further and, in the long run, will only further damage the credibility of the church and its leaders. Surely this is not the time to hide behind lawyers or to excuse our actions because they are or were based on legal advice. As people of God, we answer to a higher court. For these men of God, the question once again should not simply be how do we get out of this mess, which we have somehow created, with the least costs.

As in the Nashville case, this blaming-the-victim strategy revictimizes families in order to mitigate the church's potentially quite significant financial liability. Additionally, in the context of the church's perceived insensitivity to victims' suffering and the public's outrage and loss of trust in the church, when lawyers defend multimillion-dollar liability suits by using other aggressive and confrontational tactics that are fairly typical in such cases not involving the church, we can expect reactions to be negative and strong. People charge the church with protecting its power and assets by denying its Christian values of charity, compassion, and justice. This pattern of church actions seems to convey an overarching message: We must avoid scandal, protect the church's standing as a "sinless" institution, and preserve our power at any cost. So in defending against clergy sexual abuse allegations and suits, the ends justify the means.

A surprising and noteworthy departure from church officials' too typical use of hardball legal tactics ensued in the wake of Cardinal Law's departure from Boston in late 2002. Following the brief tenure of Law's interim successor, Bishop Richard Lennon, Bishop Sean O'Malley was installed as archbishop of Boston in July 2003. His selection was undoubtedly due, at least in part, to his prior experience in dealing with clergy sexual abuse and to his gentle, humble, and pastoral operating style. Immediately upon being appointed archbishop and assuming office, O'Malley's demeanor and public actions—for example, declining to live in palatial surroundings, reaching out pastorally to victims/survivors, and appointing a lawyer with a track record of working amicably with plaintiffs—seemed to signal his intent to settle pending lawsuits quickly and, perhaps, generously. In early September, after O'Malley's personal involvement in negotiations, lawyers for the diocese and the plaintiffs announced an $85 million settlement agreement to pay more than five hundred victims/survivors anywhere between $80,000 and $300,000 each, depending on the nature of the abuse (*New York Times*, 10 September 2003). This is possibly the highest award ever made in a clergy sexual abuse case, with prior major awards having included: $18 million by the Diocese of Lafayette, Louisiana, for a late 1980s case; over $100 million (reduced later to $31 million) by the Diocese of Dallas in 1998; $30 million (reduced to $13 million) by the Diocese of Stockton, California, in 1999; $5.2 million by the dioceses of Los Angeles and Orange County in 2001; $15 million by the Diocese of Tucson in 2002; $13.5 million by the Diocese of Providence, Rhode Island, in 2002; $10 million by the Archdiocese of Boston in the 2002 Geoghan settlement; $6.5 million by the Diocese of Manchester, New Hampshire, in 2003; and $25.7 million by the Archdiocese of Louisville, Kentucky, in 2003 (Associated Press, 10 September 2003). A significant outcome of the Boston agreement is that it provided payments for victim/survivor representation on the archdiocesan clergy sexual abuse review board and payments for treatment.

Reactions to the settlement agreement in Boston and beyond were generally positive. Many observers said that this was a watershed event in the clergy sexual abuse crisis and might serve as a stimulus and a model for other dioceses. Victims/survivors were ambivalent, on the one hand appreciating that the church had finally recognized and legitimated their victimization, and on the other hand insisting that money was never the issue. They were eager to see if church officials would go beyond money and rhetoric to acknowledge the harm they had suffered and to take steps to prevent clergy sexual abuse in the future (see, e.g., *Boston Herald*, 9 September 2003).

## The Laity

A crucial aspect of the church's external relations in dealing with clergy sexual abuse has been its relationship with its own people, the laity. In Vatican II's model of the church as the People of God, the laity are central to the church through participation in its *internal* workings and decision-making processes. The model of the church as preeminently a hierarchy, however, seems to place the laity in an *external* position: outside the inner sanctum, looking in at the workings of a clerical culture, like children expectantly and obediently worshiping their paternalistic fathers from afar. Many Catholics in Nashville and Boston, and beyond, have experienced the church's centralized and hierarchical culture as virtually excluding them from knowing about or deciding how to deal with clergy sexual abuse, a problem tearing apart their church and, often, their very lives. Clerical paternalism and its handmaiden, secrecy, relegated the laity to the role of angry and frustrated bystanders, increasingly outraged by information brought to light during court cases and in church documents finally made public by the courts.

Many Catholics judged the church decision-making processes that were coming to light to be problematic, at best, and wrongheaded, doomed to failure, and scandalous, at worst. Clergy sexual abuse allegations were often ignored, aggressively challenged, or not completely investigated, and were sometimes simply covered up. In Boston, bishops moved problematic priests from place to place during their early days as clergy sexual abusers without alerting the people and with little regard for what might happen to unsuspecting children and families. In Nashville, where church officials only learned of McKeown's and Richards's abuse many years into their priestly careers, reassignment only occurred during their final years in the active priesthood. Bishops in both dioceses refrained from reporting abusing priests to the police, but did send them for assessment and treatment, hoping and expecting to return them to priestly duty. Terminating clergy sexual abusers from public ministry seemed to be a last resort. On learning all this, as I have noted, a broad-based group of Boston Catholics decided to insert the laity into the situation by establishing Voice of the Faithful in February 2002. Nashville Catholics joined them in this now national movement in the summer of the same year. Before exploring the nature of this laity-involvement movement, it is helpful to step back and consider the context for its development.

The pre–Vatican II Catholic Church tended to operate in a decidedly paternalistic, nondemocratic fashion — even today we hear that the church is not a democracy and that the laity should pray, pay, and obey, since father knows best. After Vatican II, the church moved haltingly toward the more community-oriented, democratic, and participatory People of God model, but John Paul II's papacy has given rise to restorationist moves tending toward reversal of this trend. One should be clear at the outset that the church always had, has now, and, the clergy shortage aside, always will have fathers—from the pope, to the cardinals and the bishops, down to the everyday ground level of local priests. But there are fathers and there are fathers.

Reminiscent of Kurt Lewin's 1930s research findings on leadership styles, developmental psychology tells us there are three major parenting styles: authoritarian, permissive or laissez-faire, and authoritative or democratic (Marrow 1969; Baumrind 1968). The *authoritarian* "top-down" parent exercises coercive power from on high and expects, indeed demands, complete obedience from children, since they lack the maturity and competence to make or participate in decisions affecting their own well-being. The *permissive* parent basically abdicates the responsibility of guiding children, joins children in a "bottom-up" formless anarchy, and anything goes. Many traditional Catholics believe that the church hierarchy—inspired, in their view, by a misguided reading of Vatican II, the church's espousal of modern, democratic, essentially non-Catholic values, and the writings of dissident theologians—has been navigating a ruinous course of changing from an authoritarian to a permissive style of governing the faithful. This abandonment of the nature of the church as God ordained it to be, these critics argue, is at the heart of the clergy sexual abuse scandal and many other problems that have besieged the church since the 1960s. For example, the 16 September 2002 *Boston Globe* quoted Boston College theologian Matthew L. Lamb as saying, in an indictment of permissive dissident theologians: "No adequate diagnosis of the contributory causes of the Catholic priest abuse scandals can overlook the role of dissent among theologians. How many of the priests and bishops who have brought such suffering to minors and scandal to the public were encouraged by teachers and theologians to cut corners and dissent from the truth of Catholic faith and moral teachings? Many priests and future bishops read articles dissenting from Catholic sexual ethics in the 1960s and '70s. A climate of dissent was promoted by wholesale dissent from Catholic sexual ethics." In the same article, Christopher Coyne, Cardinal Law's spokesperson, said of priests and others raising questions occasioned by the clergy sexual abuse scandal: "Any conversation and any kind of effort towards education around the teaching of the church is always welcome. But what's important is always to be clear about what the consistent teaching and belief of the church is, and to recognize that, while we can talk about those issues, and people can raise opinions, the church's dogma and doctrine is given to us by the apostles and is not open to change."

The authoritarian/permissive, top-down/bottom-up dualisms have pervaded much of the argument and debate about how the church should understand itself as it moves into the new millennium and attempts to restore its credibility so shattered by the clergy sexual abuse scandal. Mostly missing in this debate, however, is what might be called the "third position."[7] If authoritarianism is the first or "premodern" position, and permissiveness the second or "modern" one, we must recognize that they do not exhaust the possibilities and relegate us to swinging between them pendulum style as times and contexts dictate. Indeed, there is a more mature and effective third or "postmodern" position, that of the *authoritative* parent. This democratic and participatory style of parenting focuses on persons' ever-changing authentic human development needs that require modulated and sensitively given guidance.

The authoritative parent is one who gives the type and amount of guidance or education required for empowering persons in their development toward becoming increasingly mature and competent members of the community, encouraging them to participate in decision making to the extent possible or feasible. Rather than either/or, this approach is both/and in its avoidance of dualism.

Although the parent-child-family metaphor is helpful, all metaphors are limited. In that regard, while still focusing on the need to consider the laity as mature persons, Hans Küng has argued: "All members of the church *are* church; the church belongs to all of them. . . . [T]he shepherds are . . . *not* the *fathers* of the church, in contrast to whom the laity are only minors who still cannot have any responsibility of their own for the church. The church cannot be considered a family (except as under God, the one Father): All grown-up members of the church are adult members who have an established inalienable responsibility for the whole" (Küng 1992, 83).

The founding of Voice of the Faithful (VOTF) in Boston,[8] and subsequently in Nashville and beyond, was tantamount to the laity trying to move the bishops beyond their traditional authoritarian role to become authoritative, not permissive, leaders, by urging them to embrace the laity's participation in church affairs. VOTF is concerned with many aspects of the church, including helping victims receive justice, supporting the vast majority of priests who are not sexual abusers, and seeking structural church reform through an enlarged role for the laity in church affairs. Its motto is "Keep the faith, change the church." Excerpts from its website (www.votf.org) clearly indicate what motivated its founding and what it is trying to accomplish. Its leaders describe VOTF as

> a worldwide organization of over 25,000 mainstream practicing Catholics from more than 40 U.S. states and 21 countries. Based in Newton, Massachusetts, VOTF formed in early 2002 in response to the clergy sexual abuse crisis that erupted in Boston and that has, sadly, shown itself to be not just a local problem, but a national and international scourge. . . . Our philosophy is "centrist," not extremist. We have joined together with the aim of restoring trust between the Catholic laity and hierarchy—and rebuilding the Church, not tearing it down.

We are also "inclusive," as Jesus was inclusive, and we seek to present this model to the Church hierarchy as an alternative to a closed and deeply flawed clerical culture. We are committed to providing an open and safe forum for ALL Catholics to freely and respectfully discuss the challenges of our Church, regardless of their views on specific issues. We take no position on any sex or gender issues and have no interest in doing so. Our goal is to bring the laity to the table of governance and guidance of the Church per the moral imperatives of Vatican II.

By not taking positions on controversial issues (e.g., celibacy, women priests, sexual morality) and stressing its nonradical intent, the group is trying to avoid being easily marginalized and dismissed by the hierarchy or by Catholics wary of challenging fundamental aspects of the Catholic religion.

And what has VOTF been addressing?

Voice of the Faithful is firmly committed to meaningful reform from within the Catholic Church. We do not intend or desire to found a new church. We have no interest in challenging or revising Church dogma. We have no alliances with issue-oriented interest groups. Our call for lay participation in the governance and guidance of the Church is based on the clear teachings of the Second Vatican Council, which provide a strong mandate for the laity's right and responsibility to actively guide the Church as "the People of God."

We believe that working with the hierarchy to create structural mechanisms ("structural change") through which lay Catholics can influence the temporal governance and guidance of the Church—including finances, personnel and administration at all levels—will help restore the Church to spiritual and moral health. We are convinced that the solutions to the current crisis reside largely with the whole rich spectrum of men, women and youth who live their daily lives as faithful Catholics in the real world.[9]

How has the institutional church received this group in Nashville and Boston? As we have seen, in the wake of Nashville's clergy sexual abuse scandal the bishop allowed VOTF to meet on church property and agreed to engage the group in face-to-face conversation. After the first conversation, the consensus was that the meeting, although a bit strained, was a necessary and useful development, and it has started to turn around the laity's (and the media's) negative attitude toward the church. The bishop announced he would restructure the long-standing diocesan clergy sexual abuse review panel membership to bring it in line with the U.S. bishops' call for independent laity review groups. Moreover, he said he was considering the establishment of a diocesan lay pastoral council, especially noteworthy in light of Cardinal Law's rejection of a similar move suggested by members of the laity in Boston.[10] After several months of inaction, an article in the *Tennessean* (17 December 2002) reported that VOTF had contacted the bishop urging him to move on the establishment of a council and had urged its members to contact the bishop on the matter.

VOTF's seemingly cordial reception in Nashville was not replicated in Boston. Soon after the news of VOTF's activities first hit the media, the 4 April 2002 *Christian Science Monitor* reported Pope John Paul II biographer George Weigel as saying: "A lot of people are trying to make ideological hay out of this crisis. . . . Some of these calls for what amounts to the protestantizing of the Catholic church are the result of people on an ideological joy ride." Harvard physician James E. Muller, a founder of the Nobel Prize–winning International Physicians for the Prevention of Nuclear War and a VOTF leader, replied: "We are completely mainstream Catholics—we are almost all new to this."

Muller said of VOTF's reason for being: "The faithful are designated by Vatican II to have a meaningful voice in the church; it just didn't create a mechanism. We will. . . . There are issues now that divide us, but we are united in having a democratic forum to air those differences. We have to create the structure first" (*Boston Globe*, 14 April 2002). Elsewhere Muller used Revolutionary War terminology in referring to what he called the symptom that is clergy sexual abuse: "The underlying disease is absolute power. The people of Boston know how to deal with absolute power. . . . We have donation without representation, and we have to change that" (*National Catholic Reporter*, 26 April 2002). Further: "While the media and trial lawyers held the Boston Tea Party, Voice of the Faithful is the Constitutional Convention. . . . Two hundred years ago, Americans gave representative democracy to the secular world.

We're attempting to do the same thing again, this time for the church" (*National Catholic Reporter*, 10 May 2002). What's more, the *Boston Globe* (1 May 2002) reported Muller as saying: "If I had a dream of what this would look like three years from now, our enrollment would be half of the Catholics in the world, every parish would have a chapter, and every diocese, every nation, and the world would, too, and that organization would be a counterbalance to the power of the hierarchy—it would have a permanent role, a bit like Congress." More to the immediate point, he was wary in saying: "My nightmare scenario is that the church successfully papers over the clergy sexual abuse problem and leaves intact an abusive power structure."

On experiencing VOTF's initial rumblings, Cardinal Law and officials of the Archdiocese of Boston were restive. In part, this was because the group talked about raising money outside official church channels for worthy Catholic causes. One VOTF leader was reported to have said: "What we think is going to happen is that the Cardinal's Appeal will be lucky if it raises 50 percent of its goal—that's how deep the disgust is with the Catholic laity.... What we're saying to that 50 percent that's not going to play is, don't lose sight of all the good work done by Catholic social service programs" (*New York Times*, 31 May 2002). The cardinal's top aide, Bishop Walter J. Edyvean, reportedly had asked several priests not to host VOTF meetings in their parishes, but he did meet with VOTF leaders, telling them that, although the group's intentions to support victims and nonabusing priests were worthy, its intentions to raise money independent of the archdiocese and to work toward more democracy and structural change in the church were problematic. In explaining Edyvean's position, an archdiocesan spokesperson wrote: "He underscored the fact that associations in the church, from the point of view of both theology and canon law, are meant to aid the mission of the church and that mission is carried on necessarily with and under the bishop of the diocese. Likewise, it is the diocesan bishop's role to exercise vigilance with regard to the way in which Catholic associations perform the tasks they set for themselves" (*National Catholic Reporter*, 7 June 2002). Statements like this led one of VOTF's officers to say: "In a sense, our fathers have to realize that their children have grown up" (Associated Press, 12 June 2002).

Voice of the Faithful organized and grew so quickly it was able to hold its first national conference on 20 July 2002, with some 4,000 people attending from across the U.S. and several foreign countries. In addition to having a difficult time getting conservative Catholics to join, the organization got mixed reviews from clergy sexual abuse victims/survivors. Representatives from several victims' groups did attend the meeting and were supportive of VOTF efforts; however, in explaining why a contingent of victims/survivors was protesting outside the meeting, one speaker said that protestors believed the organization's efforts were "too little, too late, and too much about you. . . . You have no right to judge them . . . or feel Catholically smug. . . . All you get is the right to beg their forgiveness." He criticized VOTF's "highly strategized, thoroughly debated, very quiet agenda" (*Commonweal*, 16 August 2002). In a similar vein, Marquette University ethicist Daniel McGuire observed: "From what I've seen so far, they're much too timid and fearful to do the job they've set out for themselves. . . . We keep hearing they're 'not dissidents.' Well, that's the whole point—dissident means you're disagreeing; you have to be a dissident to the hierarchy that promoted sexual abuse of children. . . . The hierarchical control system is the root of all evil here, and that church leadership has to change" (*Hartford Courant*, 10 September 2002).[11] But from Nashville's VOTF chapter we heard: "I certainly don't want to be part of a group that is going to alienate the bishop or the priests. We don't want to be dividers; we want to be unifiers" (*Tennessean*, 21 July 2002).

Shortly after this historic meeting, controversy arose over VOTF's intent to raise money for worthy Catholic causes. From its beginning, VOTF had talked about the need for Catholics to vote with their pocketbooks in order to express their lack of confidence in Cardinal Law's handling of the clergy sexual abuse situation and to show disapproval of the use of laity-contributed funds to settle lawsuits. "We have to gain financial power in this church. We're 99.9 percent of the church and 100 percent of the money. . . . There will be no donations without representation," said VOTF founder James Muller (Reuters, 20 July 2002).

By the middle of 2002, funds collected by the Cardinal's Appeal, the major official church fund-raising effort, were indeed down by several million dollar

and estimates were that archdiocesan budgets might be cut by 40 percent. VOTF's fear that the decreased giving would hurt the poor and other worthy groups funded through church institutions and projects marred its apparent success. So VOTF undertook fund-raising of its own on behalf of Catholic agencies, hospitals, schools, and related ministries through a mechanism called Voice of Compassion. On hearing of this turn of events, church officials contended that, although they were not trying to undermine VOTF, with whom they claimed to have had several productive meetings, they would nevertheless refuse any donations made by the organization outside official church channels. Public anger and outrage ensued.

The *Boston Globe* reported an archdiocesan spokesperson's attempt to explain the church's position on VOTF's independent fund-raising: "This is a question of how we understand ourselves as a church and how we operate as a church. Any setup that separates the role of the bishop from pastoral works is something the church can't accept. All the pastoral work of the diocese, in one form or another, should be under the guidance of the archbishop of Boston" (24 July 2002). Further: "Just as it is out of order for a bishop to carry out the pastoral work of the archdiocese without consultation with the laity, it is just as out of order for a lay church group to seek to carry out the pastoral work of the church without consultation with the bishop" (24 July 2002). The official therefore urged Catholic organizations with their own boards of directors, which presumably had the right to go counter to the archdiocese's position, to join with Cardinal Law in rejecting VOTF funds. A particularly intense controversy arose concerning whether or not Catholic Charities, an organization with a board appointed by Cardinal Law and subject to his ultimate control, could or would agree to receive VOTF donations. In December 2002, many months after VOTF's original offer, the organization's board finally voted to accept the group's donation.

Reactions to Cardinal Law's spurning of VOTF donations were quick in coming. VOTF president James Post said: "The Cardinal's Appeal failed on its own, and it failed because of the reason we all know—the scandal in the church." Victim spokesperson David Clohessy observed: "I never thought I would see the day when any Catholic official advocated any roadblock in help-

ing the poor. The mission of the church is to help the needy in every way possible, regardless of whose return address is on the check" (*Boston Globe*, 24 July 2002). Another VOTF spokesperson put it this way: "If the Cardinal's Appeal is down 30 to 40 percent, and programs have to be closed, and the public knows there's a pool of money waiting that the laity contributed to make sure organizations are up and running, and the archdiocese flat out refuses to accept it, that would be a very unfortunate situation" (Associated Press, 23 July 2002). A *Boston Globe* editorial summed up the feelings of many: "Cardinal Bernard Law's rejection of faithful Catholics who want to support the church's charitable activities but not through the archdiocesan hierarchy was remarkable for its clumsiness, even more so for the way it mirrored the church posture earlier this year that alienated so many parishioners. As with the ongoing sex abuse scandal, church leaders showed far greater concern for their own hierarchy than for the people affected by their actions" (23 July 2002). Echoing this sentiment, a *Boston Herald* editorial observed: "If ever there was a churlish and utterly pointless gesture by the Archdiocese of Boston it was the announcement that it will not accept donations from a special fund to be set up by the Catholic lay group Voice of the Faithful" (24 July 2002). As of this writing in summer 2003, Cardinal Law's successors and other officials of the Archdiocese of Boston continued to refuse VOTF offerings and urged Catholic charitable groups to do the same (the board of Catholic Charities, however, agreed to receive them).

To appreciate more fully the official archdiocesan reactions to VOTF, it is useful to look at the coverage of the clergy sexual abuse scandal by the *Pilot*, the official archdiocesan newspaper. On 15 March 2002, the *Pilot* published a special issue on the scandal, printing four times its usual number of copies. The issue contained an editorial that made headlines around the world. In it, editor Monsignor Peter F. Conley listed questions he said the scandal had occasioned:

- Should celibacy continue to be a normative condition for the diocesan priesthood in the Western (Latin) Church?

- If celibacy were optional, would there be fewer scandals of this nature in the priesthood?

• Does priesthood, in fact, attract a disproportionate number of men with a homosexual orientation?

• Lastly, why are a substantial number of Catholics not convinced that an all male priesthood was intended by Christ and is unchangeable?

He maintained that these questions "have been answered in the past but . . . have taken on a deeper intensity in more Catholic minds than prior to these sexual scandals. Even if our present woes in the archdiocese were suddenly to disappear, these questions have taken on an urgency and will not slip quietly away. Before intelligent answers can be given, we must realize that there is no panacea; that a married clergy presents its own distinctive problems and liabilities, and that more studies with concrete data will be necessary before an intelligent response can be made. Right now emotions are running too high." He then showed how these were complicated questions, not easily directly linked to clergy sexual abuse.

Conley promised to take on the issue of women priests in the next issue; however, in an editorial in the next issue, he said: "[T]he maelstrom that has whirled around [the editorial] . . . demands precedence." He said the editorial was not questioning church teachings but reporting questions that had arisen in public meetings. Further, he said: "In Cardinal Law's subsequent clarification as publisher, he acknowledged that, 'The full context of the editorial in question makes that abundantly clear. It is one thing to report the questions of others; it is quite another thing to make those questions one's own.'" Attempting to get off the hook, Conley insisted: "It was not the intention of *The Pilot* to call for changes in Church policies. Moreover, while those questions were raised in relation to the sexual abuse of minors by priests, their connection to the issue is more than dubious." He concluded: "Commentators seemed to have spent more time speculating on what the editorial might imply than what the words actually conveyed. As there is many a slip between a cup and a lip, so can there be many a slip between contextual words and an unwarranted inference" (*Pilot*, 22 March 2002).

The editorial had generated extensive coverage and widespread confusion. Was the editor of Cardinal Law's own newspaper challenging settled church positions—as the media charged but Conley denied—or was he merely reporting the questions and confusions frequently expressed by the media and the public at large? The upshot? Conley was removed from his post and returned to pastoral duties, but the archdiocese said he had been slated to leave since September 2001, and he had left with the cardinal's blessing. He was replaced as part of a budget-induced reorganization of the *Pilot*, which also involved termination of two reporters and the possible relocation of the paper's headquarters. All this may indeed be true, but it has the aura of the way many businesses and governmental agencies fire top officials who have fallen from grace. And since Conley's departure, the *Pilot* has been quite critical of VOTF, taking several occasions to question its legitimacy and motives.

In an editorial by its new editor, Antonio Enrique, the *Pilot* roundly denounced one of the speakers at VOTF's July 2002 conference: Thomas Arens of We Are the Church—a church-reform group founded in 1996 in Austria with a branch in the U.S. The editorial, titled "Boston Reform Movement Inspired by Dissident International Group," reported that Arens was appreciatively received by those in attendance when he said "the Church has to change to be an authentic representative of the message of Jesus Christ." The editorial went on in some detail to list and criticize the positions taken by the group here and abroad, maintaining that they were counter to established church teaching. It concluded: "We better understand now what is the Church model they are working for" (*Pilot*, 26 July 2002). "They" might have meant We Are the Church or VOTF or both. Whatever one's view on We Are the Church, the editorial smacked of guilt by association, seeming to associate VOTF with the agenda of an organization represented by one of the conference's many speakers.

The *Pilot* used the tactic of guilt by association more directly in another editorial critical of VOTF, titled, bluntly enough, "You Are Known by the Company You Keep" (6 September 2002). The *New Yorker* had published a long article by Paul Wilkes titled "The Reformer: A Priest Battles for a More Open Church," which described the career of Boston activist priest Walter Cuenin (2 September 2002). In addition to having the responsibility for making certain travel arrangements for Cardinal Law, Cuenin was one of the organizers of the Boston Priests' Forum, which has been trying to stand up for priests' rights during the sexual abuse scandal. The article stated that Cuenin refused to send his parish's money to one of the cardinal's budgetary funds and, particularly significant for the *Pilot*, urged his parishioners to join VOTF. In its anti-Cuenin cum anti-VOTF editorial, the *Pilot* impugned VOTF's claimed "centrist" philosophy by listing five noncentrist positions the *New Yorker* quoted Cuenin as taking:

- "Priests have been forced to remain silent about the supposedly unassailable prohibitions on birth control, second marriages, the ordination of married men and women."

- "The divorced should be allowed a front row seat, and not be told they are unworthy to approach the communion banquet."

- "Gays and lesbians should be in the other front row, and not told that their lives are 'basically disordered.'"

- "I am going to ask you not to pray for vocations. But to pray that the Church will have the strength and the courage to acknowledge the vocations we already have. Exceptional women are waiting to serve. We have married men who would make wonderful priests. We don't need more vocations—they are already here. Let's just accept them."

- "The challenge is to change the way the Church is, not just the way it looks. . . . The genie is out of the bottle. Catholics are not going back to a Church where they have no voice. I know I'm not."

What implications did the *Pilot* editorial draw?

Father Cuenin's statements further call into question the agenda for reform of those behind VOTF. While the leadership of VOTF may assert that they take no position on most matters of change in the Catholic Church, it is clear their backers do. . . . As prominent supporters continue to publicly advocate controversial positions, it grows more and more difficult for many to believe VOTF's claims that they are entirely neutral on issues of "reform."

In December 2002, Cardinal Law forbade any Catholic groups from meeting on the grounds of Cuenin's parish (*Boston Globe*, 5 December 2002). One can only speculate about the level of concern and fear that VOTF—with its widely reported push for inclusion of the laity in church affairs, its apparent impact on church fund-raising, and its rapidly growing membership—has generated in the Boston church.

The 1 October 2002 *Boston Globe* reported an exchange that captured VOTF's uphill struggle. Motivated in part by pressure from Faithful Voice, a lay group opposing VOTF, an auxiliary bishop ordered one parish not to host the organization's meetings, saying: "The activities and promotion of the Voice of the Faithful must be curtailed in order to avoid further scandal and polarity among our parishioners. . . . For the sake of unity and Catholic orthodoxy in the parish, it is inappropriate to foster these meetings and to allow the members of the Voice of the Faithful to meet with the parish councils." A VOTF leader replied: "To ban people from using church property to talk about the biggest scandal in the 500-year history of the Catholic Church in North America is ludicrous on its face. . . . If they are looking for scandal, all they need to do is look inside the chancery to find out where the real sources of scandal lie." In a later statement (*Boston Globe*, 10 October 2002), the VOTF official was quoted as saying to the auxiliary bishop that his actions "are inappropriate based on the facts of the situation and based on canon law. We believe your actions to be inconsistent with Church teaching, Christian morality, the spirit of the Vatican II Council, and contrary to your pastoral duty. . . . We might expect actions such as this from totalitarian rulers and repressive political regimes, but not from the stewards of our faith family." Referring to allegations that VOTF espoused views contrary to Catholic teaching, he said: "If you listen to slanderous accusations, fail to verify their veracity, and use unsubstantiated accusations as the justification for your public actions, you are either a participant in or a victim of an unbecoming smear campaign." To dampen down the rhetoric, an archdiocesan official said: "The dialogue with Voice of the Faithful remains open, and it is our hope to continue that. It is better to have discussions with the bishop, and not issue letters to the media. We get more accomplished that way." In mid-October 2002, Cardinal Law softened his stance slightly, reversing the auxiliary bishop's ban and allowing existing VOTF chapters to continue to meet on church property, but not so for new chapters pending further study of the VOTF organization.[12]

A VOTF official said that archdiocesan officials had only met with VOTF twice and not at all for several months. Cardinal Law finally agreed to meet face to face with VOTF leaders in late November 2002. The reported conversation was candid, but Law repeatedly said he wished the organization had gotten his permission before forming. Nothing specific came of the meeting, but observers believed that the very fact of the face-to-face meeting was significant. Several weeks later, however, after the courts forced release of additional diocesan documents that proved extremely damaging to Cardinal Law's credibility—some of which referred to acts of covering up for abusive priests into the late 1990s—VOTF president James Post described the material as constituting a "major setback to the development of any relationship between Voice of the Faithful and Cardinal Law. Relationships are based in trust, and these disclosures seriously undermine any basis for trusting the archbishop" (*New York Times*, 5 December 2002).

The crisis of trust the Boston church had been experiencing throughout 2002 finally came to a head in December. The disclosures just mentioned, which entailed particularly horrendous acts of abuse by several Boston priests and the hierarchy's characteristic cover-up, coupled with the seriously discussed possibility that the Archdiocese of Boston would declare bankruptcy because of the increasing number of civil suits, made Cardinal Law's situation untenable. Pressure for Law's resignation on the part of the media, local priests, and the laity was intense. In an unprecedented move, a group of more than fifty Boston priests publicly called for the Cardinal's resignation. Said one of the dissidents: "It feels to me like one of those pivotal moments in the history of the church, like the edict of Constantine, the Orthodox-Catholic split, the Protestant Reformation, or the Second Vatican Council. . . . [The Cardinal] needs for the well-being of the church to recognize that he has become the lightning rod, and he needs to step away, so we can bring in leadership from the outside." Theologian Richard McBrien commented that he couldn't "think of another case in modern American history, or anywhere else, where a significant number of priests have called publicly for the resignation of their bishop because of a loss of spiritual leadership" (*Boston Globe*, 10 December 2002). Significantly, regarding the laity's role in all this, VOTF decided to weigh in. A meeting of its national leadership yielded a number of resolutions. The organization called for Cardinal Law to resign and petitioned the Holy Father to appoint new leadership in Boston—an appointment that VOTF said should only occur after meaningful consultation with the Church of Boston, including the laity, priests, religious, and the hierarchy. VOTF also urged the president of the U.S. Conference of Catholic Bishops to call on the bishops to recognize and respond to the pastoral crisis in Boston. Finally, VOTF called on the president of the USCCB to ask all bishops to open to the public hidden records of known sexual abusers in their own dioceses.[13]

The result of the mounting pressure from various quarters beyond VOTF was that Cardinal Law once again made a secret visit to Rome, but this time the pope accepted his resignation, although there was speculation about how willingly he stepped down. Many observers were truly surprised, believing the Vatican would keep Law in place to avoid a domino effect whereby other heavily criticized bishops would be pressured into resigning and to avoid the appearance that the church was caving in to the laity and the force of public pressure.

Commenting on Law's resignation, James Carroll observed: "Suddenly, you faced a horrible truth about your church. Cardinal Law is gone, but you are braced for even more disturbing recognitions. The issue began as one involving, first, a small legion of perverted priests, then a shocking number of complicitous bishops, then a recalcitrant Vatican to whom the victims of abuse remained invisible. But at some point, the issue became the church itself" (*Boston Globe*, 17 December 2002).[14] Said VOTF president James Post: "In talking about the prospect for recovery, people are saying this is at least a decade-long job that stands in front of us. The pain in Boston right now is so severe that the first requirement is that someone come and begin the process of listening and consultation and dialogue with the priests, the laity, and the survivors. Renewal in Boston absolutely depends on the collaboration of all these parties" (*Boston Globe*, 14 December 2002). He added: "What got us into this mess was a system of secrecy and authoritarianism, and the only way we can get out of this mess is to turn that 180 degrees and bring sunlight and collaboration" (*New York Times*, 14 December 2002). In that regard, the Vatican named Law's interim replacement, Richard Lennon, without consulting anyone in Boston, contrary to VOTF's somewhat unrealistic desires. Lennon said that he would move toward settling the suits pending against the archdiocese, that bankruptcy was still a possibility, and that he wanted to continue earlier conversations with VOTF. He suggested that the role of the laity "could very well expand" (*New York Times*, 19 December 2002), but he neither lifted Cardinal Law's ban on new VOTF chapters meeting on church property nor agreed to accept the organization's contributions.

Meaningful participation of the laity in the clergy sexual abuse system and in other aspects of church life was a theme whose time had come across the country during the last quarter of 2002. A *Boston Globe* editorial commenting on an archdiocesan lay commission's useful and demanding recommendations geared to preventing future clergy sexual abuse put it this way: "The commission would establish two predominantly lay boards, to minister to victims and to monitor the archdiocese in any future abuse cases, a balance that has been lacking from the church. This recommendation promises to be the group's most effective. The scandal was the product of a closed clerical culture, and the openness of outside review should ensure that bishops can no longer use the cloak of denial to hide the crime of abuse" (8 October 2002). Victims and members of the Catholic community also applauded the recommendations but held their breath awaiting the hierarchy's response.

In a 24 September 2002 article, *Boston Globe* columnist James Carroll used the metaphor of the bishops desperately trying to go up a down escalator to capture the dynamics of the institutional church attempting to dig itself out of the clergy sexual abuse scandal.[15] As an antidote to this nonproductive approach, the "third-position" thinking I have suggested—an approach that encourages the laity and the hierarchy to join in common cause instead of engaging in a tug of war over the nature of the church—may be useful for helping to explore the future of the church. In the next chapter, I explore how third-position thinking has informed the development of an approach to professional ethics I call the ethics of human development and community (Dokecki 1996). In chapter 4, I detail some of the ways it has contributed to theory in human science that yields insights into ways of dealing with and preventing clergy sexual abuse (Newbrough 1992). In chapter 5, I explore how third-position thinking is consistent with an ecclesiology in which the church understands itself from *both* hierarchical *and* community-oriented People of God perspectives. Such an understanding gives rise to challenging approaches to integrating the laity into the workings of the church at all levels.

CHAPTER THREE

# Professional Ethics and the Clergy Sexual Abuse System

*Professionals have authority to put me in jail, to hospitalize me,*
*to excommunicate me, or in other ways to affect significantly*
*the structures of meaning and of freedom in my life.*

—Karen Lebacqz, *Professional Ethics: Power and Paradox*

B EYOND THEIR SACRED AND SACRAMENTAL ROLES, priests and bishops are professional persons who engage in ministerial practice. Along the way so far, I have briefly identified a number of professional ethics issues encountered in clergy sexual abuse. In this chapter, I recall these issues and offer a professional ethics analysis of what I have been calling the clergy sexual abuse system. The focus is not on the church's version of sin or sexual ethics but on the responsibilities, structures, and processes that those in the Catholic ministry (priests and church "managers" such as bishops, cardinals, and Vatican officials) have in common with other professions, such as teaching, psychotherapy and counseling, medicine, or organizational management. My intent is to provide a general value/ethical framework that can inform my analysis in later chapters, in pursuit of finding ways of ameliorating and preventing clergy sexual abuse in the Catholic Church.

## THE ETHICS OF HUMAN DEVELOPMENT AND COMMUNITY

In the introduction, I gave a brief overview of my approach to professional ethics, the ethics of human development and community (Dokecki 1996). The essence of this ethical position is that professions are social practices that ought to enhance the human development of persons (their growth and wellness) and to promote community and thereby the common good. This ethical approach challenges practitioners to work toward change in both their clients and the problematic social conditions they face (what *is*), change that helps people and the social world become more caring and competent (what *ought* to be). Enhancing human development requires confronting this *is-ought discrepancy*: We evaluate a situation as it is (interpreted through the lenses of our values); the situation ethically challenges us because we find it lacking compared with our values, our standards of what ought to be; and we act to lessen or remove the situation's value discrepancy. Actions that lessen the is-ought discrepancy include those in accord with the ethical principles of caring, telling the truth, treating persons as persons not things and respecting their autonomy, doing no harm, doing good, and being just. These principles form the basis of my analysis of the ethics of the main actors in the clergy sexual abuse system.

*Caring* is the core principle in the ethics of human development and community (Mayeroff 1971). Caring is an ethical principle and an enduring mode of interpersonal virtue that promotes the growth and development of persons. For professionals to care, they must not only have expertise and knowledge about another person but also self-awareness that allows them to evaluate whether what they are doing helps or hinders the human development of the other. They must, argues Mayeroff, "know who the other is, what his power and limitations are, and what is conducive to his growth" (13). Professionals must know and respond to the other's needs based on an accurate assessment of their own strengths and weaknesses. To care for the other, the professional must be "with the other in his world. He must be able to see from 'inside' what life is like" (42). Caring professionals treat each situation as unique and allow the "other's growth to guide what [they] do, to help determine how to respond and what is relevant to such a response" (7). Ironically, many clergy sexual abusers know their victims in this way but use their knowledge in an anti-caring, harmful fashion.

One helps other persons grow—and one in turn grows—through enabling them to care for other persons beyond themselves, to identify or create their own domains of caring, to care for themselves, and to take responsibility for their own lives. Growing, for its part, entails learning, understood not as the accumulation of facts and skills but as enlarging one's scope of understanding by increasing one's experiences and integrating them into one's meaning system. Growing also entails becoming self-determining—breaking away from slavish conformity, choosing one's values, making one's own decisions, and taking responsibility for them. Moreover, learning and becoming self-determining occur within relationships to others, not in social isolation. As professional persons, priests, bishops, and other church officials have a preeminent duty to care, to help those they encounter in the church to grow and develop, a duty honored more in the breach than in the observance in the clergy sexual abuse system.

The other principles of the ethics of human development and community build on the foundation of caring. *Telling the truth*, the principle of veracity, means that always and everywhere the presumption is that we ought to tell the truth (Bok 1978). We don't need reasons to tell the truth; we do, however, need very good reasons to lie and deceive, that is, to draw lines where lying can be convincingly defended. We have a duty to tell the truth, but we may decide to lie for a good reason, for example, to deceive someone who intends to harm our child; however, truth telling would in no way be diminished as an ethical obligation by our decision to lie to honor the competing ethical obligation of protecting the innocent from harm. Garry Wills, in *Papal Sin: Structures of Deceit* (2000) and *Why I Am a Catholic* (2002), has argued that disregard for logic, science, and the truth has come to be embedded in the structures of the church at all levels and has seriously eroded its moral authority. These structures of deceit exist in order to protect the hierarchy's top-down authority, control church decision-making, and strengthen its role as the ultimate arbiter of morality. Within this institutional context, deception and outright lying have characterized the behavior of many of the actors in the clergy sexual abuse system, from the abusing priests who lie to their victims, to church officials who deceive parishioners by keeping these priests' abuse secret in transferring them from parish to parish.

*Treating persons as persons not things and respecting their autonomy* entails the duty to treat all human beings as ends in themselves, not as means to our own or others' ends. For example, the all too common phenomenon of a professional having sex with a client is now generally understood as having little if anything to do with sex, but rather, as an instance of the professional exerting power coercively to meet his own (not the client's) needs. The professional treats the client like a pawn in a chess game, like a tool to be manipulated to fit his own agenda. As we have seen, the manipulation of clergy sexual abuse victims and their families has been part and parcel of the behavior of abusing priests and many church officials.

*Doing no harm, doing good,* and *being just* are interrelated ethical principles. They entail the Hippocratic injunction first of all to do no harm (nonmaleficence) and the more demanding duty to do good (beneficence) by actively promoting the well-being and human development of people and working toward creating a just, caring, and competent community. Nonmaleficence and beneficence relate to the duty of justice understood as being fair in determining whose harm and good are at stake—we should treat like cases alike and different cases differently (justice as fairness). This seeming truism is not as simple as it appears, since not just any likenesses and differences but morally relevant ones must be discerned in the domain of justice. These morally relevant similarities and differences are "ones that bear on the goodness or badness of people's lives" (Frankena 1963/1973, 51). Central here are needs and abilities. Ethically, treating people in relation to their needs and abilities requires discerning "whether doing so helps or hinders them equally in the achievement of the best lives they are capable of" (51). It is not that persons are equal in endowments and capacities, because they clearly are not, but that "we ought prima facie to make proportionally the same contribution to the goodness of their lives, once a certain minimum has been achieved by all" (51). The goods we promote, the harms we avoid, and our fairness in distributing these consequences involve, at base, human development and community. Clergy sexual abuse entails the unjust victimization and revictimization of abused children and their families, and harm inevitably results. Moreover, harmful acts are often rationalized as serving a good purpose—the priest tries to convince his victim, and himself, that abusing acts are really acceptable and in the best human-development and spiritual interests of the child, or church officials believe that covering up clergy sexual abuse is in the best interests of the church so it can maintain its status as a "sinless" organization, continue to exercise its authority, and carry out its mission of doing good in the community.

As we have seen, the harm caused by clergy sexual abuse and by church officials' reactions to it is extensive. Harm occurs at personal, relational, and social levels. At the personal level, in the short run, victims experience physical, psychological, and spiritual pain and damage to their basic sense of trust and personal well-being. In the longer run, many victims/survivors experience anxiety, depression, alienation, and fear of relationships and intimacy, often manifesting antisocial behavior, alcohol or drug abuse, and more general problems in living. These immediate and long-term harmful consequences pose threats to their human development.

At the relational level, clergy sexual abuse weakens the church's ability to be a caring face-to-face community. It undercuts trust in the church on the part of many victims and their families, fellow parishioners, and Catholics more generally. It threatens people's psychological sense of community—weakening their sense of membership and belonging to the church; their sense of shared values and emotional connection with others in the church; their experience of being with others in the church to help meet each others' needs for social support, meaning, and spiritual growth; and their sense of influencing and being influenced by others in using their power to affect what happens in the church. Priests who are not sexual abusers also become alienated and overly cautious about relating warmly and personally to their parishioners. By threatening the church's ability to foster spiritual growth and development, to provide social support during many of life's crises, and to promote people's psychological sense of community, clergy sexual abuse harms the church's spiritual life, threatening its very reason for existing.

Clergy sexual abuse has broader harmful consequences in the social realm beyond the harm it causes in the personal and relational realms. It shocks and scandalizes the public at large. It fuels criticism of the church from within and without. It can cause decreased charitable giving to Catholic hospitals, social service agencies, and other charitable endeavors.[1] It erodes the intellectual and moral integrity of the church's teaching authority. It causes tension between the church and the police, the courts, the legislature, and other public agencies. Moreover, the response to clergy sexual abuse by church officials, bishops, cardinals, and the Vatican has magnified the harm to the church itself many times over. The public's perception of the institutional church's secrecy, deceit, and seeming lack of concern for victims in responding to clergy sexual abuse has produced a chorus of calls for reform.

Ethical professional persons, then, should use their professional power as the means to pursue the ends of promoting human development and enhancing community by caring, telling the truth, respecting the autonomy of persons, doing no harm, doing good, and being just. They should not abuse their power for their own ends. Professionals may use their power cooperatively, for the good of others, or they may abuse power to coerce, manipulate, and harm others. Regarding justice, theologian Richard Gula has addressed clergy sexual abuse from the perspective of Catholic ministerial professional ethics and has summarized a number of the issues:

> *Justice for the victim* means providing help to regain self-esteem and trust in the church and in pastoral ministries. *Justice toward the pastoral minister* means getting help to recognize the personal and professional issues that led to the boundary violation in the first place. *Justice for the community* from which the victim and minister come means addressing its feeling of betrayal so that it can renew its trust in the church and in pastoral ministry generally. *Justice in the church* means developing policies and structures to protect against future incidents of misconduct and to respond to victims, communities, and offending pastoral ministers. (Gula 1996, 107, emphasis added)

On a related note, ethical professional persons should also use their professional power to help foster just political-economic-social arrangements, ones in which (1) community members are empowered and helped to be self-efficacious and to experience well-being; (2) communication is free and uncoerced, devoid of secrecy, deception, and the abuse of power; and (3) governance is geared to the empowerment of persons through deeply democratic and participatory political processes (Bandura 1989; Dokecki 1996; Green 1999; Habermas 1984; Prilleltensky 2001).

Judith Green, in *Deep Democracy: Community, Diversity, and Transformation* (1999), develops an approach to social reform she calls *prophetic pragmatism* (an extension of the thinking of John Dewey, Jürgen Habermas, Alain Locke, Martin Luther King, Jr., Cornel West, and other democratic social thinkers). She summarizes her extensive and careful approach to what she calls the beloved community by listing the following elements:

Respect for human rights understood as common humane values

Democratic cultural revitalization

Lifelong education within collaborative processes of rebuilding the public square

Political re-inhabitation [participatory democracy]

Shared community efficacy and commitment to mutual flourishing

Economic re-location [economics in service of the human development of persons]

A shared commitment to ecosystemic health

Shared memories and hopes

A web of caring within a consciously shared community life (217)

These elements can serve as yardsticks for evaluating the degree to which social groupings ethically measure up to the principles of the ethics of human development and community.

## THE USE AND ABUSE OF POWER: PROFESSIONALS HAVING SEX WITH CLIENTS

Dual relationships, those in which professionals have other motives in addition to working on behalf of the client's well-being, are highly problematic, and professionals should be ever vigilant of the potential for abuse of power in their work with clients. Accordingly, most professions have clear and strict ethical prohibitions against many forms of professional-client dual relationships, especially those involving sex with clients. Yet such activities persist.[2] Practicing psychotherapists treat so many victims of sexual encounters with former therapists that they often use the term "epidemic." Clergy sexual abuse, as well, sometimes seems to have reached epidemic proportions.

The phenomenon of professionals having sex with clients seems to be rampant in the United States, having increasingly come to public attention since the early 1970s. Virtually all the professions have been implicated, and the media are full of news stories and dramatized accounts of the sexual activities of teachers, counselors, physicians and dentists, psychologists and psychiatrists, lawyers and politicians, and the like. The television portrayal several years ago of *L.A. Law*'s lecherous lawyer, Arnie Becker, made the phenomenon a virtual cultural commonplace. The making of movies portraying sex between therapists and clients, such as *Final Analysis, Mr. Jones*, and *The Prince of Tides*, which have featured some of our most popular media figures, also suggests that the topic is on our collective cultural mind. And, as we have seen, the clergy, including high-level and well-known religious leaders, should be added to the list of those engaging in unethical dual relationships.

In trying to understand the dynamics of professional-client sexual relationships, consider this passage concerning adults from Stephen White's novel *Privileged Information* (1991, 2–3):

> I tell him I have fantasies of seeing him outside the office. He says, you have a pattern of enticing men to respond to you sexually. I translate: you're saying I try to get men to come on to me? He nods, stays formal. It's not necessary to repeat that pattern with me, he assures me, this relationship is different. Given your past, he says, it shouldn't surprise either of us that you are trying to generate sexual intimacy between us. But in this relationship, it's something we can work to understand, not a destructive pattern to act out again. . . .
>
> I hear him, but I don't hear him. Why?
>
> Because I need him. Because he wants me. I have to respond to that. I must. He's nurtured me, encouraged me, helped me discover me. . . . I don't want him to leave me.

The speaker here is a woman in therapy with a man, the typical arrangement in dual relationships entailing client-therapist sexual relations. As is common, and even desirable in psychoanalytically oriented psychotherapy, in which analysis of the transference neurosis is the order of the day, the client has sexual fantasies about her therapist—the phenomenon of transference. Although she fantasizes that he needs her, the passage does not indicate whether or not he has fantasies about her—countertransference. But it should not surprise us if he does have them, and let us assume that, in fact, he does.

Apart from the particular dynamics of certain forms of psychotherapy, this passage suggests a universal feature of client-professional relationships, namely, a *power differential in favor of the professional.* A client enters a relationship with a professional experiencing a need the professional is believed competent to address. The situation entails a *necessary* status differential, based on the professional's presumed training, experience, skills, and special knowledge. Unless the professional is believed to know something the client does not, there is no reason for the professional relationship to exist. Since, as Ralph Waldo Emerson would have it, "There is no knowledge that is not power," the knowledge-based status differential is also a power differential.

Professional power, argues Karen Lebacqz, is "legitimated and institutionalized power" (1985, 113). Professionals do not simply have the power to fix a problem. They also define its reality. "Professionals have authority to put me in jail, to hospitalize me, to excommunicate me, or in other ways to affect significantly the structures of meaning and of freedom in my life" (113). There is potential for distortion depending upon the way professionals use their reality-defining power. The professional's power may be used caringly and ethically, where the intent is the mutual promotion of the goods of human development and community and thereby the common good, or unethically, in manipulative, coercive, and harmful fashion, where the intent is to give priority to the professional's needs over those of the client. We can easily recognize the same general dynamics in clergy sexual abuse.

The client in White's novel candidly speaks of her dependence on the power of the therapist: "I need him. . . . He's nurtured me, encouraged me, helped me discover me. . . . I don't want to leave him." An immature and incompetent therapist could mistake her sexual interest in him to be personal, only coincidentally related to the therapeutic relationship. He could feel flattered and respond in kind, thinking that he would be innocently (and ethically) engaging in a sexual relationship between consenting adults. But he would be mistaken and would, in fact, be acting unethically—engaging in, at the very least, an unwitting but nonetheless serious abuse of his professional power. A blatantly unethical therapist, of course, could freely and manipulatively take advantage of his power advantage and her dependence to, in effect, rape her, that is, have sex with her against her will. He would be operating against what we presume her will would be if she were freed from the power of the professional relationship. In the matter of sex in the priest-child relationship, there are no consenting adults. There is just an encounter between a psychosexually immature man, perhaps a sexual predator, and a vulnerable child incapable of exercising unfettered choice. Such relationships clearly entail the unjust abuse of power and inevitably have harmful consequences.

But the client in White's novel is fantasizing about an apparently mature, competent, and ethical therapist. He recognizes that she is not sexually attracted to him apart from his professional status: "He says, you have a pattern of enticing men to respond to you sexually. I translate: you're saying I try to get men to come on to me? He nods, stays formal." He, so to speak, therapeutically interprets the transference in order to help her gain insight into her situation. Moreover, he seems to resist temptation and structures the situation in a just, competent, caring, and highly ethical fashion: "It's not necessary to repeat that pattern with me, he assures me, this relationship is different. Given your past, he says, it shouldn't surprise either of us that you are trying to generate sexual intimacy between us. But in this relationship, it's something we can work to understand, not a destructive pattern to act out again."

Stephen White, himself a practicing clinical psychologist, has packed a great deal of ethical insight into one brief fictional passage. He portrays the complexity of the client-professional transaction and the inevitability of power-related factors and motives operating within it. This mixed-motive feature of professional life's dual relationships, often leading to the unjust abuse of professional power, requires further elaboration and analysis.

James Craig and Marguerite Craig have argued that we exercise two very different forms of power depending on whether we relate to others as objects (directive power) or as persons (synergic power). Directive power is used by professionals who use their expert power to exercise control over their clients and paternalistically violate their autonomy. In doing so, they make the client dependent and powerless: "Directive power dehumanizes people because it makes them less sensitive to the fact that they cause the results of their actions" (Craig and Craig 1973, 61). It reduces their belief in their own self-efficacy. Directive power, however, is the sort of power embedded within the structures of society. If we approach clients from this unfortunately typical use of power, we will rarely help them to participate in their empowerment. This dynamic of directive power, as we shall see, characterizes many aspects of the institutional/hierarchical model of the church.

In contrast to directive power, synergic power suggests a very different view of professional power. Synergic power is "the capacity of an individual to increase the satisfaction of all participants by intentionally generating increased energy and creativity, all of which is used to *co-create* a more rewarding present and future" (62). Operating from this model, clients are partners, colleagues, and allies with whom professionals join in a cooperative relationship. Synergic power grows from trust and prudence and is caring. Its ultimate goals are to enhance people's senses of autonomy and interdependence that grow out of working together, to enhance people's view of themselves as capable of affecting their own and others' destiny, and to enhance people's view of others as capable of working together. Synergic power counters the traditional view of professionals as controlling paternalistic experts and suggests that they should work to enhance clients' human development and self-efficacy. This dynamic of synergic power permeates much of the community-oriented model of the church as the People of God.

This concept of synergic power also relates to justice and the societal distribution of power. Professionals must "seek to share power and redistribute it" (Lebacqz 1985, 131), yet there is a complex paradox in notions such as empowerment and liberation. If professionals assume that their role is to empower or liberate clients, they may be operating paternalistically (Riger 1993). Empowerment and liberation sometimes become directive when they imply that clients passively receive empowerment from professionals. The professional's use of power, therefore, must involve synergic efforts, wherein the client and the professional achieve levels of human development greater than either one alone could reach, as in what we have identified as third-position thinking.

Eugene Kennedy and Sara Charles's (1997) work on the nature of authority relates to the distinction between directive and synergic power as well as to the importance of caring in an ethical professional life.[3] For them, directive power is the essence of what they call *hierarchic authoritarianism*, while growth-enhancing synergic action defines *generative authority*. They challenge the professions and our societal institutions, including the church, to reject unjust, outmoded, oppressive, regressive, and hierarchical forms of social organization in favor of just, more historically relevant, freedom-oriented, and growth-enhancing democratic forms that are generative of both individual development and the common good. True authority is generative and caring in that it "depends for its life on healthy people maintaining healthy relationships in their personal, work, and communal lives. It survives wherever people try to help each other grow" (6).

Also related to professional power is the societal construction of gender. One of the foundational barriers to ethical professional practice across the professions, including the priesthood and the management of church matters, is that of the powerful traditional constructions of gender. Beginning in human personality, one of the enduring insights of psychoanalysis is that each person, despite his or her biological sex, has both masculine and feminine psychological characteristics. Over the course of personality development, these characteristics blend in unique ways for each person. To oversimplify, it is useful to view the "normal" male as having ascendant masculine relative to feminine characteristics in his personality, with the "normal" female in like fashion having ascendant feminine characteristics. Especially for psychoanalytic theorist Carl Jung, the major issue concerns the *degree* of dominance or ascendance of one set of gender characteristics relative to the other. If a man is so exclusively masculine that his masculine side completely dominates or submerges the feminine, and he cannot "get in touch with" his feminine side, this is a sign of immature psychological development and potential psychopathology. A similarly problematic case is that of a woman in whom the feminine totally dominates the masculine. Whatever the gender of the person, including cases of gender confusion and homosexuality, total domination of either the masculine or feminine aspects of personality indicates psychosexual immaturity. For Jung, the mature and "healthy" state of affairs is one in which gender ascendance does not mean total domination, in which a man can recognize his feminine side and a woman her masculine side, as in third-position thinking. At this level of personality development, therapists who have sex with their clients can be characterized in terms of immature psychological development and potential psychopathology, although this in no way excuses their clearly unethical conduct. Priests who have sex with adult parishioners, whether male or female, or who sexually abuse minor children, are also typically psychologically immature, but, again, this does not excuse their unethical abuse of power (Cozzens 2000, 2002; Kennedy 2001).

These personal-level issues may be understood, at least in part, in terms of psychodynamics. Simply put, having faulty or immature personality development may lead professionals to be tempted to emphasize their own rather than the client's agenda, to pursue the gratification of their own needs, rather than to enhance the client's human development and community. In that regard, research has found that therapists who have had sex with their clients tend to exhibit personally and socially problematic behavior often involving power and control, anger, and sadism (Sonne and Pope 1993). Selfishness, egotism, or narcissism may, therefore, come unduly to influence the client-professional relationship and cause the professional's needs to be given priority over fidelity to clients. Professionals may freely intend to put their needs ahead of their clients' needs and thereby exploit them, using them as means to their own ends, or they may inadvertently do so because of psychopathological factors. In either case, society expects professionals to be mature enough to be ethical and not to succumb to these self-centered concerns.

Professionals should both (a) have been carefully chosen for entry into their profession on the basis of their virtue or strength of character, making it highly likely they can be trusted to strive in the highest ethical fashion to work unselfishly on behalf of their clients, and (b) have been helped to become aware of their faults and immaturities and take steps to correct them during the process of professional socialization. Problems on either of these two counts raise serious ethical concerns. As I noted in chapter 1, the Catholic Church has claimed to have instituted changes in the selection and education of priests in American seminaries regarding psychosexual issues, although controversy still exists between conservative and liberal Catholics about the ideal form of preparation for the priesthood.

The gender-based analysis of individual personality development may be extended to the societal level. Different societies and different historical periods display different blends of the masculine and the feminine in their values and modes of societal organization. David Bakan (1966) has argued that modern Western society has come to be heavily imbued with masculine (*agency*) values—enacted through directive and manipulative power and mastery—to the virtual exclusion of feminine (*communion*) values—enacted through more caring forms of power. We must rectify this exaggerated situation, says Bakan, by *mitigating agency with communion*, in effect, mitigating masculine values with feminine values. This would not entail a war between men and women, and the goal is not to replace male dominance with female dominance. This hostile "war-like" approach would merely be another extreme version of the either/or (and incidentally agentic/masculine) logic and power strategies, as with first/second position thinking, that have characterized our societal norms and mores, including those of the church. Rather, the goal is to help society be in better balance through encouraging the expression of *both* masculine *and* feminine values, an expression that would not take the form of a shouting match but of a dialogue or a reflective conversation, as with the third position. In this way, men and women as individual persons would be enabled to develop more fully, and community and societal development would also be enhanced. Moreover, the resulting state of affairs would be more conducive to ethical professional practice than the masculine value position that has traditionally dominated the social-institutional context, including that of the church, surrounding the professional-client relationship. This gender-based analysis begins to identify personality and cultural factors at the heart of professional practice and many other aspects of our society, including the clergy sexual abuse system.

These personality and cultural perspectives infuse the life persons live in community. To appreciate more fully the professional ethics dimensions of clergy sexual abuse from the perspective of the ethics of human development and community, it is helpful to look more closely at the nature of community, and central to understanding community is third-position thinking.

## THE THIRD POSITION AND THE COMMUNITY OF PERSONS

To understand community from the third position is to integrate the classically opposite perspectives on social life of *Gemeinschaft*, the theory of the village, and *Gesellschaft*, the theory of the city (Dokecki 1992; Dokecki, Newbrough, and O'Gorman 1993; Newbrough 1992; Newbrough, O'Gorman, and Dokecki 1993; O'Gorman, Dokecki, and Newbrough 1993). *Gemeinschaft* entails an *organic* and communal emphasis on *the one*; *Gesellschaft* has a *mechanistic* and individualistic focus emphasizing *the many*. The third position requires a double rather than a single intention: A moral action is one that intends the goal of improving the community and, at the same time, the goal of enhancing the human development of individual persons (Macmurray 1961).

The third position stresses the importance of communication in the development and maintenance of community. Jürgen Habermas's (1984) theory of communicative competence, moreover, suggests that community is the active process of free and uncoerced conversation in pursuit of the public interest and the common good.

The common good is not utilitarianism's greatest good for the greatest number. Rather, from Jacques Maritain's perspective in *The Person and the Common Good* (1947), it is *what is good in common for each and every person* — for Maritain (and Aquinas), eternal life with God; in the present context, human development and community. Personality theorist Erich Fromm, in *The Sane Society* (1955), argued that the common good of the person entails meeting universal needs (relatedness, transcendence, rootedness, sense of identity, and frame of orientation and devotion) that grow from the human situation. Moreover, Fromm argued that modern society is "insane" because it poses many obstacles to meeting these needs. In his last book, *To Have or To Be?* (1976), Fromm argued that any society that stresses the accumulation of things (having) over living lovingly and caringly with other persons (being) will fail to enable its members to meet those universal human needs, and thereby will make a meaningful life in community impossible to achieve. It is interesting to note that Pope John Paul II used a similar argument in the encyclical *On Social Concern*, where he distinguished between the *under*development characteristic of poverty and the *over*development characteristic of affluence, both of which derive from societal distortions arising in the having orientation that stand in the way of authentic human development and community (Baum and Ellsberg 1990).

## HISTORICAL PERSPECTIVES ON THE THIRD-POSITION THEORY OF COMMUNITY

In chapter 5, I explore the issues involved in rethinking the nature of the church in the context of the clergy sexual abuse scandal as informed by this chapter's ethical analysis and the next chapter's human science analysis. It is useful to view the upcoming ecclesiological matters from the standpoint of intellectual history. A historical excursion at this juncture also helps in the further development of the rationale for the ethics of human development and community.

Beyond attempting to avoid the *Gemeinschaft/Gesellschaft* dualism, third-position theory is a critique both of premodernity's organic and of modernity's contractarian political and ethical theories (Macmurray 1957, 1961). This double critique yields a third position in which ethics entails the pursuit of an ever more developed community of persons rationally participating in everyday life — personal, relational, social, economic, and political. The purpose of community life, so conceived, is *generativity*, the improvement of the local situation (as an interdependent ecology) and the improvement of the people who live there (as persons to be developed). The third position suggests a normative ideal of an integrated social ecology that honors liberty, equality, and fraternity[4] — balanced in a dynamic tension to develop a good society (Newbrough 1992).

The movement toward an ethics intending human development and community, J. R. Newbrough argues (1992), should be understood in the context of intellectual history, and he uses Stephen Toulmin's *Cosmopolis: The Hidden Agenda of Modernity* (1990) to help develop the third-position theory of community. Toulmin identified the modern period as beginning in 1648 when the Peace of Westphalia brought the Thirty Years War to a close. It had been a bitter, vicious time of conflict between Catholic organic (communion) interests and Protestant more individualized (agency) interests. It was also a time of social and economic disasters—crop failures, plagues, and the lack of strong political leadership. This war came after the full blooming of the Renaissance in the 1500s, when there was great interest in understanding and supporting human persons and their development.

The Renaissance humanists, such as Erasmus, Montaigne, and Shakespeare, were urbane, open-minded, and skeptically tolerant. The Peace of Westphalia, argued Toulmin, eschewed much of this humanism in the process of redefining the primary political entity as the nation-state to protect against the power of the Catholic Church. Much of the agenda of modernity, then, has entailed a retreat from humanistic values, and, in the face of the terrible social conditions that prevailed in Europe during much of the seventeenth century, the Renaissance attitudes of open-mindedness and tolerance were viewed as allowing, even encouraging, religious conflict to continue. The times called for clear, distinct, and certain ideas. Enter Descartes, who developed the method of systematic doubt as a means for establishing certainty and, thereby, moving to resolve religious conflict. Through continuous doubting, people could arrive at the foundation of truth. Descartes located that foundation in rational thought and Euclidian geometry. Logic and mathematics became the preferred method in a world that Newton conceived as physical and mechanical. Certainty could be achieved in a confusing and conflict-ridden world through a powerful and agreed-upon method. The search for and extension of this method eventually gave rise to science as the prevailing Western mind-set, and to logical positivism as the dominant philosophy of science.

Logical positivism, articulated in the early twentieth century by the Vienna Circle and debated throughout much of the twentieth century, was devoted to establishing abstract and universal, not practical, knowledge. Toulmin described four intellectual moves that brought it about: (1) from the oral to the written, (2) from the particular to the universal, (3) from the local to the general, and (4) from the timely to the timeless. The driving motivation was a quest for certainty through prediction and control entailing sensory experience and mathematical reasoning. It should be obvious, moreover, that a written, universal, general, and timeless view of knowledge and culture is not particularly conducive to community, which relies mainly on face-to-face oral communication about concrete particular matters in particular times and local places.

We are, however, no longer true believers in logical positivism. The briefest possible summary of its fate is that the proposition it was trying to prove—transcendent metaphysics is meaningless—came to be seen as a meaningless proposition by its own methodological lights. In addition, intellectuals were disillusioned by the Holocaust and the bomb, interpretable as the ultimate outcomes of logical positivism and the scientific attitude. Historically minded philosophers of science (e.g., Stephen Toulmin, Norwood Hanson, Thomas Kuhn) argued that science was more socially and politically contextual than the searchers for abstract universals could ever defend. To state it in terms of intellectual history, we may say that the modern age ended with the collapse of logical positivism, and we are now searching for new grounds for rationality and ethics.

The contemporary world, argued Toulmin, is in a situation similar to that of Europe during the Thirty Years War. In this our time, uncertainty and processes of deconstruction and change abound. There is a great yearning for community, but we have tended to lose faith in many of the institutions that have traditionally helped provide it, including the family, the neighborhood, and, recently fueled by the clergy sexual abuse scandal, the church. We also yearn for certainty and stability, but we have lost faith in the ability of both traditional science and religion to provide them.

Science and philosophy, however, are shifting gears. Rather than speaking of *the* scientific method, we now talk of *multiple* methods. Proofs are giving way to knowledge claims subject to rational argument among community members (Polkinghorne 1983). In the social and behavioral sciences, qualitative methods and the use of narrative are becoming acceptable, under the rubric of human science. We are rediscovering practical knowledge (Aristotle's *phronesis*), with a resurgence of interest in the Pragmatism of Charles Sanders Peirce, William James, and John Dewey (Bernstein 1971, 1976, 1983, 1992; Dokecki 1987; Menand 2001). Thus, the quest for community—the mitigation of agency with communion—is taking place at a time of more openness in science to multiple methods and sources of knowing (Dokecki 1992). There are parallels, of course, between the call for tolerance and open-mindedness in method and the call for these charitable attitudes in our life together in community. Vatican II was the Catholic Church's attempt to begin addressing these issues.

Toulmin's (1982) is a constructive position. While many today are methodologically deconstructive, arguing that we must live and pursue our intellectual goals without any overarching stories (Lyotard 1984), Toulmin argued from a methodologically constructive position that postmodernism's anti-cosmological viewpoint arose from our initial love affair and subsequent disillusionment with logical positivism and scientific rationality. He asserted that it is unreasonable to dismiss the possibility of a coherent and comprehensive outlook that shows both how all the pieces fit into the whole and where we fit in the grand scheme of things. We need to search tentatively for an overarching story, a root metaphor (Pepper 1942)—a *cosmology*—that is intellectually defensible and that holds the promise of meeting what Fromm identified as the basic human need for a frame of orientation. Toulmin's nomination for this return to cosmology is *ecology*. Ecology entails the argument, from a living systems standpoint, that living creatures must be understood in the context of the total environment, which itself is structured in interdependent fashion. This is similar to Erik Erikson's (1950) theory of generativity as the "Ethics of Human Ecology" (Browning 1973, 151) and John Dewey and Arthur Bentley's (1949) transactionalism, which views human action as an interdependent function of person-in-environment.

Thus far, my exposition of third-position theory using Toulmin has mostly dealt with community as social environment. There are two important person-level psychological dimensions of a meaningful theory of community. These are (1) the degree to which we experience our social world as community, the *psychological sense of community* (McMillan and Chavis 1986; Sarason 1974), and (2) the degree to which we experience ourselves as competent and effective community members, our beliefs of *self-efficacy* (Bandura 1989). Members of communities as viewed through the lens of third-position theory would not only be expected to grow "objectively" as persons, but also to report the experience of being connected, supported, and cared for in their social relationships. And intertwined with this psychological sense of community is the belief that we are powerful and self-efficacious, that is, in control of our lives and capable of intentionally affecting others. Central here is the phenomenon of empowerment.

## EMPOWERMENT

Empowerment is beginning to have the status of a buzzword. Yet helping clients identify and develop their power and use it in pursuit of their self-determined ends remains a valid and useful way of describing professionals' ethical use of their own power. Empowering clients in today's world, however, requires a fundamental reassessment of professional roles (Schön 1983). Donald Schön describes two very different models of professional roles: Model I (technical rationality) and Model II (reflection-in-action).

Technical rationality is the received view in modern institutional and professional life. In Model I, the major professional role of the technically rational expert is problem solving. Problem setting, the "process by which we define decisions, ends and means," is typically overlooked (Schön 1983, 39). A danger clearly inherent in this Model I approach is arbitrarily cutting the practice situation to conform to professional knowledge in Procrustean-bed fashion. The professional assumes the role of the expert, the one who knows all. The expectation is that clients will passively and docilely comply with the professional's advice. Therefore, Model I describes the traditional treatment-focused, top-down approach to professional action. In this version of the professional role, the professional has virtually all the power and all the answers, as in the traditional model of the hierarchical church. The professional's role—be it that of a therapist, physician, priest, bishop, or pope—is to "fix" or indoctrinate the individual client or parishioner.

In contrast, Model II (reflection-in-action) entails reframing both the professional's and the client's role expectations. Model II, using third-position thinking, calls for *complementarity*: The client and the professional enter a partnership that involves joint exploration of the situation. The professional has some expertise yet realizes that this knowledge is incomplete without the unique perspective of the client. This version of the professional's relationship with the client "takes on the form of a reflective conversation, where the . . . practitioner tries to discover the limits of his expertise," instead of imposing predetermined knowledge upon the client (Schön 1983, 300).

Model II embodies what I have called *reflective-generative practice* (Dokecki 1996). When the professional enters transactions with clients, he does so possessing some expert knowledge and a theory of professional practice. Unlike the Model I professional, however, the Model II reflective-generative practitioner does not assume the traditional expert role. Instead, there is a reflective relationship with the client that involves exploring multiple perspectives and sharing responsibility for both problem setting and problem solving. The client-professional partnership "incorporates recognition of the autonomy of those being served but also includes solidarity with them," writes Lebacqz (1985, 57), in a discussion of the ethics of the ministry.

Movement from the more typical Model I to Model II requires changes of perspective on the part of both professionals and clients. Tables 3.1 and 3.2, adapted from Schön, show the dimensions of these changes. They depict the changes in outlook required in the professional's move from Model I "expert" to Model II reflective-generative practitioner and in the client's move from the traditional Model I contract to Model II's reflective-generative covenant.

The contrasting professional perspectives on the client-professional transaction depicted in table 3.1 suggest the need for significant, personally demanding change. Model I's all-knowing, objectively distant, and status-conscious role would be shifted to Model II's appreciation for the limits of one's knowledge, connection with the client as a person at both the intellectual and the emotional level, and relation with others in a more genuine, less status-directed fashion, as in the third position. There are direct implications for the church if we contrast Model I and Model II views of the roles of priests, bishops, cardinals, and popes. This is the same contrast as that between the traditional hierarchical model of the church and Vatican II's People of God model.

+ + + + + + + + + + + + + + + + + + + + + + + + + + + + + + + + + + + + + + + + + + + + + + + + + + + + + + + + + + + + +

TABLE 3.1 *Contrasting Professional Perspectives*

| MODEL I | MODEL II |
|---|---|
| *Expert* | *Reflective-Generative Practitioner* |
| I am presumed to know, and must claim to do so, regardless of my own uncertainty. | I am presumed to know, but I am not the only one in the situation to have relevant knowledge. My uncertainties may be a source of learning for me and for them. |
| Keep my distance from the client, and hold onto the expert's role. Give the client a sense of my expertise, but convey a feeling of warmth and sympathy as a "sweetener." | Seek out connections to the client's thoughts and feelings. Allow his respect for my knowledge to emerge from his discovery of it in the situation. |
| Look for deference and status in the client's response to my professional persona. | Look for the sense of freedom and of real connection to the client, as a consequence of no longer needing to maintain a professional facade. |

Source: *Dokecki (1996, 95), as adapted from Schön (1983, 300).*

+ + + + + + + + + + + + + + + + + + + + + + + + + + + + + + + + + + + + + + + + + + + + + + + + + + + + + + + + + + + + +

From the client's perspective, the change from Model I's traditional contract to Model II's reflective-generative covenant also requires significant, personally demanding change (table 3.2). Many clients may be intimidated by reflective-generative practitioners. They will have been socialized into a role of having faith in professionals and wanting them to guarantee security, being unquestioningly compliant, and expecting unerring professional expertise. A relationship with a professional entailing client participatory involvement, interdependence, and discovery will require some getting used to, and this in turn will require the professional to be willing to engage in mutual learning and exploration with the client. Changed modes of professional education will be necessary. Again, the contrast between Model I and Model II views as applied to the laity has direct implications for the church. Model I describes the hierarchical model's pray-pay-obey view of the laity; Model II describes the People

+ + + + + + + + + + + + + + + + + + + + + + + + + + + + + + + + + + + + + + + + + + + + + + + + + + + + + + + + + + + +

TABLE 3.2 *Contrasting Client Perspectives*

| MODEL I<br>*Traditional Contract* | MODEL II<br>*Reflective-Generative Covenant* |
| --- | --- |
| I put myself into the professional's hands and, in doing this, I gain a sense of security based on faith. | I join with the professional in making sense of my case, and in doing this I gain a sense of increased involvement and action. |
| I have the comfort of being in good hands. I need only comply with his advice and all will be well. | I can exercise some control over the situation. I am not wholly dependent on him; he is also dependent on information and action that only I can undertake. |
| I am pleased to be served by the best person available. | I am pleased to be able to test my judgments about his competence. I enjoy the excitement of discovery about his knowledge, about the phenomena of his practice, and about myself. |

*Source: Dokecki (1996, 96), as adapted from Schön (1983, 302).*

+ + + + + + + + + + + + + + + + + + + + + + + + + + + + + + + + + + + + + + + + + + + + + + + + + + + + + + + + + + + +

of God model's view of an empowered and active laity participating in all aspects of the life of the church.

Two concepts come to mind in considering needed changes in client and professional role expectations: *partnership* and *shared responsibility*. "Partnerships are valued over paternalistic approaches because the former implies and conveys the belief that partners are capable individuals who become more capable by sharing knowledge, skills, and resources in a manner that leaves all participants better off after entering into a cooperative arrangement" (Dunst, Trivette, and Deal 1988, 9). This emphasis on partnership is complemented by Robert Moroney; in his book *Shared Responsibility* (1986), he makes the concept of need central to his analysis of social policy. He illustrates his notion of shared responsibility with a marvelous negative object lesson. While on a visit to the United Kingdom, Moroney accompanied a local authority social worker carrying out a survey of handicapped persons. An elderly couple, the husband 80 years old and disabled from a stroke, the wife caring for him despite severe arthritis, was asked in the course of the interview what needs they had and what problems the local social services agency might help them with. By any number of standards, the couple had many professionally defined needs. They lived in a second story flat with the toilet in the backyard. The apartment was heated by a single fireplace and three space heaters. They were able to move about with difficulty but were visited by their neighbors. The couple told the social worker that they would like some assistance. The wife pointed to a large tree outside the bedroom window and said that they were worried that a large overhanging branch might strike the window and break it. If this were to happen in the winter, they might freeze to death. Neither she, her husband, nor the neighbors could do anything about it, and she wondered if the social worker could arrange to have the branch cut off. The professional response was not atypical: "That's fine, but let's talk about your real needs." (155–56)

In this story, the clients had a keen understanding of their needs. The professionals, however, were enacting a role and assuming a character that made them insensitive to their clients. One can almost hear an echo of the cry, "They just don't get it," uttered so frequently by the critics of the church hierarchy during the 2002 clergy sexual abuse scandal.

## THE INSTITUTIONAL CHURCH'S MANAGEMENT OF CLERGY SEXUAL ABUSE

"They just don't get it" has often been said of many aspects of the church's legal and managerial attempts to deal with clergy sexual abuse over the years. What "they" don't get is that the virtually unchecked and unfettered power that inheres in their roles as priests and members of the hierarchy is too easily subject to misuse and abuse. Misuses and abuses of power have been at the heart of the clergy sexual abuse scandal—from the hierarchy's exercise of power and control in relating to both the laity and priests as an aspect of the church's corporate culture; to the offending priests' abuse of power in molesting children; to the Vatican's, the cardinals', the bishops', and other church officials' power tactics in dealing with abuse once discovered. Lord Acton's well-known nineteenth-century dictum about power corrupting and absolute power corrupting absolutely is part of conventional wisdom. It is less well known, however, that the subject of his observation was the Catholic Church. Here it is instructive to recall the charges made by some observers that the Diocese of Nashville and the Archdiocese of Boston used legal strategies, widely interpreted as blaming the victim, that attempted to implicate victims and their families in the harm caused by clergy sexual abuse. These strategies badly served the mission of the Catholic community in Nashville and Boston since they raise serious ethical issues.

In Nashville, for example, the diocese advanced what could be judged as an ethical legal argument that the actions of church officials during the 1980s pointed to the diocese's lack of fault for Edward McKeown's subsequent child abuse in the mid-1990s. Also within ethical bounds was the legal argument, with which courts have so far agreed, that the number of years that had elapsed between McKeown's association with the diocese and the abuse in question in the civil suit relieved the diocese of fault or liability. Continuing in an ethical vein, the diocese argued that, should diocesan fault be found anyway, several government officials should share comparative fault if they knew about McKeown's predilections and failed to report him to the appropriate authorities. It was quite a different matter, however, to include McKeown's victims and their families in the attempt to spread the fault and reduce the diocese's financial exposure.

Since victims of sexual abuse by *any* professional person experience harm, intimidation, and deep feelings of guilt, fear, and anxiety, no one should fault them *in any way* for their reluctance to identify their professional victimizers publicly. Moreover, if it is thereby unconscionable for *secular* organizations to blame victims for sexual abuse committed by professionals by claiming the victims have an obligation to go public by reporting their abuse, then it is even more ethically problematic for the church to do so, in light of its moral position of concern for the weak and the victimized. Nashville diocesan lawyers pushed otherwise-ethical strands of argument in defense of the diocese across a moral/ethical line when they blamed McKeown's victims for failure to report their own abuse. A merely legal stratagem, therefore, became a morally/ethically flawed attack on innocent and injured persons, and, in effect, victims were revictimized in the interests of preserving the church's power, its standing as a "sinless" institution, and its financial assets. Moreover, the counterargument—that the church's ethics should not be questioned here because this is the kind of thing attorneys routinely do to protect their clients' financial interests—overlooks the fact that attorneys speak for their clients. Attorneys are agents of their clients. In other words, not merely the attorneys but the diocese itself blamed the victims.

Blaming the victims of clergy sexual abuse has taken a number of forms over the years throughout the country in addition to claiming that victims have or share legal liability for their own abuse. Abusing priests have sometimes claimed that their victims seduced them, an argument advanced by some defenders of the church as well. On bringing their abuse to the attention of church officials, many victims have reported aggressive, even hostile, interrogation by church officials, ostensibly to get at the truth, but they have experienced it as an attempt to intimidate them into silence. They have felt humiliation, anger, and frustration and have reported that the experience is tantamount to being abused once again. Dioceses have even threatened to use their power to bring countersuits against reported victims and to embroil them in lengthy and costly litigation.

Although blaming the victim is a typical strategy many societal institutions use when facing vexing social problems—to solve a given social problem, identify the victims and blame them for the problem (Ryan 1971)—it is particularly problematic when the Catholic Church does so regarding clergy sexual abuse. Blaming the victim is not consistent with the church's caring mission, since it enhances neither the victims' nor the church community's growth and development. The blaming-the-victim defense is often a deceptive ploy, made up as part of an aggressive legal strategy to lessen the church's financial exposure. This strategy violates victims' autonomy in that it treats them as things to be manipulated for the church's purposes rather than as persons worthy of respect in their own right. Blaming victims harms them, and the personal toll it takes far outweighs the intended good of protecting the church's assets. When the church uses its power in this strategy to intimidate already vulnerable and suffering victims, the injustice in such a confrontation is blatant. In short, when church officials blame the victims of clergy sexual abuse, they come up seriously wanting relative to all the principles in the human-development and community-ethical framework.

The use of the blaming-the-victim strategy is instructive regarding the general approach the institutional church has taken in managing clergy sexual abuse. Relative to the church's mission of promoting the spiritual well-being of its members, one would think that the last thing Catholic Church officials would do is revictimize the vulnerable victims of its priests. But many bishops and other church officials have used legal tactics inconsistent with Catholic values and ethical precepts. As much as possible, sometimes in line with that aspect of their ministry that stresses their fiduciary responsibility to husband church financial resources, they have attempted to minimize the loss of funds due to possible and actual clergy sexual abuse civil lawsuits. On their view, allowing the existence of abuse and the identity of abusers to be made public had to be avoided at all costs in order to avoid giving scandal. Scandal would weaken the church's authority and its ability to carry out its many good works. It would cause people to question their faith and undermine their trust in the clergy, the hierarchy, and institutional Catholicism more generally. So abusing priests were protected behind the shield of secrecy and moved from place to place unbeknownst to parishioners and to future victims and their families.

The well-being of the People of God, then, did not appear to be the first priority of many bishops and church officials, that honor often having gone to preserving and protecting church funds and the hierarchical church and its clerical culture—ends in themselves that seemed to justify virtually any means. Officials embroiled in the clergy sexual abuse scandal often seemed not to care about victims and their families. They used deceptive tactics. They often treated victims and their families, and the laity more generally, as pawns on the hierarchical and clerical chessboard, not as the People of God. Much harm was done in the name of doing good. Justice was in scarce supply, a victim of concern for money and the avoidance of scandal, and the abuse of church power. In handling clergy sexual abuse, then, the church's call to promote human development and community went generally unheeded.

In conclusion, I have tried to show the usefulness of looking at the clergy sexual abuse system from the standpoint of professional ethics, in particular the ethics of human development and community. As Catholic moral theologian Richard Gula has written: "The perspective of professional ethics is the most inclusive one for assessing sexual conduct in the pastoral relationship. . . . [It] underscores the moral significance of one's professional character, the duties that belong to one's professional commitment, and the inequality of power in the professional relationship" (Gula 1996, 103). In the next chapter, I build on the ethics of human development and community by using human science concepts and findings to go more deeply into the dynamics of clergy sexual abuse.

CHAPTER FOUR

# Human Science Perspectives on the Clergy Sexual Abuse System

*Participation, cooperation, collaboration of the laity in the decisions of the*

*church?. . . [A]s long as I can contribute advice and work but am excluded from*

*decision making, I remain, no matter how many fine things are said about my*

*status, a second-class member of this community: I am more an object that is*

*utilized than a subject who is actively responsible. Persons who can advise and*

*collaborate but not participate in decision making in a manner befitting*

*their status are not really the church but only belong to the church.*

—Hans Küng, *A Democratic Catholic Church*

CLERGY SEXUAL ABUSE, as we have been discovering, is a complex personal, relational, and social system. In comparing Nashville's McKeown and Richards cases and Boston's Geoghan and Shanley cases, we saw four unique persons whose individual stories nonetheless bore significant similarities. The two unique dioceses also displayed similar patterns—from the settings they provided for the specific acts of abuse; to the strategies they used to manage the priests, the victims/survivors, the laity, and the media; to the consequences that followed for parishes, the broader church, and the public. In the course of developing the primary database for this book, studying more than

2,500 media and other Internet sources from the United States and across the world, I rarely found anything new or startling after the first dozen or so cases. In fact, except for Cardinal Law's high-profile and media-intensive special situation, what emerged during 2002 were patterns of action similar to the patterns described by Berry (1992/2000) and Bruni and Burkett (1993/2002), who reported on many clergy sexual abuse cases that emerged during the 1980s and early 1990s. Priest by priest, bishop by bishop, criminal or civil case by case, an image emerged of generally predictable structures and processes — the image, of course, was based on reported cases, and we must keep in mind that there are undoubtedly exceptions to it. The purposes of this chapter are to clarify the existence and operation of these structures and processes in the clergy sexual abuse system and to analyze them from the perspectives of a number of human science disciplines.

Because values imbue all aspects of scholarly work, the exploration of the ethics of human development and community in the previous chapter is both the overture and the first act of my human science analysis of clergy sexual abuse. With that analysis in mind, let us turn to perhaps the critical and most value-laden aspect of the clergy sexual abuse system: the use and abuse of power.

Looked at from the perspective of professional ethical principles, we have discerned a number of problematic phenomena within the clergy sexual abuse system. Caring for those outside the church's clerical culture (and increasingly within that culture as well) is often in short supply. Much of the truth of clergy sexual abuse is shrouded in secrecy, both justified and unjustified, and deception. In the institutional church, "the first intuition, or reflex, of the institution is secrecy . . . [which] is invoked not so much to protect the privacy of the individuals [as] to reinforce the power of the institutional arm. . . . So secrecy serves control in official Catholicism; as in every institution, it is prized as an instrument of expediency and as a veil that blurs the goals of justice or truth" (Kennedy 2001, 90). Church officials have often manipulated clergy sexual abuse victims and their families and denied them their humanity. Harmful and unjust victimization and revictimization of abused children and their families have been common occurrences, often resulting from the church's too prevalent tendency to place the good of the institutional church above the good of its people. "The bureaucratic response of the Church as an Institution is . . . directly opposed to the pastoral response of the Church as People" (Kennedy 2001, 145).

From the perspective of professional power issues, we have seen offending priests and many church officials unjustly abusing their professional power by using it directively, in an authoritarian fashion, for their own ends, by coercing, manipulating, and harming others. An example here is the church's use of victim-blaming to preserve its power and resources. This is in tension with using power and authority synergically as the means to promote the ends of human development and community and thereby the common good. Moreover, these contrasting power dynamics map onto the tension between the model of the church as preeminently institutional and hierarchical (directive power) and the communal model of the People of God (synergic power). Interestingly, these dynamics also relate to the earlier identified gender tension between masculine agency and feminine communion and the tension between Model I and Model II modes of professional-client behavior, as shown in table 4.1.[1]

+ + + + + + + + + + + + + + + + + + + + + + + + + + + + + + + + + + + + + + + + + + + + + + + + + + + + + + + +

TABLE 4.1 *Types of Power and Related Human Science Concepts*

| Directive Power | Synergic Power |
| --- | --- |
| Authoritarianism | Authority |
| Agency | Communion |
| Masculine orientation | Feminine orientation |
| Model I expert practitioner | Model II reflective-generative practitioner |
| Model I traditional contract | Model II reflective-generative covenant |
| Institutional/hierarchical model of the church | People of God model of the church |

*Source: Dokecki (1996, 96), as adapted from Schön (1983, 302).*

+ + + + + + + + + + + + + + + + + + + + + + + + + + + + + + + + + + + + + + + + + + + + + + + + + + + + + + + +

Since no person or organization is perfect, pure expressions of either the right or the left side of table 4.1 do not exist. I have used the word "tension" to suggest a "both/and" blending that is conducive to promoting human development and community (although Model II already represents such a blending). I use this table and the third-position approach in searching for ways to ameliorate and prevent clergy sexual abuse in the remainder of this chapter and in the next, which takes a turn toward ecclesiology. In the following sections, I review research on the church's organizational culture, ideology, and patterns of authority so we can understand the stage on which the clergy sexual abuse scandal has been playing out.

## THE ORGANIZATIONAL CULTURE OF
## THE CATHOLIC CHURCH

In characterizing the organizational culture of the Catholic Church, former seminary rector Donald Cozzens, in his *Sacred Silence: Denial and the Crisis in the Church* (2002), stresses the role of clericalism, the crucial yet destructive modus operandi characterizing much of the way the church pursues its mission. Clericalism, says Cozzens, is "always dysfunctional and haughty, crippling the spiritual and emotional maturity of the priest, bishop, or deacon caught in its web" (117). He cites a 1983 report prepared by the Conference of Major Superiors, titled *In Solidarity and Service: Reflections on the Problem of Clericalism in the Church*. The report presented a vivid picture of clerical culture. Clericalism entails the "concern to promote the particular interests of the clergy and protect the privileges and power that have traditionally been conceded to those in the clerical state." The Major Superiors added that "clericalism arises from both personal and social dynamics, is expressed in various cultural forms, and often is reinforced by institutional structures. Among its chief manifestations are an authoritarian style of ministerial leadership, a rigidly hierarchical worldview, and a virtual identification of the holiness and grace of the church with the clerical state and, thereby, with the cleric himself" (quoted in Cozzens 2002, 117–18). How has clericalism been manifest in the clergy sexual abuse system, especially in the clerical episcopal subculture?

Barbara Balboni's dissertation *Through the "Lens" of the Organizational Culture Perspective: A Descriptive Study of American Catholic Bishops' Understanding of the Sexual Molestation and Abuse of Children and Adolescents* (1998) explores some of the ramifications of clericalism by presenting the findings of a carefully conducted set of in-depth interviews with six abusing priests and twenty American bishops. Balboni's intent is to describe and analyze the church's understanding of clergy sexual abuse that occurred from the 1970s through the mid-1980s, prior to the time of major national media exposure or general public awareness. Her work provides the opportunity to learn about the culture of the church as an organization in the words of abusing priests and the bishops themselves. Much of the American church's earlier approach persists even today, although church officials did develop and attempt to implement, with uneven success (Steinfels 2003), meaningful clergy sexual abuse policies in the early 1990s and have undertaken an agonizing reassessment as a result of the 2002 scandal.

Balboni's six priest-perpetrators came from the New England area, had mostly been sexually involved with pubescent boys, were not currently active priests, and were either the subject of out-of-court settlements or had some form of civil or criminal legal entanglement. Overarching themes in the interviews of the priests were that they (1) saw clergy sexual abuse as a moral failure and (2) continued to experience the permanency of their calling to be priests—their desire to serve the church and its people and their commitment to preserve the church as an institution. For example, one priest said: "The hardest things are the little things. My name and picture were left out of the diocesan book, the one that comes out every year with all the priests' pictures. I wasn't invited to the diocesan priests' day of recollection. . . . I asked for the (diocesan paper). If I hadn't I probably wouldn't have gotten that either. I asked to get the newsletter for priests that comes out monthly, otherwise I wouldn't be getting that. After all, I'm still a priest" (132). Another priest observed: "You know what I think the problem is, the problem about whether these guys, guys like me, can go back into the ministry. The Bishop wants to hear, 'they're cured,' because they're told by lawyers this is what's necessary. . . . But the treatment guys won't say that. They say, there's no treatment for sexual addiction. All there is is control. . . . We will take him back, if. . . . But, no one will do this. No one will say, 'he's cured.' The bishops are under the influence of lawyers. They're telling them what to do. . . . I'm not going to fade into the background. The Church would be happy if I did. . . . I won't be laicized. They say I should resign for the good of the Church, but I'm part of the Church" (148–49). Balboni used the picture painted by the priests she interviewed as the background for her study's major focus on the organizational culture of the church as seen through the eyes of the bishops she interviewed.

Balboni's twenty bishops were active and retired members of the National Conference of Catholic Bishops (NCCB), now the United States Conference of Catholic Bishops (USCCB), from across the country. Of the forty-eight bishops she asked to participate, twenty-eight declined. Her questioning focused on the clergy sexual abuse situation during the 1970s and 1980s. She took pains to point out that all bishops are not alike, quoting one bishop as saying, "I don't pretend to know all the different kinds of responses. . . . Some bishops have probably been superior to others and some inferior to others. Some are probably more enlightened, more responsible, and so on" (169).

The overarching theme, one that continues to prevail, was that bishops understood defending and preserving the church as an organization to be their main mission and saw their responses to clergy sexual abuse as good-faith efforts to be faithful to that mission. In the early days of the clergy sexual abuse crisis, bishops attempted to avoid exposing the church to scandal and to protect their priests, rather than to give priority to the plight of victims. They saw clergy sexual abuse as sinful, and laicization was not an option. As Balboni notes:

> All sin was perceived as a moral failing for which the punishment was prayer, penance, and a firm resolve not to sin again
> - will power, not treatment, was considered the remedy
> - bishops looked at priests' religious not psychological motivations
> - psychological profiles on priest-perpetrators had not been developed or were not readily available
> - bishops did not understand the addictiveness of the priests' attraction to children and adolescents; for example, priests that were "good with youth" were seen as a "plus"; immaturity was not viewed with suspicion, it was seen as "docile"

- confidentiality was the norm; the seal of confession bound bishop and priest, and bound as well bishop and the victims' families

Laicization was not considered an option; once ordained, a vocation to the priest[hood] was considered permanent
- reassignment within the diocese was the norm; on occasion a priest with a problem might be sent to a neighboring diocese of a friend-bishop
- the bishops' treatment of the priests paralleled the way families treated their own problem children and adults
- the Catholic population was more homogenous; the congregations were mostly immigrant, blue-collar families, with very traditional values, one of which was to respect the Church and the priesthood (22–23)

In addition, given bishops' sole responsibility for, and autonomy in, their dioceses, and given their duty to report directly to the pope, they kept their clergy sexual abuse cases pretty much to themselves, unless forced to go public by media exposure. Said one bishop: "Given the way bishops have operated for several hundred years, with a patriarchal, heavy male, nobody-can-tell-me attitude, you have a kind of built-in system where they're going to hold their cards close to their chest" (170). Another bishop linked secrecy with the diverse characteristics of bishops and dioceses, saying: "I don't think a public discussion of the issue would have taken place [in the past], and that's a shame, but that's the way it is. Even now, even though there have been a lot of times when we've talked about it publicly, the idea that we would have a national policy dealing with this, is just not something that is our way of thinking. Most people think that the Catholic Church is a monolith, but each diocese is so different. The way we deal with things is so different. It's unbelievable" (170–71).

Compounding the problem of vast diversity across dioceses are perceived problems in the area of collegiality. As one bishop put it: "I just think that the collegiality is not as healthy as I'd like to see it become. And I honestly believe that it is not as healthy as it once was. . . . There are some sharp differences among the bishops. . . . My personal feeling is that it's a deeper question than language; it's a question of ecclesiology and Christology that we need to come together on, in ways that would allow us to get beyond fighting the battle on that level. . . . [W]e need to have an honesty and openness that will allow us to come to a better understanding of deeper things than language, as important as language is" (174). These bishops' 1998 statements highlight how momentous was the adoption of a national policy by the American bishops in the midst of the 2002 scandal.

Based on her understanding of the church's organizational culture during the early days of the clergy sexual abuse crisis, Balboni contrasted the way things were in the 1970s and 1980s with the way they should have been in hindsight. Seminary training should have adequately dealt with celibacy and helped young men be more psychosexually mature. Bishops should have been stricter with their priests and more willing to send them for treatment. Bishops and non-abusing priests should have been more responsive to clergy sexual abuse allegations and more aware of the addictive aspects of the offending priests' problem.

Balboni found that the bishops she interviewed were unanimous in saying that, today, a compassionate pastoral response of reaching out to victims is their highest priority. But, during the 1970s and 1980s, they had very little contact with victims, and then only with their parents. The families, moreover, typically requested that the matter be kept confidential and did not demand the removal of the priest, who was often a close family friend, from the parish; they demanded only that he be kept away from young people. Bishops also lacked the means and the will to investigate cases thoroughly, even when accounts differed, and they tended to minimize harm done to the children, saying "They'll get over it" (24). Said one bishop: "Our first . . . inclination was to be with the priests. And not to be with these people . . . not even to believe them. And they've been indignant and they have a right to be indignant, but it is still a struggle on the part of every bishop on how do I stand with the victim when I've got this priest right next to me and he's critically ill" (199). Another bishop said: "I think the biggest mistake we made was to try to hide ourselves from the victims. . . . I think we were too concerned about the legal ramifications and the financial ramifications of being taken to court. I think we were probably in denial. A lot of us thought . . . priests don't behave this way. The hell they don't" (198). And yet another said: "Now hindsight is a lot better. I think that we were shocked by it and so taken aback by it, that we didn't do what I think we should have done, and that is talk about it openly. Instead it was always in Executive Session. It was always, kind of we'll just talk about it among ourselves, lest the people become scandalized. Mistake" (198).

Balboni reports that the bishops she interviewed were unanimous in saying that lawyers—for the diocese, for the insurance companies, and for the victims—"profoundly affected" the way they dealt with clergy sexual abuse (208). One bishop said: "If the victim is over 20, the chances are the victim is very, very angry, and is looking for some 'big bucks.' And the lawyers want us to keep away from them because we might say the wrong thing" (213). Recalling one highly visible case, a bishop said: "The papers were after me because the publicity was enormous. So I wrote a statement apologizing to people who had been abused and how it affected me, and that sort of thing. The lawyers weren't totally happy because I was admitting and so on, but the papers and the people were super. I got all kinds of good feedback. Why? Because I was pastoral" (210). Another bishop said: "I think many times the lawyers would not allow the bishop, or would warn the bishop not to give pastoral care in a certain situation, because were they to do that, they would jeopardize the diocese" (211). These bishops' words nicely capture the tension between Catholicism's preeminent value of caring for weak and vulnerable people and the organizational church's motivation to protect its reputation and financial assets.

Balboni concludes her 280-page dissertation by highlighting a key feature of the church's current organizational culture. She recalls findings from Eugene Kennedy's extensive empirical study of the American priesthood, *The Catholic Priest in the United States: Psychological Investigations* (1971), commissioned by the American bishops in 1967. Using Erik Erikson's human development framework to categorize his data, Kennedy classified the developmental level of the priests he studied as follows: 8 percent maldeveloped, 66 percent underdeveloped, 18 percent developing, and 7 percent developed. In other words, almost three-quarters of the priests were found to be developmentally immature, only 7 percent having achieved maturity. Despite these eye-opening and disturbing findings, Balboni claims that the bishops "did little, if anything with the recommendations" from a study they themselves commissioned (225).[2]

Balboni quotes two questions Kennedy posed to the bishops. First: "Do you put first priority on assisting American priests to achieve greater personal maturity and, therefore, greater effectiveness as priests?" Second: "Do you rather put priority on American priests' adjusting themselves to the expectations of the institutional priesthood even at the price of not developing themselves?" (Kennedy 1971, 173). Balboni's perception of the bishops' refusal to answer these questions concerned her greatly in light of the clergy sexual abuse situation in the church. One bishop she interviewed said about Kennedy's work: "It gave clear evidence that we had a big problem. The Bishops . . . just totally refused to look at those studies. And if they had done something right then to meet the problems that were revealed by those studies, we probably could have avoided some of the problems that we got into" (Balboni 1998, 230). Balboni's conclusion is important:

> It seems to me that the bishops were unwilling to admit to the dilemma that [Kennedy's] study raised. Bishops knew the truth of this study—that priests, and bishops are first priests, are ordinary men. They are called to a life of service and they have been put on a pedestal because of that calling, but most, if not all, recognize their own frailty. The Church's scripture and tradition take the sinfulness of the People of God—both laity and priests—into account. But the bishops did not choose to identify themselves or their presbyterate with human weakness. They chose to ignore the fact that the church is the means to salvation and in need of salvation. The church is *ecclesia semper reformanda*, "always in need of reform." . . . In the end, the bishops answered neither of the two questions posed. They would have run a risk by choosing the first and assisting the presbyterate with the achievement of their own personal maturity. They would have run a risk by putting first the institutional needs of the church. But to have done nothing, served no one well. Making tough choices, said some bishops, is something bishops don't like to do. . . . At the risk of overstating, the bishops' lack of attention to their presbyterate seems wantonly neglectful. Contrary to the opinion that the bishops were protecting the clergy in clergy abuse cases, it seems they were protecting themselves. (234–35)

This conclusion, based on human science inquiry, echoes themes we have already encountered in earlier chapters and helps set the stage for my ecclesiological analysis in chapter 5.

Viewing Balboni's findings through the lens of table 4.1, and at the risk of overgeneralizing, the organizational culture of the church during the early days of the clergy sexual abuse crisis often seemed to be more directive and controlling than synergic and caring in the exercise of power; it seemed more authoritarian than grounded in legitimate authority; more individual-focused and agentic than truly communal; more masculine than feminine in orientation; more Model I than Model II in terms of the bishops' style of management and how they treated victims/survivors and the laity; and more in line with the institutional/hierarchical model of the church than with the People of God model. As we have seen in earlier chapters, many of these features of the church's organizational culture continue to characterize its handling of the clergy sexual abuse crisis in the present.[3] I now turn to broader ideological issues that provide the larger political and social context for Balboni's findings about the church's organizational culture.

## THE IDEOLOGY OF THE CATHOLIC CHURCH

As we have just seen, Balboni's main finding was that bishops saw defending and preserving the church as an organization to be their main mission, and it provided the rationale for their handling of clergy sexual abuse. Sociologist Gene Burns, in *The Frontiers of Catholicism: The Politics of Ideology in a Liberal World* (1992), argues that preserving the Vatican's power to control the church as an organization was the foundational reason for the development of the Catholic Church's currently reigning ideology. The issues of what the church's ideology is, could be, and should be are central to the development of meaningful clergy sexual abuse policies, particularly regarding the role of bishops vis-à-vis the Vatican and the laity vis-à-vis the bishops.

The notion "Catholic ideology" is an oxymoron for many traditional Catholics because they believe the church is founded on and embodies God-given, absolute, objective truth, whereas ideology suggests false consciousness and distortion based on value biases and political interests. For Burns and many other human scientists, however, ideologies are omnipresent and necessary bases for all political, economic, and social systems, including religious systems. It is not that there is one Platonic ideal organization and all the rest have ideologies; rather, all organizations have ideologies that we must analyze if we are to truly understand them. Burns's analysis of Catholic ideology entails the interrelationship of the sociological constructs of (1) structures, (2) power, and (3) ideology.

*Structures* are "impersonal organizational and social patterns that constrain our freedom of movement" (Burns 1992, 6). Structures are like social life's buildings that help give shape to our knowledge and predictability to our life world. Persons socially construct these patterns, but they come to know and experience them as "objective." Structures outlive those who constructed them and are difficult to challenge and costly to change. There are, according to my interpretation of Peter Berger and Thomas Luckmann's social phenomenology (1966), three cyclical moments in developing our knowledge of the structures of the social world: The person externalizes (constructs) the meaning of social reality that has been experienced; the person objectifies this externalized construction; and the person internalizes the once externalized and now objectified construction in ongoing socialization and social living.[4] Some people attend too much to the objectifying moment of this process and are naively realistic with a fundamentalist view of social structures. They reify (from the Latin *res, rei*—thing; therefore, to reify is to "thingify") structures that have been socially constructed, turning them into unchangeable things. Others overemphasize the externalizing/constructive moment and are subjectively idealistic, relativistic, and even solipsistic about the structures of the social world. They fall prey to the intellectually and ethically corrosive relativistic view that any social construction is as good, bad, or indifferent as any other. Thinking, reasoning, and ethics thereby become highly problematic, and we are left being ethically relativistic, skeptical, even nihilistic. To be scrupulously avoided, then, are an objectivism that reifies social reality and an idealism that relativizes it (Bernstein 1983).

Full appreciation of the three moments of this process of social construction yields a sophisticated view of reality as *both* there, to be known with confidence, *and* continually interpreted and reinterpreted. We are, Berger and Luckmann argue, born into an already existing social world with social structures that are for us simultaneously humanly constructed, objectively experienced, and socially produced. Our world, writes psychologist George Kelly, "is a real world, not a world composed solely of the flitting shadows of people's thoughts. But . . . people's thoughts also really exist, though the correspondence between what people really think exists and what really does exist is a continually changing one" (Kelly 1955, 6). We construct social reality, including our religious reality, and can and must reconstruct it, in order to develop humanly and find meaningful community in the social world.

Returning to Burns's analysis, the degree of power given persons or organizations have relative to others determines how they participate in social structures. *Power* is the capacity to act on one's own agenda and the "ability, if necessary, to enforce one's will. . . . [It] includes the ability to control the agenda and prevent undesirable issues or problems (e.g., resistance) from arising in the first place" (Burns 1992, 7–8). Power comes from the *resources* a person or organization commands—for example, money, arms, allies, knowledge and skills—and from the person's or organization's *autonomy*—freedom from being influenced by the actions or decisions of others.

An *ideology*, according to Burns, is a belief system arising from interactions with others in the social world. An ideology is one of the forms a social structure may take, and the constraints it provides may either empower people to live efficiently, productively, and happily in the social world or curb their freedom in unwelcome, onerous, and aversive fashion. Relative to an organization's power, which derives from its degrees of resources and autonomy, ideology as social structure and power transact in a complex and dynamic fashion:

> An ideology is not simply a list of beliefs. It is more a hierarchy of issues; people with the greatest power within the ideological structure will attempt to control the content of those issues at the top of their hierarchy more than those issues they place on the bottom. *An ideology is a hierarchy of issues enforced through the exercise of power*, but it always includes various spaces of autonomy and is always potentially an object of political struggle. An ideology can exist only if social interaction (including political interaction) continually reinforces its hierarchy of issues. It is, however, empirically *not static*, as the very exercise of power can alter patterns of autonomy and the distribution of resources. (Burns 1992, 12, emphasis added)

The fluid and changeable rather than static and permanent nature of an ideology's hierarchy of issues is of crucial importance as we attempt to understand the Catholic Church's ideology relative to the clergy sexual abuse system.

An organization that overlooks the need for change and development in its ideology and related structures does so at the peril of being out of touch with and irrelevant to ever-changing social realities. Burns argues that "distributions of power shape ideological structures. Changes in power distributions are thus fundamental channels of ideological change" (13). Relative to ideology, I have argued elsewhere (Dokecki 1996), we encounter a tension at the heart of many social issues, such as the clergy sexual abuse crisis. On the one hand, ideologies serve to legitimate the existing power structure of social institutions—a *conservative* function. On the other hand, ideologies can and must change to foster social change, requiring adjustment in the power structure, in order for an organization to survive, grow, and flourish in the interests of the human development and sense of community of its members, and thereby the common good—a *progressive* function. From the perspective of the ethics of human development and community, an organization's actions relative to its ideology, following third-position logic, should *both* maintain and legitimate its social harmony and community stability *and* effect meaningful, sometimes even revolutionary, social change or community development. The church must acknowledge this tension between the need for legitimation and maintenance and the need for social change, as it started to do in Vatican II. The ethical challenge for all in the church, from the People of God to the hierarchy, is to get the right mixture, to manage the tension in pursuit of human development and community and, thereby, the common good. This is one of the unfinished items on the Vatican II agenda and a major source of controversy in the church today. With these underlying issues in mind, we can begin to appreciate Burns's identification and analysis of the specifics of the Catholic Church's ideology.

If, as Burns suggests, an ideology is "a hierarchy of issues," the task is to identify the individual value issues composing the church's ideology and their hierarchic order of priority. The subtitle of his book, *The Politics of Ideology in a Liberal World*, refers to the church's nineteenth-century ideological response to the age of classical liberalism—the decline of most monarchies and of the *ancien regime*, the rise of nation-states and democratic political forms, the decline of feudalism and the emergence of capitalism as the preeminent economic system, and religion's loss of status to the Enlightenment's preference for reason and science as the arbiters of truth. Especially important was the church's reaction to losing the papal states and being forced to forfeit all claims to temporal political power. This political development, according to Burns, forced the Vatican to turn its attention from its external worldly power to the development and exercise of its power within the church. Thus, the situation in the nineteenth century can be stated succinctly:

> Liberal, anticlerical states, particularly in Italy and France, were resentful of the Church's historical influence and had the power to suppress its operations in their countries; indeed, the pope lost his kingdom to the newly unified republic of Italy. To avoid conflict, the papacy came to gradually deemphasize doctrine that had specific, controversial implications for state policy. Instead, Rome increased emphasis on the *faith* and *morals* of Catholic individuals and families as the basis of its religious authority. Faith and morals were ideologically peripheral issues for secular states, mostly irrelevant to their own power. Thus they were happy to allow the Church autonomy over such concerns. . . . [S]imultaneously the papacy had obtained autonomy over one category of issues (more purely "religious" issues) while becoming politically excluded from another category of issues ("temporal" issues). . . . Rome no longer had any political reason to participate actively in the legitimation of state policy. This had interesting implications for papal ideology on temporal issues. Such ideology, most of which fell under the category of *social doctrine*, became a less binding level of doctrine. It also addressed the topic of state policy only in vague terms, in contrast to the Church's style while it still had temporal power. By avoiding specificity, Rome avoided ever condemning particular state policies. (Burns 1992, 17–18, emphasis added)

Especially important here is that the church changed its long-standing understanding of itself in response to external political and social forces, despite the claims of ahistorical traditionalists that the church has never changed.

For the last 150 or so years, then, Rome has been presiding over the development and enforcement of a Catholic ideology for the modern, liberal era, one that comprises the religious issues of *faith* and *morals*, preeminently important at the top of the church's value hierarchy, and the temporal issue of *social doctrine*, decidedly less important at the bottom. This ideological hierarchy, Burns argues, both arose from the Vatican's directive, authoritarian, and patriarchal position that gave it the power to develop and enforce it, and helps maintain that power as the members of the church accede to and follow it. The Vatican insists that Catholics are bound, under pain of sin and threat of losing their immortal soul, to believe in the tenets of the Catholic *faith* (as articulated, for example, in the Apostle's Creed and extending to matters such as papal infallibility and primacy, and the insistence on a male and celibate priesthood). Catholics are similarly bound in the realm of *morals* to behave in certain prescribed and proscribed ways, especially regarding sexual matters (e.g., the prohibitions against sex outside marriage or for purposes other than procreation, as well as those against artificial birth control, abortion, remarriage after divorce, and homosexual acts). Rome thereby exerts an extraordinarily powerful influence on the private thoughts, beliefs, and actions of individual Catholics throughout the world. As Richard Sipe has observed: "The validity of the aphorism 'Control a person's sexuality and you control the person' was not lost on the power system of the church as it struggled for the hearts, minds, and welfare of its priests and people" (1995, 99).

Although Catholic ideology is also manifest in the church's *social doctrines* (e.g., pronouncements on forms of government, the ethics of war, the nature of labor and workers' rights, the economy, social justice), these doctrines are of decidedly less importance and do not bind Catholics in the same way as do matters of faith and morals. They are open to discussion and debate and generate wide differences of opinion among the faithful. Areas of ambiguity exist between the two apparently separate levels of the ideological hierarchy, since the Vatican insists that matters of faith and morals constrain the development of Catholic positions on social issues. For example, although abortion is a controversial topic of social and political discussion, the Vatican's position on the right to life and the prohibition of abortion as a matter of faith and morals is said to trump arguments in favor of freedom of choice. So although the church claims it does not bind Catholics in the realm of political matters, it does seem to bind them regarding abortion policies, and this tension has been the bane of many pro-choice Catholic politicians and public figures.

Where does the clergy sexual abuse crisis fit in all of this? Many American Catholics of both conservative and progressive stripe began voicing their disquiet concerning the behavior of abusing priests and the church hierarchy's handling of the situation in 2002. Although they may have had different understandings of the causes and the needed remedies, these disquieted Catholics seemed to agree in their dissatisfaction with and loss of trust in those in the uppermost echelons of the church. Voices of concern have even evolved for some into actions of protest, and we have seen the rapid growth of Voice of the Faithful (VOTF), starting in Boston in early 2002 and spreading throughout many dioceses in the United States.

Church leaders' responses to clergy sexual abuse have been within the context of the Vatican-controlled Catholic ideology. As we have been seeing with the help of Burns's analysis, in the church today, the pope and Vatican officials preside over Catholic ideology at the top of the church's power hierarchy, followed by the bishops, with the clergy, members of religious orders, and the laity subject to the power of either the Vatican or local bishops, depending on what matters are at stake. In the clergy sexual abuse crisis of 2002, the American bishops were pressured by widespread public anger and outrage into developing policies, and they did so by their own lights, with priests, victims/survivors, the media, the public, and the Catholic laity looking over their shoulders as spectators. The bishops' autonomy, however, was severely constrained since they had to submit their policies to the Vatican for approval, and the Vatican expressed concern about approving a set of policies that might be counter to universal church law, might be giving too much say to the laity, and, although responsive to the American situation, might be inappropriate for the rest of the church throughout the world. And where were the disquieted members of the laity? Burns's description of the status of the laity is sobering when applied to the clergy sexual abuse system: "The laity's power in the church is weak and almost wholly indirect. . . . Within what can be called Catholic ideology, the laity are more acted on than they are actors" (Burns 1992, 16). And many Catholics fear that the more things in the church need to change, or even appear to be changing, in some progressive fashion, the more things stay the same, with the church's conservative and intransigent ideology continuing to exert its usual influence in preserving the "natural" order of things about who is in charge.

But what about the need of any organization, including the church, to resolve the conservative-progressive tension at the heart of ideology in order to change so as not to become irrelevant to ever-changing political, economic, and social conditions? And what role might the laity (and priests) play in such a change process? As Burns suggests: "The future of the Catholic Church, like any social institution, very much depends on how its members attempt to defend or expand their autonomy and power within the institution" (196). Further: "It is very unlikely, however, that any such process will develop rapidly or dramatically in the Church as a whole. There is too much at stake. Within contemporary Catholic ideology, the hierarchical control of faith and morals is a central component of the political structure of the Church." Although attempts may be made to reform the church by utilizing the strengths of the laity, argues Burns, they will "depend primarily on the hierarchy's initiative. More likely to force changes are constraints from outside the Church that the hierarchy cannot easily avoid" (201). The outside constraints Burns refers to here are the changes in the church and its ideology brought about by events such as the wresting of control of the papal states by the emerging unified Italian republic.

Possible hyperbole aside, when Catholic theologian Thomas Groome said, "This is our September 11" (*Los Angeles Times*, 2 February 2002), referring to the then-emerging clergy sexual abuse scandal, might he have been identifying an event that could precipitate significant change in the supposedly changeless Catholic Church? In the clergy sexual abuse situation of 2002, there were indications that the church was experiencing "constraints from outside the Church that the hierarchy cannot easily avoid." Relentless media coverage and a constant drumbeat of criticism by columnists, analysts, theologians and other noted academics, victim/survivor spokespersons, and members of the laity, as well as many priests, created a situation unprecedented in church history, perhaps more fraught with peril for the church power structure than even the Reformation. Because of the instant communication that technology has made possible, the resulting crisis of confidence and trust in the church hierarchy took on worldwide proportions virtually overnight. Moreover, with the call for Cardinal Law's resignation by a group of his own priests, and the widespread unrest in the laity, manifested in part by the rapid rise of VOTF, the church found itself pressed for change *inside the church* as well. The clergy sexual abuse scandal of 2002 has caused serious questioning of the authority of the Vatican and church officials in America and throughout the world. Crucial to the survival and future development of the Catholic Church is the way in which the members of the church grapple with the inside/outside calls for reform and the authoritarian/authority tension identified in table 4.1, a matter I subject to further analysis in the next section.

## AUTHORITARIANISM OR AUTHORITY?

In the discussion of the human-development and community-ethical framework in chapter 3, I introduced the distinction between directive and synergic power (Craig and Craig 1973). One uses *directive power* in treating a person as a thing, as a pawn in one's own chess game, as an instrument for achieving one's own agenda, as a means to one's own ends. "Directive power dehumanizes people because it makes them less sensitive to the fact that they cause the results of their actions" (61). One uses *synergic power* in treating a person as a person not as a thing, as someone worthy of respect in her or his own right, as someone whose autonomy, goals, purposes, and agenda must be respected. Synergic power is "the capacity of an individual to increase the satisfaction of all participants by intentionally generating increased energy and creativity, all of which is used to *co-create* a more rewarding present and future" (62). Such power grows from trust and prudence and entails caring for others; its ultimate goal is the enhancement of (a) others' feeling of self-efficacy in being capable of affecting their world, (b) their psychological sense of community, (c) their senses of both autonomy and interdependence, and (d) their view of other people as capable of working together in community.

As we saw earlier, Eugene Kennedy and Sara Charles, in *Authority: The Most Misunderstood Idea in America* (1997), developed a distinction between authoritarianism and authority that closely resembles the directive/synergic power distinction. Their idea of authoritarianism entails directive power; authority entails growth-enhancing synergic power. True authority is generative and caring in that it "depends for its life on healthy people maintaining healthy relationships in their personal, work, and communal lives. It survives wherever people try to help each other grow" (6). Their use of the word "power" is different from that of Craig and Craig, for example, when they say that because people "do not distinguish clearly between authority and authoritarianism, authority is confused with power when power is actually a function of authoritarianism" (1). Craig and Craig do not confuse authority and power; rather, they distinguish between two kinds of power: one, directive, which is at the heart of authoritarianism; the other, synergic, which helps define the nature of true and natural authority. Recall table 4.1, where authoritarianism is also related to the masculine/agency orientation, the Model I expert practitioner and traditional contract, and the institutional/hierarchical model of the church; and where authority relates to the feminine/communion orientation, the Model II reflective-generative practitioner and covenant, and the People of God model of the church.

For Kennedy and Charles, authoritarianism coerces people through the use of oppression and control into a static state of conformity that severely impedes their freedom and human development. Its base "lies not in love but in power." It "serves the purposes of the few who would dominate the many" and makes "laws and regulations ends in themselves" (5). Authoritarians preside over people from their privileged position at the top of hierarchies, and the phrase *hierarchical authoritarianism* names their leadership philosophy. "Natural authority," on the other hand, "is a positive, dynamic force ordered to growth" (2). Through the medium of liberating and growth-enhancing human relationships, natural authority facilitates people's human development and expands their freedom—as when mature and effective parents "author" their children's development, mature spouses within a marriage "author" each other's generativity, competent teachers "author" their students' learning, or caring pastors "author" their parishioners' spiritual development. Authority necessarily entails three dynamic aspects: (1) a person who is the author or agent of the growth-enhancing energy, (2) another person who actively receives the author's growth energy, and (3) a creation or achievement that results from the author-recipient personal relationship—for example, children's development, spouses' generativity, students' learning, parishioners' spiritual development. This might also characterize the relationship between an authoritative and loving God and God's people on earth. Regarding the tripartite nature of authority, if any one element drops out or if the balance among them is not maintained, authority ceases to exist, and authoritarianism, social chaos, or stagnation may ensue. Persons who exercise authority work with other persons in face-to-face community-like relationships, and the phrase *generative authority* names their leadership philosophy.

The basic argument Kennedy and Charles advanced in their book is that our society is experiencing a crisis of authority—for example, the prevailing situation in the business world related to Enron and other corrupt companies and the situation in the church regarding clergy sexual abuse. The crisis derives in a major way from the fact that *hierarchies don't work anymore*, if they ever really did, for the needed exercise of mature and effective authority in social and organizational affairs. This is because we are in an age of space exploration, technology, and instant worldwide communication that guarantees the failure of hierarchical authoritarianism's attempts to constrain and control knowledge and information and to deny mature people a role in organizational decision-making. In a 2 August 2002 *National Catholic Reporter* article criticizing the U.S. bishops' newly developed charter and norms for dealing with clergy sexual abuse, Kennedy writes: "All hierarchical institutions rummaged for candles or hurricane lamps when the Space/Information Age short-circuited the elaborate grids along which top-down hierarchies transmitted their power, leaving them literally in the dark about how to regain control over that power again." And regarding the Boston situation, he writes: "As authoritarianism withered, those who had gained power from its exercise, including the most powerful of American princes, Bernard Cardinal Law, discovered, like a man using a bent key to start a 1910 Bentley, that the age of transportation has changed radically and that his outmoded vehicle is fit only for museum showings and antique car rallies." Kennedy goes on to criticize the bishops for taking a legalistic, mechanistic, authoritarian, and ultimately uncaring approach in their clergy sexual abuse policies, an approach that gives testimony to the hierarchy's lack of natural, mature, and effective leadership.

Regarding the relationship between authority and the ethics of human development and community, Kennedy and Charles write that "authority's effects are as positive as its intentions are *moral*. It nourishes the sound *develop-ment* and maturity of the individual, but it also exists to enhance the common good, that is, to build *communities* to accommodate a broad range of citizens. Authority is not authority unless it enlarges the healthy freedom of men and women. In the same way that breathing, curiosity and the need for love are in-tuitively understood as natural, so too is authority, as the impulse to give and enrich life in others" (Kennedy and Charles 1997, 4). Again, these ideas help us understand God as a loving authority in contrast to understandings of God as a fearsome authoritarian force in the lives of people. Kennedy and Charles go on to analyze society's moral crisis of authority in the realms of marriage, family life, education, work, the professions, governmental and business institutions, the law, and religious institutions, especially the Catholic Church's situation since Vatican II, held during the early 1960s.

In Vatican II, Kennedy and Charles argue, the church finally responded to the challenges of the modern world "by reorganizing itself, restoring the fun-damentally nonhierarchical collegial pattern established by Jesus Christ in his relationship with his apostles" (198). Actually the church's new course was fraught with ambiguity, since the traditional institutional-hierarchical model was seen as necessarily coexisting with the more communal People of God model, and experimentation would be required to work things out (Dulles 1974/1987; Kennedy 2001). *Collegiality*—organizational and liturgical forms characterized by more egalitarian, community-like human relationships in which "people associated in cooperative local relationships"—was the key to moving away from the dominant hierarchical approach in the church (Kennedy and Charles 1997, 199). The pope and the bishops were to work to-gether collegially, and national churches were to operate collegially through conferences of bishops, as were the clergy and laity in local dioceses and parishes. Among a number of influential societal developments, the informa-tion age and the success of Catholic education, especially in developed coun-tries, had created a laity quite capable of participating in collegial relationships to help the church make its decisions and carry out its mission. We saw the rise of parish and diocesan councils affording laypeople a voice in church gover-nance, and we saw a major increase in laypeople performing formerly clergy-dominated ministries (see also Steinfels 2003).

Vatican II, under the influence of the People of God model, also ushered in significant changes in the liturgy. While the theological and ecclesiological subtleties of Vatican II might have eluded some in the laity, no Catholic who attended church on Sunday missed the many obvious and dramatic liturgical reforms. Rather than celebrating mass throughout the universal church using Latin—the language of the hierarchy, the clergy, and the highly educated— the new liturgy was in the vernacular, and those attending were active participants using the local language everyone could understand. Although liturgical specifics differed somewhat from place to place, for the most part, the priest, who had formerly presided at an altar at the far end of the church with his back to the people, now faced them from an altar placed nearer to them. Many communion rails separating the priest from the people disappeared, and it became common for priests to abandon the pulpit to roam among the people while delivering their homily. The priest had formerly placed the Eucharistic bread on the tongue of persons receiving Holy Communion, but now recipients had the option of having the bread placed in their hand so they could feed themselves in grown-up fashion rather than be fed like children, and they were permitted to drink from the communion cup as another sign of their maturity. Moreover, laypeople, including women, often distributed Holy Communion and served as lectors, and altar boys were joined by altar girls in serving mass. Newly built and remodeled churches tended to have more circular than linear seating patterns to facilitate face-to-face relationships among the members of the church community. Moreover, many dioceses and parishes undertook to develop small faith-sharing communities as a way of enhancing parishioners' sense of community in otherwise large and impersonal congregations. The cumulative real and symbolic effects of all these outward changes were powerful in helping Catholics transform their lives in the church from serving as passive cogs in the hierarchical machine to assuming their identity as mature persons in the community of the People of God.

Given all that has changed since Vatican II, Kennedy and Charles write, "one could argue that the transition to the positive authority of collegiality is irreversible; indeed, evidence abounds that the long 'baroque' era marked by the exaltation of papal and religious figures has already ended" (199). As I have mentioned, however, there has been a backlash against Vatican II over the last decade or two, a backlash led by Pope John Paul II and Cardinal Joseph Ratzinger. Optimistically, Kennedy and Charles claim that "Pope John Paul II's reaction—to reestablish hierarchy vigorously and uncompromisingly—is destined to fail precisely because of the nonhierarchical environment created not by heresy [as some church traditionalists claim] but by the Space/Information Age. The effort to restore hierarchical forms has, in fact, failed because it has diminished the attention of believers, that is, their readiness to listen to what hierarchs say" (200). Kennedy and Charles amplify their optimistic assessment of the inevitable decline of the institutional and hierarchical in favor of the People of God model in claiming that, "despite the effort to restore hierarchy, the Pope and the bishops will eventually make a transition away from the obsolete hierarchical model into the center of a collegial church" (201).

My own experience in working with collegial and participatory structures in the church has been very uneven, and it is only with the rise of laity concern occasioned by the clergy sexual abuse crisis that I have become cautiously optimistic again about the future of the People of God model. In the early 1970s, just as the effects of Vatican II were being felt in my diocese, I was elected to the local parish board of education and served on the parish council as well, energized greatly by the rising interest in lay participation in church governance. In Kennedy and Charles's terms, I began to feel that I had authorship in the church. The bishop subsequently appointed me as a founding member of the diocesan education board, and, spurred on by certain church officials supportive of laity involvement, we eventually established a commission covering all aspects of education in the diocese, which many believed could have served as a national model. The bishop and other church officials, along with many laypersons, were members of the commission, which I presided over as chair. The level of collegial interaction was high and personally very satisfying to other lay members. I subsequently sat on the diocesan planning commission and chaired the committee overseeing diocesan staff benefits. I was then selected to be a member of the National Association of Boards of Education (NABE), a division of the National Catholic Education Association (NCEA), and eventually served as NABE president and as a member of the NCEA board of directors.

Very heady stuff for a lowly Catholic boy from Brooklyn, but things started to change in the mid-1980s, not so much at the parish level but at the levels of the diocesan, national, and universal church. NABE was the voice of lay participation in Catholic education, but it had to fight to maintain its position in NCEA, and I constantly fought off attempts to cut its budget and reduce its influence. At the diocesan level, the once-heralded education commission eventually went out of existence, and by the mid-1990s, lay involvement in diocesan affairs was pretty much restricted to business and financial professionals who counseled the bishop about budget and investments. In talking with other members of the laity who had been involved in church governance, we tended to agree that our diminished participation seemed to be related to the Vatican's pulling back from the collegial aspects of Vatican II, a feeling shared by many bishops as well in terms of their recent disappointing collegial relations with the Vatican. In the wake of the clergy sexual abuse scandal of 2002, however, the issue of the authorship of the laity in pursuit of restoring the authority of the church is back on the agenda with a vengeance. Central to VOTF's mission, as we saw in chapter 2, is the belief that changes in church *structures* regarding the participation of the laity in church decision-making are central to the possibility of restoring trust in the church's authority.

## THE STRUCTURES OF THE CLERGY SEXUAL ABUSE SYSTEM

The concept of structure, central to Burns's analysis of ideology and power discussed earlier, is also key in sociologist Anson Shupe's research in the area of the sociology of religion and religious deviance (Shupe 1995, 1998; Shupe, Stacey, and Darnell 2000). The clearest and most systematic exposition of this human science research program appears in his 1995 book *In the Name of All That's Holy: A Theory of Clergy Malfeasance.* There Shupe identified virtually all of the phenomena we have encountered so far in this book, including those found in the human science efforts of Balboni, Burns, and Kennedy and Charles. Unlike these authors, however, he developed a systematic theoretical framework with testable hypotheses for understanding clergy malfeasance — defined as *"the exploitation and abuse of a religious group's believers by the elites of that religion in whom the former trust"* (Shupe 1995, 15, emphasis in the original). Clergy malfeasance, a form of elite crime, is an umbrella concept covering a variety of types of church-related deviance and crime, including clergy child sexual abuse. Shupe's intent was to identify the social and structural, rather than personal and psychological, aspects of religious organizations that account for the perpetration of clergy malfeasance and the response to it by both the organizations and the victims.

In Shupe's words: "The sociological reality is that all religions are hierarchies of social status and power, just as they are hierarchies connecting spiritual realms of supernatural powers and entities with subordinate, supplicating mortals. . . . Moreover, that power is disproportionately held by leaders who are ecclesiastically trained, ordained, or 'called' to receive it. It is a power that is often undergirded by the loyalty and respect of rank-and-file believers who are taught or encouraged to expect that their leaders possess in large measure some special discernment or spiritual insight and have the benevolent, ethical treatment of believers always uppermost in mind" (25–26). Reminiscent of the inevitable power discrepancy in favor of professionals in relationships with clients, the asymmetrical power distribution favoring religious leaders (priests and bishops in the Catholic context) over followers (the laity), which grows from the social structures of religious organizations, is central in Shupe's account.

Religious tradition attaches moral weight and the capacity for moral persuasion to priests' powerful role, and parishioners thereby grant them a special kind of entrée into their lives. The resulting priest-parishioner relationship is the source of priests' ability to foster parishioners' spiritual development, but it also renders parishioners vulnerable and creates major barriers to reporting abuse, if it should occur. As we have seen, in the clergy sexual abuse system, powerless victims/survivors face powerful abusing priests, bishops, and other church officials bent on protecting the church, avoiding scandal, and maintaining their power and the church as an institution. Daunting as these barriers to reporting may be, paradoxically, the situation is made worse by the otherwise positive force of the reverence and respect that lay members of the church community have for their priests, because it can lead them to become defensive and protective. They often deny the allegation of abuse, in the first place, or blame the victim for making the allegation public once they come to believe the abuse did occur. "Accusations of abuse can alienate faith community believers from each other, just as occurrences of abuse can alienate victims and their sympathizers from churches" (Shupe 1995, 26), a phenomenon much in evidence over the years in the hostile relationship between the church hierarchy and victim advocacy groups such as The Linkup and the Survivors Network of those Abused by Priests (SNAP).

Citing 1 Corinthians 4:20–21 ("The kingdom of God is not a matter of talk but of power"), Shupe offers five axioms about the power inherent in church structures as the contexts for clergy sexual abuse and other forms of clergy malfeasance (27–31). First, as mentioned above, religious organizations are hierarchies with unequal distributions of power. The clergy's (priests' and bishops') greater share of power, relative to the laity, derives from their presumed special access to wisdom and spiritual experience based on their training and "calling," their special insights, and their responsibility for the entire church organization. Second, members of the clergy possess the moral power and authority to deny the laity spiritual privileges, such as church membership, reception of the sacraments, the forgiveness of sins, and even salvation. Third, churches are "trusted hierarchies," in that the laity has a high degree of trust in the clergy's "good intentions, nonselfish motives, benevolence, and insights/wisdom" (29). Fourth, since churches are trusted hierarchies, they provide the clergy with "opportunity structures" that, given the laity's vulnerability and lack of power, make it relatively easy for certain members of the clergy to violate the laity's trust and to manipulate, coerce, and abuse members of the church community if they should choose to do so. The clergy's betrayal of the essential trusting or fiduciary relationship they have with the laity is the ethical heart of the clergy sexual abuse system. Fifth, instances of manipulation, coercion, and abuse of the laity by the clergy should be understood as resulting not from the pathology of a few "rotten apples" among an otherwise healthy, dedicated, and well-functioning clergy, but from the fact that the church as a trusted hierarchy "*systematically provides opportunities and rationales for such deviance and, indeed, makes deviance likely to occur. . . .* Organization, not psychology, is the emphasis here" (30–31, emphasis in original).

Shupe identifies a typology of church structures to develop and test his theory and ultimately uses the dichotomy between "hierarchical" and "congregational" to investigate the structural contexts of clergy malfeasance and responses to it by the church and by victims. Churches characterized as *hierarchical*, including the Catholic Church, are those with centralized authority structures in which an ecclesiastical hierarchy executes a top-down chain of command, and the laity has little if any power. *Congregational* churches have flat organizational structures, are laity- or member-centered, and stress the authority of particular local congregations. These structural contexts differentially affect how the clergy sexual abuse system operates in the social world. Although it would be folly to suggest that the Catholic Church should become totally congregational in structure, given my emerging focus on the laity, Shupe's use of the hierarchical/congregational distinction yields useful hints for further development of a rationale for increasing laity participation in church decision making.

## Structures Facilitating the Perpetration of Abuse

Two key aspects of the perpetration of clergy sexual abuse are recidivism, the tendency for a clergy sexual abuser to abuse again and again, and normalization, the tendency for an abuser to rationalize his acts of abuse so as to preserve his positive self-image. Shupe finds support for his hypotheses that hierarchical churches are more likely than congregational churches to promote recidivism and more likely to discourage normalization.

In the Catholic Church, with its hierarchical structures, the permission for and tolerance of clergy sexual abuse recidivism is, first, the result of indirect structural conditions—how highly children and laypeople trust their priests, and how many trusted opportunity structures the church provides in which priests may have access to potential victims. Second, there are direct structural conditions supporting recidivism—the invisibility of acts of clergy sexual abuse and the church's handling of it, with a consequent lack of accountability, achieved through the exclusion of the laity from the church's inner workings. Shupe writes: "Hierarchical groups, through the enhanced status of their

clergy and greater invisibility of clerical accountability, are more able to transform protected places into opportunity structures for clergy malfeasance . . .
[witness the] avalanche of claims of clergy abuse reaching back to the mid-
1960s in hierarchical churches, and less frequently in congregational ones"
(Shupe 1995, 58).[5]

Regarding normalization, although individual priests may attempt to rationalize their abuse to themselves to preserve their self-concept, and church
officials may similarly attempt to minimize the extent of an abuse scandal to
preserve the church's positive image, the fact remains that clergy sexual abuse
is counter to the long-standing norms of the Catholic Church. Despite the
many violations of Catholic sexual morality by its priests that have come to public attention, celibacy is nonetheless the church's long-prevailing official norm.
Moreover, the church has a clear structure for the laity to air its grievances concerning norm violation, although this structure "does not always satisfy victims
and their advocates because . . . religious bureaucracies tend to operate so as to
protect the interests of functionaries over those of clients/laity" (60).

In effect, the same structural dynamics in the Catholic Church that support
abuse recidivism also work against abuse normalization, although the mere
existence of norms and policies does not necessarily discourage actions proscribed by them. One could extrapolate from Shupe's findings here that it is
likely that more laity involvement in church affairs would decrease abuse recidivism because an informed and active laity would be a deterrent to furtive
abuse perpetration and its cover-up by church officials. Moreover, laity involvement would increase the likelihood that church norms proscribing clergy
sexual abuse, important and praiseworthy as they might be in theory, would be
put into practice rather than serve as window dressing, would be honored more
in the observance than in the breach.

## Structures Influencing Organizational Response

If crises jointly entail threat and opportunity, then church leaders must absorb
and deal with the crisis created by the clergy sexual abuse scandal, and two possible organizational responses come to mind. First, bishops may defensively at-

tempt to control or neutralize the damage in order to preserve or restore their and their priests' integrity, spiritual authority, and trustworthiness. Second, more positively and proactively, they may enact structural reform measures that both alert all involved, clergy and laity alike, about the nature of clergy sexual abuse and its consequences and provide effective means of detecting, processing, and, better yet, preventing, future cases of abuse.

A typical form of organizational response for reducing the impact of clergy sexual abuse is *neutralization*, which Shupe has found is more likely to be associated with hierarchical than congregational church structures. It is "an organizational strategy employed by religious elites and administrators, in the face of victimization claims, to protect either their own prerogatives or the larger group itself" (Shupe 1995, 80). Neutralization serves the interests of the hierarchy, not those of victims and the laity. "Neutralization is rarely victim-friendly" (81). Church officials attempt to neutralize clergy sexual abuse by (1) using organizational inertia (a slow-moving and often noncooperative bureaucracy wears complaining victims/survivors down); (2) appealing to sentimentality (silence about abuse is for the good of "our" church); (3) reassuring people and reconciling them to their faith (claiming that the matter of clergy sexual abuse is already being effectively addressed and all that remains is to resume being a faithful member of the church); (4) bargaining (offering money and services); and (5) intimidating people into silence (making coercive and manipulative spiritual or legal threats). I have already discussed the Catholic Church's use of ethically problematic legal and administrative strategies, such as blaming the victim, but I should note here that Shupe concludes his discussion of religious organizational response to clergy sexual abuse and other forms of clergy malfeasance by observing that "it is for ethicists to determine whether such short-run tactics ultimately compromise the spiritual goals of the religious institution and belie its claim to spiritual authority" (115).

## Structures Conducive to Victim and Laity Empowerment

In line with the emerging focus of this book on the laity, the theory of clergy malfeasance also addresses how church structures may or may not lead to the empowerment of victims/survivors and the laity in the clergy sexual abuse system. Shupe hypothesizes and finds that, paradoxically, although victims in hierarchical as compared to congregational churches are less likely to "blow the whistle" about their abuse, they are more likely to become empowered and call for structural reform in their church (119). If we recall that the personal harm clergy sexual abuse causes individual victims/survivors spreads to relational harm experienced by the broader church community, we will see that these whistle-blowing and empowerment dynamics apply to victims and the laity alike. If we wish to find evidence in support of Shupe's hypothesis, we need look no further than the 2002 Boston clergy sexual abuse crisis in which victims only came forward, usually quite reluctantly, many years after their abuse by Catholic priests, and there was a very visible and vocal presence of Catholic victim/survivor advocacy groups, such as The Linkup and SNAP, and of the emerging laity involvement movement represented by VOTF.

The dynamics of victim and clergy empowerment in the clergy sexual abuse system are two sides of the same structural coin. On one side, hierarchical churches ward off grievances and challenges to their legitimacy by means of their sharply defined, traditional, and often authoritarian norms and ways of operating. Consequently, victims and others affected by clergy sexual abuse are initially reluctant to question the church's power or to scale its daunting bureaucratic heights. But victimization has three levels: (1) victims/survivors in the clergy sexual abuse system are ambivalent and experience fear, guilt, and shame; (2) they suppress or even repress the emotional pain caused by clergy sexual abuse; and (3) they eventually mobilize and become empowered to reform the church's structures and ways of managing the clergy sexual abuse system. The first and second levels relate to authoritarian and traditional church structures that make victims/survivors less likely to blow the whistle in the clergy sexual abuse system. Because of the other side of the structural coin, however, victims are virtually driven to move to the third level. In a telling passage, Shupe asserts:

> The irony is that . . . hierarchical administrators, with their emphasis on control and structure, are less likely to tackle claims of abuse and malfeasance directly and more likely to retreat to formal guidelines of procedure, protocol, and legality [recall Kennedy 2001, mentioned earlier]. These tactics ultimately prove dysfunctional, for they alienate the laity. Perceiving their treat-

ment to be the result of spiritual bankruptcy or insensitivity within the institution's leadership, the laity adopt mirror strategies: retaining attorneys, instituting lawsuits, and abandoning normative appeals in favor of remunerative or coercive strategies. The fundamental issue, however, is rarely one of financial settlement, even if the courts are brought into the picture. The money is only a punitive factor raised by frustrated victims. The real goal is reform and justice. (Shupe 1995, 127)

Shupe did not see the motivation of empowered victims/survivors and laypersons as antireligious, specifically anti–Catholic Church, but rather as reformist. This statement by Shupe captured well the clergy sexual abuse scandals in the Catholic Church from the 1980s until the mid-1990s and foresaw what would happen in Nashville's McKeown case and the 2002 scandal in Boston and beyond. The problem of "spiritual bankruptcy or insensitivity within the institution's leadership" is key because a church leader's task is to promote human development and community, outcomes put at extreme threat in the clergy sexual abuse system (Dokecki, Newbrough, and O'Gorman 2001).

## PSYCHOLOGICAL SENSE OF COMMUNITY IN THE CLERGY SEXUAL ABUSE SYSTEM

My own human science work in the field of community psychology over the last fifteen years has been at the intersection of human and community development, professional ethics, spirituality, and ecclesiology (theology of the church).[6] Together with my colleagues community psychologist J. R. Newbrough and pastoral theologian Robert O'Gorman, I have been conducting a consultation project in a Catholic parish (the St. Robert Project). We have been using liberation theology concepts and pedagogical techniques to further the pastor's and his lay co-leaders' goals of developing community and promoting members' spirituality and psychological sense of community in their large urban parish. This book's analysis of the clergy sexual abuse system has grown naturally from these earlier and still ongoing efforts.

In the St. Robert Project, we have been consulting regularly with the pastor and key members of the laity. Early in our work, we came to view the fact and

the process of leadership as key to community development and the consequent enhancement of people's psychological sense of community (Dokecki,
Newbrough, and O'Gorman 1993; Newbrough, O'Gorman, and Dokecki 1993;
O'Gorman, Dokecki, and Newbrough 1993). We defined leadership as "an
influence relationship among leaders and followers who intend real changes
that reflect their mutual purposes" (Rost 1991, 102). Our findings led us to propose leadership-for-community principles at the parish level, which also have
relevance for understanding the bishop-as-leader-for-community at the diocesan level. These principles help elaborate the leadership and authority issues in
the clergy sexual abuse system.

The first leadership-for-community principle is that the goal of church leadership must be to help enhance community life and the psychological sense of
community in contemporary society, since atomization and community fragmentation are the norms. Second, at the core of the contemporary atomized
and fragmented community is a crisis of spirituality; therefore, the essence of
leadership-for-community is to attend to the authentic human-development
needs of persons-in-community, often masked by the lack, or overvaluing, of
material goods. Third, leadership-for-community is a matter of enhancing people's human development, community, and psychological sense of community
through integrating them into church life. This entails promoting collaborative and mutual patterns of community participation. Fourth, leadership-for-
community at its best is a transforming process through which church leaders
enable community members to minister to each other, to find meaning in their
individual and collective lives, to live practical yet spiritual lives, and to experience a meaningful psychological sense of community. Fifth, leadership-for-
community enables the church community to develop stabilizing structures
that encourage community members to become stewards of human, material,
and fiscal resources and to operate according to church law so the church is
fiscally and legally sound. Sixth, the process of leadership-for-community requires situation structuring that entails planning, the use of rituals, and many
other means for clearly communicating the expectation for collaborative and
reflective effort between church leaders and the people. Seventh, and finally,
since revitalizing the church community is not an achievement but an ongo-

ing task to be mastered, the leadership-for-community process must be continually revitalized to ensure both continuity and change in church community development. This requires that ongoing attention be given to the development of processes integral to the parish that enhance spirituality and maintain a vital psychological sense of community. An example might be the founding of small faith-sharing communities and their integration into the ongoing life of the church community.

This model of leadership-for-community suggests a transformation in typical thinking about leadership in the church. While preaching, conducting ritual, and overseeing economic and legal matters are important leadership functions, this transformation grounds leadership in the realities of a present society where atomization militates against community. This transformation reorders pastoral leadership priorities so that community development is central among other interrelated and still necessary functions. It identifies the "crisis of spirituality" that causes contemporary atomization and community fragmentation to produce the political, economic, and social forces that alienate people and diminish their psychological sense of community. It orients the leader to develop community participation as mutual action or ministry, involving the pastor or the bishop, other pastoral leaders, and members of the church community. In the context of the clergy sexual abuse system, the implication is that, if bishops and priests as leaders operated in the spirit of these leadership-for-community principles, then they would be significantly more effective than they have been in dealing with and preventing the personal, relational, and social harm caused by clergy sexual abuse.

Regarding society's and the church's "crisis of spirituality," Newbrough, O'Gorman, and I have been working toward a conceptual framework that places spirituality and psychological sense of community at the center of both community psychology and pastoral theology (Dokecki, Newbrough, and O'Gorman 2001). The theme of spirituality explicitly entered our work through the St. Robert pastor, who saw spirituality as a theme central to the transformation of his parish from a moribund organization to a true community. He introduced us to an article by Sandra Schneiders, who defines spirituality as:

"The experience of consciously striving to integrate one's life in terms not of isolation and self-absorption but of self-transcendence toward the ultimate value one perceives. . . . Spirituality as lived experience is, by definition, determined by the particular ultimate value within the horizon of which the life project is pursued" (Schneiders 1989, 684). She notes that there are two approaches to spirituality. The first, that of academic theology, begins with the belief that one receives a spiritual experience as a gift, given to a receptive person by the Holy Spirit. The second, anthropological tradition begins in experience "from below": persons find spirit, authentic human development, and psychological sense of community in the process of reflecting on their experience. Spirituality here centers on the most basic questions about our everyday lives and goes to the realms of values, ethics, and intentionality.

In a vein related to Schneiders's work, Catholic theologian and environmentalist Thomas Berry sets spirituality in, not apart from, the dynamics of the larger human community: "This public spirituality is . . . much more significant than the cultivated spirituality of marginal groups or individuals engaged in intensive prayer and meditation apart from the dynamics of the larger human community. . . . [T]he ultimate spiritual issues are those dealt with within the cruel and compassionate world of active human existence, in the marketplace, in the halls of justice and injustice, in the places where the populous lives and works and suffers and dies" (Berry 1988, 110–11). Traditional Christian spirituality, Berry argues, negates the natural world as the place for the meeting of the divine and the human. The natural world becomes less capable of communicating the divine presence, and one's sense of being an integral member of the earth community is thereby severely weakened. He contrasts this with an equally problematic American spirituality, which has provided inspiration for science and technology: Everything needs to be transformed; nothing in its natural state is acceptable. This spirituality leads to the compulsion to use and consume. One can see that consumption is sacred from the central position it now occupies in society. The diminishment of the grandeur and fertility of the natural world, for Berry, is not simply an economic loss. It also entails the elimination of a profound psychic experience, restricting imaginative power (i.e., loss of narrative), and ultimately leads to the loss of unique modes of divine presence. It can also be an obstacle to having a meaningful psychological sense of community.

Berry argues that neither the modern scientific mode of consciousness (American spirituality) nor our traditional spiritual consciousness (traditional Christian spirituality) is concerned with the integral functioning of the earth community. The greatest single need at present is the intercommunion of all the living and nonliving elements of the universe. From the beginning, the basic characteristics of the universe manifest the unique and irreplaceable qualities of the person inseparably bonding with every other being in the universe.

Spirituality, according to Berry, is a matter of story. Traditional Christian spirituality's dualism of the sacred/spiritual and the secular has shaped our fundamental values and the means for their attainment in our society (see also Kennedy 2001). One of the major reasons there is a lack of community settings and the psychological sense of community today is because we live in two cultural worlds that shape our story—the sacred/spiritual, where the physical is excluded; and the secular, where the sacred/spiritual is excluded. "An integral story has not emerged, and no community can exist without a unifying story" (130).

The contemporary quest for community and the achievement of psychological sense of community, then, can be seen as a spiritual quest. It has been the subject of work by educators, theologians, and social scientists within the tradition of liberation theology (e.g., Azevedo 1987; Boff 1986; Dokecki 1982; O'Gorman 1990). The liberationists, complementary in many ways to Berry's approach to spirituality and community, have been emphasizing the development of small, local, mutual, intentional communities in the reconstruction of church life in Latin America. Their approach entails a "bottom-up" participative reconstruction of the church and the community.

The work of the Latin American liberationists has been in response to the recent transformation in community life in Latin America. Rapid changes have produced major dislocations. Modernity and its cultivation of the atomized individual came to Latin America only in the last fifty years. The result has been the immediate and keenly felt loss of community. In the crisis resulting from this disrupted way of life, it became necessary to recapture community. The liberationists responded by developing a new form of church—the small Basic Ecclesial Community (BEC). In the BEC, the people practice "theology at sunset." They relate the experiences of their day—wages insufficient to provide food, shelter, and clothing, no medical care, inadequate education, political brutality—to experiences in the Scriptures. This reflection and religious consciousness-raising call forth response—action seeking a change in the oppressive structure of the status quo. Their education is an interplay of knowledge-use and knowledge-generation: they use biblical texts to understand their situation and give it new spiritual meaning by their actions.

Beyond introducing the BEC as a new form of church, the liberationists have contributed to our understanding of the nature of the church more generally and have helped develop further the model of church as the People of God. Over the last fifteen or so years, many dioceses and parishes throughout the United States have created small BEC-like faith-sharing communities to complement the Sunday liturgy and expand Catholics' experience of church. The enhancement of people's spirituality and psychological sense of community that comes from engaging with others in these groups suggests the power of face-to-face communicative encounters in the relational realm. This entails a process of risking the self in true face-to-face conversation so that one is willing to be transformed and converted to deeper levels of faith and spirituality (Cowan and Lee 1997). Church leaders who facilitate the development of these communities are working in the spirit of the Model II reflective-generative practitioner.[7] They invite parishioners into communion in Model II covenant-like relationships with themselves and their fellow Catholics. They thereby experience the meaning of their Catholic faith in authoritative (not top-down authoritarian) fashion, through its synergic (not directive) power to inform daily life.

The clergy sexual abuse scandals since the mid-1980s, and especially the 2002 Boston fiasco, have led many Catholics to reexamine the nature of their spirituality and their religious lives. Once they began to appreciate the many interrelated aspects of the clergy sexual abuse system, they experienced an erosion of trust in church officials' exercise of authority. An expanding number of faithful Catholics have been taking steps to increase their influence and authorship in the church, in groups like VOTF, so they can feel more empowered and lead more meaningful and spiritual lives. Suspicion of their once respected and trusted priests and bishops has threatened the psychological sense of community they look for in the church. For many, their sense of membership and belonging to the church has weakened, although the majority of Catholics appear to have remained faithful to the church while hoping for, and sometimes working for, meaningful reform. Their sense of shared values and emotional connection with others in the church, especially church leaders, has diminished. Their experience of being with others in the church to help meet each others' needs for social support, meaning, and spiritual growth has been challenged: Will imperious church leaders really allow them to relate fully in this way? Perhaps most importantly, their always fragile sense of influence, of believing they can use their power and authorship to affect what happens in the church, has become a matter of serious concern.

VOTF is one voice among many questioning church structures that disenfranchise the laity and arguing for the need to wake the laity from its inactive, even depressed, state. In that regard, and in the spirit of liberation theology, theologian Paul Lakeland writes:

> The first step in emergence from structural oppression is for the laity to move from depression to recognition of their oppression and the prerequisite for this is to be able to name their own oppression. In liberation theology, such a step is called "conscientization," and it is the primary awakening of a community, through which it begins the struggle to pass from being object or victim of history, as defined by someone else, to subject of its own history. Through conscientization, people begin to take charge. In whatever context, it represents achieving or reclaiming adulthood from those who reinforced the infantilization of the victims. In whatever context, it is the moment at which the patriarchs, patronizers, or "parents" are challenged to abandon their stranglehold on power, and, all too frequently, the moment at which they often redouble the strength of their hold. (Lakeland 2003, 197–98)

This statement captures well the tension between the communal and institutional views of the church that has been so apparent in the clergy sexual abuse crisis. The call to liberation theology in helping to analyze and reform the clergy sexual abuse system suggests that two interrelated levels of reform must occur. First, the church must transformatively change its structures so as to promote the wellness of its members, free them from hierarchical oppression, and liberate them to develop spiritually as mature members of the church community—a *political* task. Second, many members of the church will require consciousness-raising, perhaps through participation in small church communities in the spirit of liberation theology's basic communities to become empowered to assume their rightful role in church decision-making—a *psychological* task.

## CONCLUSIONS FROM HUMAN SCIENCE ANALYSIS OF THE CLERGY SEXUAL ABUSE SYSTEM

The several strands of human science analysis presented in this chapter converge on the key ethical issue identified in chapter 3, namely, the use and abuse of power and the consequent threat to human development and community. Throughout the book so far, we have seen that clergy sexual abusers have abused their power in molesting their victims, and bishops have abused their power in covering up these acts of abuse and denying the laity any real say in these or other matters. These abuses of power highlight the importance for the church, or any organization, of achieving a just distribution of power in which all members—members of the hierarchy, the clergy, and the laity—participate in influencing what happens in the life of the organization. Participatory decision-making is a prerequisite for members' development of a meaningful psychological sense of community.

Balboni's (1998) research showed that bishops operated in the clergy sexual abuse system by using their power to create an organizational culture in which maintaining the church as an organization trumped virtually any other concern, including the pastoral care of victims and the protection of children as potential abuse victims. Burns's (1992) analysis showed that the church's ideology grew from the Vatican's need in the modern world to preserve its power over church governance and over the intimate lives of the faithful. Kennedy and Charles (1997) showed that the church's power-asserting and power-maintaining hierarchical approach to governance, in an age when hierarchy no longer

said: "They're telling us we can't stand here, we can't stand there. This is like 10 years ago, when the bishops didn't want to see us or hear us" (*New York Times*, 12 November 2002). Would Pope John XXIII have created such a climate? How did the bishops and the laity get to this place of mutual suspicion and mistrust, and what new understandings of the nature of the church having human-development and community-enhancing possibilities are available to the church in the future?

## *Cardinal Law Secretly Meets with Pope John Paul II*

Seven months before the November 2002 Washington USCCB meetings, an unprecedented and controversial series of events began to unfold that clearly demonstrated how an institutional/hierarchical church conducts its business. In mid-April 2002, Cardinal Law, barraged by protests and strident calls for his resignation because of his mishandling of the Boston clergy sexual abuse situation, met secretly with Pope John Paul II in Rome. This arrogant and sometimes flamboyant prince of the church had assumed an uncharacteristically low profile during his journey, seeming to go hat in hand to throw himself on the mercy of his holy father. Said Holy Cross professor David O'Brien: "The secrecy of going over there like that is really weird—you'd love to know how they got him out of town without being noticed" (*Boston Globe*, 17 April 2002).

Law reported that the Vatican was "very conscious of the gravity of the situation." He came back at least partially vindicated, however, saying that, although "the fact that my resignation has been proposed as necessary was part of my presentation," after speaking with the pope he felt "encouraged" and said he would remain in office "as long as God gives me the opportunity." The fact that the pope didn't force Law to step down or encourage him to resign, at least at this juncture, suggested to Notre Dame professor Scott Appleby "that the Vatican has decided that they don't want a domino effect . . . that if Cardinal Law should resign, other bishops who made egregious errors in reassigning priests also might have to resign" (*New York Times*, 17 April 2002).

## U.S. Cardinals Summoned to Rome

Law's secret Vatican visit was the prelude to a highly trumpeted summit meeting held in Rome on 23–24 April 2002 between the pope and U.S. cardinals. The meeting apparently resulted from an earlier Vatican visit by USCCB's Bishop Gregory and Bishop William Skylstad, who said he told church officials about "the loss of moral credibility of the church, the tremendous pain and hurt on the part of victims and the impact upon families, the feeling of so many of our priests who are doing wonderful exemplary work and yet really feel touched by this whole thing and are embarrassed and angry" (*New York Times*, 16 April 2002). Vatican officials claimed that the American cardinals were not being called on the carpet but were meeting with the pope to provide advice and information about the scandal, which heretofore had been considered by the Vatican to be almost exclusively a problem of the U.S. church. Theologian Richard McBrien said of the cardinals: "These are cheerleaders, these are not bona fide advisers. These are the kinds of people who the church is confident will approve what they've already decided to do." Priest and author Donald Cozzens said of the focus of the meetings: "I don't expect much. . . . This is a moral problem in the eyes of the Vatican. To admit it has systemic/structural dimensions is almost unthinkable to them" (*Boston Globe*, 18 April 2002). McBrien predicted: "If they give the usual rationalizations—that it's primarily an American problem, that it's media-driven, that these are old cases and that most bishops have already addressed it—then the problem is not going to go away and the Catholic faithful and Catholic priests are still going to be very upset."[5]

Pope John Paul II opened the summit by addressing the assembled cardinals in words that would come to provide the sometimes ambiguous and confusing context for developments concerning the church's emerging response to clergy sexual abuse over the next seven months:

> The abuse which has caused this crisis is by every standard wrong and rightly considered a crime by society; it is also an appalling sin in the eyes of God. . . .
> It is true that a generalized lack of knowledge of the nature of the problem and also at times the advice of clinical experts led Bishops to make decisions

which subsequent events showed to be wrong. You are now working to establish more reliable criteria to ensure that such mistakes are not repeated.
At the same time . . . we cannot forget the power of Christian conversion, that
radical decision to turn away from sin and back to God, which reaches to the
depths of a person's soul and can work extraordinary change. Neither should
we forget the immense spiritual, human and social good that the vast majority of priests and religious in the United States have done and are still doing. . . . People need to know that there is no place in the priesthood and religious life for those who would harm the young. They must know that
Bishops and priests are totally committed to the fullness of Catholic truth on
matters of sexual morality, a truth as essential to the renewal of the priesthood
and the episcopate as it is to the renewal of marriage and family life. (Reuters,
23 April 2002)

According to the pope, therefore, clergy child sexual abuse, perpetrated by a
very small minority of priests, is a crime and, presumably, fair game for civil
authorities. These criminals do not belong in the priesthood, suggesting a no-
nonsense, zero-tolerance approach. Further, American church officials must
make up for their errors that exacerbated the scandal by crafting careful policies dealing effectively with these priest-criminals and protecting their potential victims from harm. The pope's words imply that the bishops' errors were
not a function of the workings of the church but of understandable ignorance
and bad advice given to the bishops by "experts" on sexual abuse.

Dropping the other shoe, the pope reminded the cardinals that clergy child
sexual abusers have also sinned, and the church should be open to forgiving
these sinners. Their sin concerns sexual morality, a domain the bishops must
deal with effectively to renew the hierarchy, the priesthood, and society more
generally. The pope may be implying here, among other things, that bishops
have been lax in dealing with homosexuality and violations of celibacy in seminaries and priestly life, both volatile and highly controversial matters for the
American church. "Blaming homosexuals is becoming like the anti-Semitism
of the Catholic Church. They are raising it although there is no proof that there
is any connection between homosexuality and child abuse. And there are many
fine homosexual priests," said Eugene Kennedy, whose recent book *The Un-*

*healed Wound* is highly critical of the church's thinking on human sexuality. Chicago Cardinal Francis George commented: "The left doesn't like celibacy, the right doesn't like homosexuality, so off we go to the races. Everybody has an agenda" (*New York Times*, 25 April 2002).

Additionally, the pope's address emphasized the high value the church places on its priests for the good they do. The Vatican would come to stress the importance of safeguarding priests' rights, believing that U.S. bishops were not being vigilant enough in doing so in their recent vigorous attempts to meet public pressure to remove clergy sexual abusers from the priesthood. How is this to be accomplished while protecting innocent children from harm? And how far should the church go in cooperating with civil authorities regarding clerical criminal-sinners? Are they in or out of the priesthood? Is it zero-tolerance or something less? What criteria and processes should the church use to decide which priests to select for church discipline? What role should a priest's sexual orientation play in all this? How should identified cases be adjudicated? What punishment should those found guilty receive, and what should be their ultimate fate in the church? What happens when church and civil judgments differ?

The summit continued into its second day with the pope lunching with those in attendance and repeating his position on the clergy sexual abuse crisis. The summit's lengthy deliberations ended with a press conference presided over by USCCB's Bishop Gregory. He underlined the issue that seemed to be uppermost in people's minds: "There is a growing consensus, certainly among the faithful, among the bishops, that it is too great a risk to assign a priest who has abused a child to another ministry; that's clear. But it was not within the competence of this particular meeting to make that final determination, although the topic was clearly addressed" (*New York Times*, 24 April 2002). Addressed, yes; clearly addressed, hardly. Zero tolerance or not? Clarity on this issue, so important to victim advocates, would have to await the June 2002 USCCB meetings in Dallas.

Before, during, and after the Vatican meetings, the media was full of anxious and concerned statements by American priests. They worried they were being sacrificed to public opinion and the desire to protect the hierarchy's power.

They feared the possible development of an uncaring and legalistic zero-toler-ance policy, which could be too quickly and unthinkingly executed in witch-hunt, McCarthy-like fashion. The cardinals realized they owed their priests an explanation, so they drafted a letter, assuring their priests: "At our meeting, you have been very much in our minds and hearts, for we know the heavy burden of sorrow and shame that you are bearing because some have betrayed the grace of ordination by abusing those entrusted to their care. We regret that episcopal oversight has not been able to preserve the church from this scandal. The en-tire church, the bride of Christ, is afflicted by this wound—the victims and their families first of all, but also you who have dedicated your lives to 'the priestly service of the Gospel of God' (Romans 15:16)" (*New York Times*, 24 April 2002). This vague expression of concern did not help. Further clarification of the treatment of priests would also await the June Dallas meetings and, as it would turn out, many months after that.

For more general consumption, and to provide a framework for the Dallas meetings, the cardinals released a statement affirming a number of basic prin-ciples. (1) Clergy child sexual abuse is both a crime and a sin. (2) Pastoral care of victims is a priority. (3) Most known cases of clergy sexual abuse have in-volved the abuse of adolescents, not true pedophilia. (4) Science does not sup-port a link between celibacy and pedophilia, and priestly celibacy remains the church's teaching. (5) Because doctrinal issues are involved in clergy sexual abuse, (a) pastors must affirm the church's teachings on sexual morality, (b) seminaries will receive Apostolic Visitations to improve both their selection processes and their moral teaching regarding sexual morality, and (c) there should be a national day of penance and prayer related to the spiritual dimen-sions of clergy sexual abuse. (6) Catholics should faithfully heed the teachings contained in the pope's address to the cardinals (Reuters, 24 April 2002).

The cardinals also described proposals they had made to Vatican officials concerning the agenda of the June USCCB meetings in Dallas. They pledged to develop national clergy sexual abuse standards for Religious Institutes and Dioceses for submission to Vatican review (*recognitio*); to develop "a special process for the dismissal from the clerical state of a priest who has become *no-torious* and is guilty of the serial, predatory, sexual abuse of minors"; and to supplement Code of Canon Law clergy dismissal procedures by developing "a special process for cases which are *not notorious* but where the Diocesan Bishop considers the priest a threat for the protection of children and young people, in order to avoid grave scandal in the future and to safeguard the common good of the Church" (Reuters, 24 April 2002, emphasis added).

The "notorious"/"not notorious" distinction was an attempt to recognize both the wide degree of severity of abusive behavior encountered in identified cases and the need to respect the rights of both victims and accused priests, especially where the time elapsed since a reported case of abuse is great or there are convincing indications of reformed behavior. The distinction, however, made victims/survivors and other observers nervous. They feared church officials might be refusing to adopt a zero-tolerance policy by calling for an ambiguous and difficult to establish discrimination that would open the door to the exercise of the same kind of hierarchical discretion that had caused the crisis in the first place. Said *America* editor and Vatican expert Thomas Reese: "Where there is disagreement is over what to do with a priest who was involved in nonserial abuse 20 or 30 years ago and has been clean ever since" (Associated Press, 25 April 2002). In that regard, Washington's Cardinal Theodore McCarrick addressed such a hypothetical case, noting that if such a priest "since then has never had any trouble and the people know and they say, 'He's a good man, we don't have to get rid of him, we'll monitor him, we'll take care of him,' do I say, 'You're out?' I've got to pray about it." Victim advocate David Clohessy, however, called the distinction "more arbitrary hairsplitting. It attempts to minimize the problem by focusing on the egregious abusers, when all abuse is egregious" (*New York Times*, 25 April 2002).

Not surprisingly, the Vatican summit's inevitable failure to live up to expectations and its resulting ambiguities and unanswered questions left nearly all those concerned with clergy sexual abuse confused or disappointed. Not only did the meetings fail to slake the anger and frustration of victims/survivors, priests, many rank-and-file Catholics, the media, and the general public, it also added fuel to the scandal's fire. Not only were the outcomes unclear and disappointing, but many also saw the process as problematic and symptomatic. The process was an object lesson in how the institutional/hierarchical church typically functions. All roads lead to Rome—Cardinal Law secretly went to Rome, the pope summoned the cardinals to Rome, future policy-development efforts were to proceed within Rome's framework, and the final product was to be cleared with Rome, as it would turn out, not once but twice. An Associated Press photo appearing on the webpage of a 24 April 2002 *Boston Globe* story covering the summit is metaphorically instructive. Its caption read: "Pope John Paul II delivers his remarks on sexual abuse to American Catholic leaders yesterday in his private library in the Vatican." The pope, clad in white and seated beneath a massive El Greco painting, is addressing the black-and-scarlet–robed cardinals arrayed in a semicircle around him, creating a large empty space in the foreground. The void calls attention to the people who are not there—victims/survivors, priests, and members of the laity.

## U.S. Bishops Meet in Dallas

The USCCB webpage addressing the clergy sexual abuse system bears the title "Restoring Trust: Response to Clergy Sexual Abuse." The bishops met in Dallas on 13–15 June 2002 to do what they could to "restore" and "respond" so as to stem the hemorrhaging of trust in the hierarchy. They attempted to allay the mounting concerns about the scandal, loudly expressed inside and outside the church, here and abroad. In the weeks preceding the Dallas meetings, virtually every U.S. media outlet—print, broadcast, Internet, and otherwise—provided what the computer age calls "24/7" coverage. Academicians, theologians, Vatican and American church representatives, abuse experts, politicians, journalists, lawyers, people on the street, priests, the laity, and victims/survivors voiced their opinions or expressed their anger, frustration, and outrage. As had been the case over the years, conservative and progressive groups differed markedly on their understanding of causes and needed remedies, but they were virtually unanimous in criticizing many church officials for their lack of accountability, understanding, and transparency in their ill-fated attempts to deal with and prevent the sexual abuse of children by priests. For example, a spokesperson for the conservative organization Roman Catholic Faithful said: "It's clear that the church hierarchy in this country is in meltdown. A bishop can do practically anything and remain in good standing" (Associated Press, 2 December 2002). The best face anyone seemed able to put on the scandal was that God would bring good out of it, either if there was a renewal of spirituality and increased fidelity to church teachings, or if there was movement toward fundamental church reform. Others were extremely pessimistic about the future of the church. The bishops were clearly under siege. The question of the hour was, Would they continue to display their characteristic defensive siege mentality?

The ubiquitous Bishop Wilton Gregory held a press conference on the eve of the Dallas meetings. He said his role in the meetings would be "to moderate what promises to be a series of lively discussions and debates over the next two days" (USCCB, 12 June 2002). He claimed that bishops had been listening to others in preparation for this discussion and debate and referred to the unprecedented decision of the bishops to hear from two representatives of the laity, three victims/survivors, and a treatment professional. A promising prelude.

In his presidential address opening the meetings, Gregory continued in a decidedly open and nondefensive vein, saying: "What we are facing is not a breakdown in belief, but a rupture in our relationship as Bishops with the faithful. And this breakdown is understandable. We did not go far enough to ensure that every child and minor was safe from sexual abuse. Rightfully, the faithful are questioning why we failed to take the necessary steps." He said penance was required and structured the rest of his remarks around the Catholic understanding of the sacrament of penance: "The Penance that is necessary here is . . . the responsibility of the Bishops ourselves. Both 'what we have done' and 'what we have failed to do' contributed to the sexual abuse of children and young people by clergy and Church personnel. It is we who need to confess; and so we do." He then listed the bishops' sins:

• We are the ones, whether through ignorance or lack of vigilance, or—God forbid—with knowledge, who allowed priest abusers to remain in ministry and reassigned them to communities where they continued to abuse.

- We are the ones who chose not to report the criminal actions of priests to the authorities, because the law did not require this.

- We are the ones who worried more about the possibility of scandal than in bringing about the kind of openness that helps prevent abuse.

- And we are the ones who, at times, responded to victims and their families as adversaries and not as suffering members of the Church.

And quite significantly, regarding what the bishops needed to do to rectify their misdeeds, he spoke of "our corporate need for and this grace-filled opportunity of *working more collaboratively* with our devoted laity, religious, and clergy" (USCCB, 6 November 2002, emphasis added). Pope John would have approved.

At his closing press conference Bishop Gregory spoke of the charter and norms that he and his fellow bishops had drafted, saying we "agreed to bind ourselves in a mandatory charter, to protect children and minors from sexual abuse from priests and deacons; to acknowledge and reach out to victims and their families; to ensure that all priests are worthy of the trust of their people; and to ensure that Bishops are answerable and that the actions they take are transparent and consistent." Bishop Gregory characterized the charter's provisions as follows:

> The sum total of those actions means that Bishops will not tolerate even one act of sexual abuse of a minor. There will be severe consequences for any act of sexual abuse. No free pass. No second chances. No free strike. For those who think or say that this is not *zero* tolerance, then they have not read it carefully. . . . As Catholics, we do believe in forgiveness. We do believe in the power of conversion. An abuser, who recognizes the profound harm he has committed, and who has shown remorse, can indeed be forgiven for his sins. He just doesn't get a second chance to do it again. Period.

Diplomatically and dramatically he concluded: "Our actions today are not a panacea. The Charter is not perfect. More work needs to be done. As the victim/survivors told us, 'Listening is easy. Talk is cheap. Action is priceless.' That is our challenge. Ultimately, that is how we will be judged" (USCCB, 12 November 2002). But what kind of action? Referring to Bishop Gregory's attempt to do penance in his opening address, James Carroll trenchantly observed that Gregory apologized "despite the fact that he presided over the Dallas meeting that never took up the question of the bishops' own responsibility for the sex abuse crisis. Indeed, several bishops have apologized profusely, with little apparent inclination to attack the clerical culture that is the obvious problem" (Carroll 2002, 106).

I detail the specifics of the bishops' work in the next subsection in analyzing how the Dallas charter compared with what the bishops finally decided on, after Vatican intervention, in their November 2002 meetings in Washington, D.C. It is worth mentioning at this point the provisions of the Dallas charter that pertained to laity involvement in addressing clergy sexual abuse. In the spirit of his opening remarks, Bishop Gregory reported that, at the diocesan level, "[e]very Diocese will have a review board, the majority of whose members will be lay persons, not in the employ of the diocese. The Review Board will assist the Diocesan Bishop to assess allegations, to make recommendations on the fitness for ministry of priests or deacons. I[t] will also regularly review diocesan policies and procedures for dealing with sexual abuse of minors both for past cases and for the future" (USCCB, 12 November 2002). In addition, the USCCB also created an Office for Child and Youth Protection and a new lay National Review Board, to include parents, chaired by Frank Keating, Governor of Oklahoma. This board would monitor the work of the Protection Office and the diocesan implementation of the charter and would be empowered to conduct "a descriptive study and an historical study of the nature and scope of the problem within the Catholic Church in the United States, including statistics on perpetrators and victims." This last was significant because critics have long complained about the church's failure to document the extent of the clergy sexual abuse problem. Gregory did not detail the precise roles and functions of these diocesan and national review boards, and their standing would come to be the subject of confusion and debate. For example, as the National Review Board started its work, particularly the study of the clergy sexual abuse situation in local dioceses, Governor Keating said: "Some of these dioceses have very little in the way of definite records. They are slovenly to the point of reckless in some cases, and that's why I think that some of the information is suspect." As matters would develop in late spring 2003, Keating became so frustrated by his interactions with certain bishops that he publicly likened them to the mafia in their secretive ways of dealing with the review board. Many bishops, others in the church, and several members of the board criticized Keating for underestimating the bishops' degree of cooperation and for his indelicate and blunt language, and he eventually resigned his post. And Leslie Lothstein, who had participated in an earlier aborted study in the mid-1990s, said: "This new study will never be completed. I've been there, done that. They won't do this study because done correctly it will put them at risk in discovery proceedings in court suits" (*New York Times*, 8 December 2002).

Responses to the Dallas meetings were quite varied. Victims/survivors were encouraged but still skeptical and critical. They were grateful that several of their number had been invited to address the bishops, but they did not see the charter as expressing an iron-clad zero-tolerance policy for clergy sexual abusers. Experts disagreed with each other, some saying the bishops had finally faced up to their responsibility and taken very promising steps, although more work needed to be done. Others criticized the bishops for not being truly accountable for their mishandling of clergy sexual abuse, since they had called for neither the resignation nor the disciplining of any offending bishops, such as Cardinal Law. Law had been remarkably quiet during the sessions. In addition, many priests felt their rights were being placed in further jeopardy and the bishops were hanging them out to dry. Still others maintained that the bishops had failed to address fundamental issues, such as celibacy, women priests, homosexuality, and church governance. Outcomes aside, the process was more transparent and open and less defensive than in the past. On the other hand, many felt that the bishops were merely caving in to public pressure and doing whatever it took to keep the media and critics off their back. The true test of the church's resolve to deal meaningfully with the clergy sexual abuse system, however, would await the Vatican's response to the Dallas proposals and how the bishops would deal with it.

## The Vatican Responds, the U.S. Bishops Revise

After four months of press leaks and endless speculation, on 18 October 2002, Bishop Gregory announced the formation of a Mixed Commission of four Vatican officials and four U.S. bishops to address the Vatican's concerns with the bishops' Dallas proposals.[6] In Dallas, the U.S. bishops had produced two clergy sexual abuse documents: the *Essential Norms for Diocesan/Eparchial Policies Dealing with Allegations of Sexual Abuse of Minors by Clergy or Other Church Personnel*, and the *Charter for the Protection of Children and Young People*. According to the USCCB, "the Essential Norms provides church sanction and support for the complementary implementation of the USCCB's Charter" (USCCB, 14 November 2002). The relationship between the norms and the charter was not entirely clear and has been a topic of continuing confusion and controversy.

In a letter to the U.S. bishops reporting the Vatican's concerns, Cardinal Giovanni Battista Re, Prefect of the Vatican's Congregation of Bishops, after praising the bishops for the overall spirit of their work, said that "despite these efforts, the application of the policies adopted at the Plenary Assembly in Dallas can be the source of confusion and ambiguity, because the 'Norms' and 'Charter' contain provisions which in some aspects are difficult to reconcile with the universal law of the Church" (Vatican, 14 October 2002). Bishop Gregory said the Mixed Commission's charge would be "to reflect further on and consider revision of certain aspects of the Charter accepted by the Bishops in Dallas and the Norms proposed to the Holy See for *recognitio*" (*National Catholic Reporter*, 18 October 2002). He outlined three areas the Vatican had identified "in order to guarantee that our plan of action for the protection of our children will avoid misinterpretation and be in full accord with the universal law of the Church." As an example of the first concern, he identified the need for clarification of the standing, role, and functioning of the diocesan lay review boards. Second, the definition of sexual abuse, borrowed from the Canadian bishops, was a "source of confusion and ambiguity" and needed to be clarified. Third, the bishops' proposed process for "dealing with a priest who is known to have abused a minor" needed to be brought into harmony with the Code of

Canon Law and other relevant church legal procedures (USCCB, 10 November 2002). These examples of what U.S. bishops had to address, both through the Mixed Commission and the subsequent USCCB deliberations and interactions with the Vatican, went to the heart of the Dallas proposals—lay involvement, the definition of clergy sexual abuse itself, and zero tolerance and due process. Was the Vatican asking for a fine-tuning or a massive overhaul?

Bishop Gregory knew that the Vatican response would raise concerns that the pope was reprimanding the American bishops for their efforts and vetoing locally responsive policies from afar—in effect, violating the principle of subsidiarity. To allay these concerns, he reported an exchange he had with a Vatican official, who commented about the Mixed Commission that, "when you describe the work before us to others please stress that it does not represent a conflict between the Holy See and your Episcopal Conference. Our task, he said, is one in which we will exercise 'deep communion' in order to achieve 'common agreement'" (USCCB, 10 November 2002). Governor Keating's National Review Board, for its part, released a positive and optimistic statement, saying that members were "comforted by the overall support given by the Vatican to the efforts of the American bishops" (USCCB, 18 October 2002).

## U.S. Bishops Meet in Washington, D.C.

In light of the Vatican's reputation for glacial working speed, the Mixed Commission remarkably finished its work in time for the mid-November USCCB meetings, scarcely one month after receipt of the notice of Vatican concerns. Much of the charter remained unchanged except for the definition of clergy child sexual abuse and the processes entailed in identifying and dealing with abusers, matters the commission dealt with in detail in its revision of the norms.

The USCCB website (18 November 2002) presented a side-by-side comparison of the original Dallas norms and the commission's suggested (mandated?) revisions. Significantly, although religious order priests (those who belong to a religious order, such as the Jesuits, in contrast to those who belong to a diocese), who constitute about a third of priests in the U.S., were not covered by the Dallas norms, unbeknownst to the Conference of Major Superiors of Men, they were now included in the norms.

Consideration of the differences in the two definitions of abuse illustrates the difference in mind-set between the bishops, operating under the gun and in the spotlight in Dallas, and the Vatican, operating in the unhurried safe harbor of the Roman Curia. The Dallas norms cited the definition used by the Canadian Conference of Bishops (1992, 20) in *From Pain to Hope*, namely, that sexual abuse entails "contacts or interactions between a child and an adult when the child is being used as an object of sexual gratification for the adult. A child is abused whether or not this activity involves explicit force, whether or not it involves genital or physical contact, whether or not it is initiated by the child, and whether or not there is discernible harmful outcome." The Mixed Commission's definition was more church-like, moralistic, and legalistic: "[T]he norm to be considered in assessing an allegation of sexual abuse of a minor is whether conduct or interaction with a minor qualifies as an external, objectively grave violation of the sixth Commandment." In each diocese, the bishop, "with the advice of a qualified review board" would "determine the gravity of the alleged act." The Vatican-inspired definition, then, called the American church away from its secular understandings and back to God and the church's view of objective sexual morality. Practically, however, clear decisions about which acts are "external" and "objectively grave" instances of abuse would, in certain instances, be difficult to make; and leaving the ultimate say to a bishop, albeit presumably with the advice of a diocesan review board, would give him the kind of discretion critics say caused much of the scandal in the first place. Managing complex systems such as the clergy sexual abuse system requires managerial discretion; however, we grant discretion to those we trust, and a key aspect of the scandal has been the erosion of trust in the bishops. (I address the issue of the church's managerial discretion in chapter 6.)

The revised definition mentioned one of the more controversial aspects of both the Dallas and Mixed Commission norms—namely, the standing, role, and functioning of the diocesan lay review boards. Both versions specified that the membership of a board would include at least one priest and a majority of laypersons who are not employed by the diocese, although the commission added that the lay members must be "in full communion with the Church." The Dallas norms said: "To assist the diocesan/eparchial bishop in his work, each diocese/eparchy will have a review board." The Mixed Commission, how-

study of the reasons for this scandal? In short, will we know the full truth or won't we?"[7]

O'Brien's questions about the efficacy of the commission's work referred to the role of the Vatican and canon law in the process of identifying and dealing with abusing priests, a convoluted process in which the laity's influence would undoubtedly be even further diluted. The Dallas norms said that a "credible allegation" of abuse would result in the accused being "relieved of any ecclesiastical ministry or function" and subsequently investigated according to the principles of canon law. The accused would be encouraged to seek both civil and canon law representation. The commission's revised norm was more complicated. An allegation would first be investigated according to canon law principles, with the accused encouraged to have civil and canon law representation; the reputation of the accused would be carefully protected; the Vatican Congregation for the Doctrine of the Faith would be notified if the allegation was shown to have merit; the bishop would then follow canon law and "remove the accused from the sacred ministry . . . and prohibit [his] public participation in the Most Holy Eucharist pending the outcome of the process." In the Dallas norm, the sequence was: (1) receive a credible allegation (though the meaning of "credible" was not specified), (2) remove the priest from active ministry, and (3) then investigate. For the commission, the sequence was (1) receive an allegation, (2) investigate, (3) inform the Vatican, (4) then deactivate the priest. Since an investigation might take a long time, the commission's process would mean that an abusing priest might remain in active ministry for a protracted period rather than being immediately removed as in the Dallas version. Moreover, in addition to inserting the Vatican into the diocesan process, the commission's approach could be interpreted as favoring priests' over victims' rights.

Additional evidence that the commission's revisions paid more attention to priests' rights than did the Dallas norms concerns the role of treatment professionals. The Dallas norms said that the bishop "*will* ask [an abusing priest] to undergo appropriate medical and psychological evaluation and intervention, if possible," while the commission stipulated that "[t]he alleged offender *may* be requested to seek, and *may* be urged voluntarily to comply with, an appropriate medical and psychological evaluation" (emphasis added).

What happens when a priest admits to having abused minor children or, after investigation, is found to be a clergy child sexual abuser? In the Dallas norms, for "even a single act of sexual abuse of a minor—past, present, or future—the offending priest or deacon will be permanently removed from ministry." In certain instances (e.g., old age or infirmity), however, an abusing priest might not be dismissed but might be expected "to lead a life of prayer and penance. He will not be permitted to celebrate Mass publicly, to wear clerical garb, or to present himself publicly as a priest." This was as close to zero-tolerance as the U.S. bishops were willing to go, and after the norms were released in June 2002, victim advocates complained that they had not gone far enough.

The commission's revisions stated: "When even a single act of sexual abuse by a priest or deacon is admitted or is established after an appropriate process in accord with canon law [presumably requiring a trial by a secret church tribunal], the offending priest or deacon will be removed permanently from ecclesiastical ministry, not excluding dismissal from the clerical state, if the case so warrants." Significantly, the commission removed the Dallas phrase "past, present, or future," and much debate followed, since it turned out the commission was saying, in effect, that according to canon law's statute of limitations, victims must make abuse allegations about past abuse by age twenty-eight. This outraged victims/survivors because the trauma of clergy sexual abuse is so great and long-lasting that virtually every victim's charge of clergy sexual abuse to date had come from victims older than twenty-eight. Many victims' ability to report their abuse, said canon lawyer Thomas Doyle, was "seriously impeded by pathological bond to their abuser and to the institution that caused such a degree of duress that they were paralyzed from disclosing. This duress is grounded in the fear that the abuse victim was the only one as well as the fear that to speak ill of a priest would result in grave spiritual punishment" (*Worcester Telegram and Gazette*, 6 December 2002). Church officials said that this statute of limitations problem was mitigated by the commission. But, using highly technical canonical language, the commission inserted the Vatican's Congregation for the Doctrine of the Faith into the process. That Congregation would ordinarily return cases to the local bishop for adjudication by a tribunal, but if something like the statute of limitations might disqualify certain victims' allegations, the bishop can go back to the Vatican and ask for an exception (derogation). That the commission's approach was neither victim- nor laity-friendly was shown by the fact that the crucial words "statute of limitations" never even appeared in the commission document, and figuring out what all this meant required someone versed in canon law. Moreover, as we shall see in reviewing the Canon Law Society of America's attempt to clarify the meaning of the norms, the commission's removal of the Dallas phrase "past, present, or future" leaves in doubt to which accused priests the norms would apply—any priest *ever* accused of clergy sexual abuse, only priests accused within a certain time frame, or, perhaps, only priests accused after the norms go into effect.

One victim advocate claimed that the overall process intended to hold the bishops accountable "is going back into the secrecy of the courts run by the clergy." Regarding the use of clergy-run secret courts, Chicago's Cardinal Francis George said: "The point is that it not look as if the bishop is jury, judge and executioner" (*New York Times*, 14 November 2002). These courts or tribunals were also problematic in that the church had no experience in adjudicating cases of clergy sexual abuse and it might take years to deal with the backlog of pending cases. Said one lawyer representing victims/survivors: "These secret trials are absolutely incompatible with the American system of justice. I see a major confrontation coming in this country between the Constitution of the United States and the church's Canon Law. In this country, we do not operate in secrecy" (*Worcester Telegram and Gazette*, 4 December 2002).

As with the Dallas norms, not all abusing priests would be removed from the priesthood in the commission's version. Those with conditions such as "advanced age or infirmity" would be expected to "lead a life of prayer and penance" out of the public eye. In addition, the commission added provisions not present in the Dallas norms. The local bishop has the administrative power, as executive of the diocese, "to remove an offending cleric from office, to remove or restrict his faculties, and to limit his exercise of priestly ministry" and "in exceptional cases, the bishop/eparch may request of the Holy Father the dismissal of the priest or deacon from the clerical state ex officio, even without the consent of the priest or deacon."

The next area addressed in the two sets of norms proved to be very controversial by virtue of the change of only a few words. Regarding the always contentious issue of the church's duty to report known cases of clergy sexual abuse to civil authorities, the Dallas norms said that the church *"will report to the public authorities any allegation* (unless canonically privileged) of sexual abuse of a person" whether a minor or an adult, and will " cooperate with public authorities" (emphasis added). This would have represented a major change of policy and practice for many dioceses. The commission, however, said that the church *"will comply with all applicable civil laws with respect to the reporting* of allegations of sexual abuse of minors to civil authorities and will cooperate in their investigation" (emphasis added). Unlike the Dallas norms, which required reporting to state authorities in every instance of abuse, the commission's norms required reporting only in states that required the church to report, and, it turns out, not every state requires the church to do so. Critics saw this as a weakening of the idea that clergy sexual abuse is a crime that always requires the involvement of civil authorities; however, the bishops stated that, irrespective of what the norms said, they would adhere to the *charter's* provision requiring reporting to civil authorities in every instance. Again, we see the call to bishops' discretion, and, with the suggestion that the charter might trump the norms, the potential for confusion was great.

Next, the norms addressed an issue that is a major aspect of the current scandal, namely, procedures the church must follow in the possible transfer out of a diocese of a priest known to be a sexual abuser. Both versions said that bishops must not transfer clergy sexual abusers under any circumstances without making full disclosure to the new diocese or place of residence. The commission's version was, if anything, even stronger, clearer, and more detailed than the Dallas version. The all too typical pattern of a bishop transferring a priest from place to place within the Catholic Church with his status as a sexual abuser unknown to his new superiors—as happened, for example, when Cardinal Law transferred Paul Shanley—would no longer be permitted. The issue of how to protect potential victims in the abusing priest's new place of residence, however, was not addressed.

Finally, both sets of norms affirmed the importance of protecting the rights of alleged victims and alleged abusing priests. And so, with very little discussion

The *Norms* are not retroactive. . . . While they do provide for the possibility of obtaining a dispensation from the law regarding prescription, nothing else in the *Norms* has retroactive effect. This means that the determination that for the good of the Church "any priest in the United States who has committed even one act of sexual abuse of a minor . . . shall not continue in active ministry" (*Norm* 9), cannot be applied to offenses committed before the *Norms* take effect [1 March 2003]. Any offense committed before the *Norms* take effect is subject to the applicable laws at the time, not the new norms. . . . Since the sexual abuse of a minor by a cleric has consistently been reserved to the Congregation of the Faith, . . . any question involving the application of penalties at the present time for past incidents can only be resolved by the Congregation. Hence, when questions arise concerning past offenses, the diocesan bishop/eparch must refer the case to the [Congregation] which will direct him how to proceed. (2)

When the norms are placed in their universal church law context, then, one can see that it is uncertain how soon, if ever, a clergy sexual abuser who abused a minor prior to March 2003 will be removed from contact with potential future victims. It is almost as if all the furor during 2002 and early 2003 did nothing more than return the church to the status quo ante regarding known cases of clergy sexual abuse. Despite the CLSA's valiant efforts to make the *Norms* clear, their inherent ambiguity remains, confusion continues to reign, and the U.S. church will have to look to Rome to know what is the right thing to do in these significant past aspects of the clergy sexual abuse system. It took the *Guide*'s analysis to penetrate the bishops' well-intentioned language and return us to the reality of the Vatican's control of many matters of immediate and vital concern to U.S. Catholics.[10]

## Concerns over Process

Beyond these ambiguous and problematic outcomes of the institutional church's attempts to address the clergy sexual abuse system, the omnipresent question of process has loomed large. The church has not met John XXIII's challenge of mitigating the institutional/hierarchical vision of church with the more community-like People of God vision. It has not made progress toward John's "new order of human relationships." If anything, divisions within the church about the role of the laity and collegiality in church governance have been widened not narrowed. To an unknown extent, the bishops may have maintained their managerial discretion relative to the Vatican in removing abusing priests from the active ministry, but since discretion is predicated on trust, the scandal-induced erosion of trust in the bishops has produced feelings of suspicion and concern. The church's damaged credibility continues to be a victim of the abuse scandal.

Concerned Catholics have yet to mitigate the Vatican's and the bishops' authoritarian control by achieving a more just distribution of power within the church, reflected in moving toward all levels of the People of God having an opportunity to participate in church governance—although Cardinal Law finally stepped down due, at least in part, to pressure brought by the laity and, especially, some of his priests. The institutional church has continued to view clergy sexual abuse virtually exclusively as a moral problem with no structural aspects. Fundamental issues such as celibacy, women priests, homosexuality, and church governance have remained unaddressed (Cozzens 2002). The Vatican has exerted control over the U.S. bishops by means of a document that was not only unknown to the priests, victims/survivors, and the laity but was also kept secret from many of the bishops themselves. Regarding the Vatican's approach, canon lawyer Thomas Doyle has commented: "It feels like the last item on the agenda is the protection of children and the top of the agenda is power, power, and power" (*Boston Globe*, 29 November 2002). Even the church's vaunted new policy-development efforts and changes made to existing policies, purporting to deal definitively with hundreds of identified clergy sexual abusers, may have turned out to be no change at all with respect to those who abused minors prior to March 2003, which means virtually every currently known abusing priest. In the words of James Carroll: "[A] power structure that is accountable only to itself will always end by abusing the powerless. Even then, it will paternalistically ask to be trusted to repair the damage"

(Carroll 2002, 15). Many Catholics have refused to grant this trust and have demanded that the church recognize them as adults who, while they respect their authoritative elders, have left behind the rule of their erstwhile authoritarian parents.

## THE CHURCH'S UNDERSTANDING OF ITSELF

### *Vatican II Reforms Related to the Clergy Sexual Abuse System*

The clergy sexual abuse scandal has given the world a vivid demonstration of how a church that understands itself through the lens of the institutional/hierarchical model conducts its business—from Pope John Paul II's promulgation of secret norms related to clergy sexual abuse in April 2001; to Cardinal Law's secret meetings with the pope in Rome; to the pope's summoning of the U.S. cardinals to meet with him in Rome; to the bishops' meetings in Dallas to craft clergy sexual abuse norms; to the Vatican's critique of those norms, resulting in the Mixed Commission's revisions of them; to the bishops' adoption of these revisions in their November 2002 meetings in Washington, D.C.

As we have seen, the institutional/hierarchical model tends to be conceptually related to (1) authoritarianism, (2) the use of directive and coercive power, (3) an agentic (patriarchal and masculine) orientation to the social world, and (4) the adoption of a Model I top-down style of ministerial practice in which the clergy-as-experts tend to view those with whom they work as docile and dependent children. The People of God model, on the other hand, mitigates these tendencies by movement toward (1) the exercise of natural and true authority, (2) the use of growth-enhancing synergic power, (3) a more communion-like (feminine) orientation to the social world, and (4) the adoption of a Model II style of ministerial practice in which bishops and priests interact with those with whom they work in a mutual partnership of mature adults.

As a product of Catholic education from the mid-1940s to the early 1960s, graduating from a Catholic college on the eve of Vatican II, I always viewed the church as institutional/hierarchical. I had no reason to doubt that it would always be that way—was, is, and ever shall be, world without end, Amen. For this

Brooklyn-born and -bred Catholic, Catholic education gave me virtually no appreciation for Church history and biblical scholarship as they might relate to the emerging drumbeat of criticism within the church of the prevailing ecclesiology. This theological criticism led to Vatican II's vigorous debate about the nature of the church and the need for reform.

Pius XII was the very visible pope of my childhood, and I was unaware of the legacy of his like-minded predecessors—especially, late-nineteenth-century Pius IX with his *Syllabus of Errors* and early-twentieth-century Pius X with his condemnation of Modernism. These popes fought to strengthen the institutional/hierarchical church and stamped that model on the very being of most Catholics throughout the world socialized into the Catholic faith during their pontificates. When the affable John XXIII succeeded Pius XII in 1958, I had no idea that "he was conscious of the limits of his role and spoke candidly to his clergy of the evils of authoritarianism (which 'represses legitimate initiatives, is unable to listen, confuses harshness with firmness, inflexibility with dignity') and paternalism ('a caricature of paternity' that 'keeps people immature in order to maintain its own superior position,' 'speaks protectively, and does not accept true collaboration'—the word despised by Pius XII") (Cahill 2002, 163). These convictions of Pope John infused Vatican II and inspired me to ask the rhetorical question, What would John XXIII do?[11]

As monumentally important as Vatican II was in opening the church to new ways of thinking and acting, befitting Pope John's call for openness and sensitivity to the actual experiences of Catholics and their church throughout the world, its documents were typically more like agendas for future thinking and development than definitive pronouncements. This was certainly true concerning how the church might understand itself theologically, the domain of ecclesiology, and the pastoral reforms that might flow from this or that vision of the nature of the church. Given the 2000-year history and tradition of an organization as vast as the Catholic Church—often fraught with theological and political disputes—and the fact that the council took place in the volatile and disputatious political environment of the postwar/cold war mid-twentieth century, it would have been too much to expect a clear and concise statement about the nature of the church. Further, the delegates and experts who attended the council sessions represented very different theological approaches, ranging from the quite conservative, even fundamentalist, to the progressive, even radical. Much political infighting preceded the opening of the council, and Pope John was masterful in assuring that the council would entail truly open discussion rather than merely serving as a rubber stamp for entrenched positions. But open discussion meant controversy, and since human beings run the church, the council documents were often products of political compromise.

The key Vatican II document regarding the nature of the church is *Lumen Gentium* [Flannery] (the Dogmatic Constitution on the Church) promulgated by Pope Paul VI on 21 November 1964. This is the document most frequently cited by church critics regarding needed reform to address the clergy sexual abuse system. It began by emphasizing the church as mystery and sacrament, and in order to illuminate its sacred meaning, the council would follow "faithfully the teaching of previous councils." This almost guaranteed ambiguity and compromise, since one previous council, the nineteenth-century's Vatican I, had been controversial in its insistence on the institutional/hierarchical nature of the church. Vatican II was seen as the occasion for necessary rethinking to enable the church to be more relevant to the modern world. The document mentioned many metaphors for understanding the mystery of the church — sheepfold, village, building of God, mother — but concentrated on three: mystery and sacrament, the People of God, and hierarchy. Many observers believed it was significant that *Lumen Gentium* presented the mystery and sacrament and newer People of God visions first, followed by the prevailing hierarchical understanding.

Before turning to Avery Dulles's analysis of these and related models, it is useful to see how *Lumen Gentium* presented the role of the laity in the church. In the following excerpted paragraphs, one begins to grasp the potential for controversy:

> The laity should, as all Christians, promptly accept in Christian obedience decisions of their spiritual shepherds [the hierarchy], since they are representatives of Christ as well as teachers and rulers in the Church. . . .
>
>     Let the spiritual shepherds recognize and promote the dignity as well as the responsibility of the laity in the Church. Let them willingly employ their

prudent advice. Let them confidently assign duties to them in the service of the Church, allowing them freedom and room for action. Further, let them encourage lay people so that they may undertake tasks on their own initiative. Attentively in Christ, let them consider with fatherly love the projects, suggestions and desires proposed by the laity. . . . However, let the shepherds respectfully acknowledge that just freedom which belongs to everyone in this earthly city.

A great many wonderful things are to be hoped for from this familiar dialogue between the laity and their spiritual leaders: in the laity a strengthened sense of personal responsibility; a renewed enthusiasm; a more ready application of their talents to the projects of their spiritual leaders. The latter, on the other hand, aided by the experience of the laity, can more clearly and more incisively come to decisions regarding both spiritual and temporal matters. In this way, the whole Church, strengthened by each one of its members, may more effectively fulfill its mission for the life of the world. . . . All the laity as a community and each one according to his ability must nourish the world with spiritual fruits.

Thus, the laity have dignity and responsibility and should have the freedom to take initiative, engage in dialogue with the hierarchy, and work to fulfill the mission of the church community. The laity, however, are sheep/children/subjects who should obey their shepherds/fathers/rulers and be relegated to the role of offering advice regarding decision making. One can see here some of the seeds of the conflict between the Voice of the Faithful and many bishops concerning the role of the laity in dealing with clergy sexual abuse.

A subsequent Vatican II document further developed the church's view of the laity—*Apostolicam Actuositatem* [Flannery] (the Decree on the Apostolate of the Laity), promulgated by Pope Paul VI on 18 November 1965. This document identified at length the many ways in which the church needed the "apostolate of the laity"—the laity as co-participants with members of the church at all levels in advancing the work of the apostles—to help improve the temporal order according to the Christian virtues of charity and justice. It paid little attention to the role of the laity in church governance, and when it did touch on such matters, the tone was mostly paternalistic and hierarchical, while at the same time claiming to value the laity's contributions. For example, while "the laity should accustom themselves to working in the parish in union with their priests, bringing to the Church community their own and the world's problems as well as questions concerning human salvation, all of which they should examine and resolve by *deliberating in common,*" it must be kept in mind that the laity "should be incorporated into the apostolate of the whole Church according to *a right system of relationships.* Indeed, union with those whom the Holy Spirit has assigned to rule His Church . . . is an essential element of the Christian apostolate. No less necessary is cooperation among various projects of the apostolate which must be suitably *directed by the hierarchy.*" But in a more accommodating statement, "Bishops, pastors of parishes, and other priests . . . should keep in mind that the right and duty to exercise this apostolate is *common to all the faithful,* both clergy and laity, and that the laity also have their own roles in building up the Church. For this reason they should *work fraternally* with the laity in and for the Church and take special care of the lay persons in these apostolic works" (emphasis added).

## Models of the Church

Much spirited theological and pastoral work developing the church's understanding of itself and the role of the laity followed the conclusion of Vatican II in 1965. An important book that integrated and analyzed much of the emerging ecclesiological thinking was published nine years later by Jesuit theologian (recently named Cardinal) Avery Dulles. His *Models of the Church* (1974, expanded edition published in 1987) became a classic by clearly laying out the many ways of understanding the church beyond the institutional/hierarchical vision that had dominated Catholic thinking for years before Vatican II. He begins the book with this caveat: "I take a deliberately critical stance toward those ecclesiologies that are primarily or exclusively institutional. But . . . I insist that the institutional view is still valid within limits" (10).

Influenced by H. R. Niebuhr's *Christ and Culture* (1951), which comparatively analyzed the relationship between Christianity and culture, Dulles compares six models (images or metaphors) for understanding the church—the church as (1) institution, (2) mystical communion (People of God or Body of Christ), (3) sacrament, (4) herald, (5) servant, and (6) community of disciples.

Rejecting "either/or" in favor of "both/and" third-position thinking, he stresses that the complexity of the mystery of the church requires the simultaneous use of all these interrelated models and perhaps others. Calling attention to the fact that Vatican II had led Catholics to see the value of theological pluralism, his purpose is to help bring about a healing and unifying pluralism rather than a divisive and destructive pluralism. To foster his healing and unifying approach, Dulles compares the models using seven criteria: (1) foundation in scriptural sources, (2) foundation in the church's tradition, (3) ability to give Catholics a sense of identity and mission, (4) ability to foster Christian values and virtues, (5) relevance to people's contemporary religious experience, (6) ability to stimulate theological development, and (7) ability to promote interfaith or ecumenical dialogue. He believes these criteria would be generally acceptable to the adherents of each of the models, allowing us to see their relative strengths and weaknesses in pursuit of more complete understanding.

Dulles juxtaposes the institutional/hierarchical and People of God models as follows: "Persons drawn to the institutional model will show a particularly high regard for values such as conceptual clarity, respect for constituted authority, law and order. They reject other models, and perhaps especially the [communion or People of God model] as being too vague, mystical, and subjective. Partisans of the communion model, on the other hand, find the institutional outlook too rationalistic, ecclesiocentric, and rigid. They label it triumphalist, juridicist, and clericalist" (191).

An often misunderstood phrase used to characterize the institutional/hierarchical church is *perfect society*. Although some non-historically-minded Catholics believe the church is perfect in that its officials can do no wrong—Garry Wills's *Papal Sin* (2000), among other works, convincingly corrects this belief—the phrase actually refers to the belief that the church is institutionally complete, being subordinate to no other institution and lacking nothing for achieving its divinely established purpose. Operating from the analogy of political society, the view of the church as perfect society emphasizes such features as governance, laws, hierarchical structures of authority, and the powers of its officials—necessary features, Dulles argues, of any institution or organization. He distinguishes, therefore, between the church as institution and *in-*

*stitutionalism*, a view that sees the necessary institutional aspects of the church as *preeminent*. He argues further that institution, papacy, law, and dogma do not automatically imply institutionalism, papalism, legalism, and dogmatism. "Institutionalism is a deformation of the true nature of the Church—a deformation that has unfortunately affected the Church at certain periods of its history, and one that remains in every age a real danger to the institutional Church" (35).

Institutionalism sees the hierarchy as preeminent in exercising the church's three functions of teaching, sanctifying, and governing—hierarchical church officials compose the church teaching, the church sanctifying, and the church governing; ordinary church members compose the church taught, the church sanctified, and the church governed. Regarding the nature of authority, this model, monarchical and oligarchical in its political outlook, needless to say, does not define the church as a democratic society, but one in which rulers reserve power to themselves and perpetuate it "by cooption" (38). The major characteristics of such a church are clericalism (the church's clergy has the power), juridicism (the church emphasizes law and penalties), and triumphalism (the church is an army at war with Satan and evil in the world).

The assets of the institutional/hierarchical model, according to Dulles, are: its harmony with official Catholic positions on the nature of the church for the last few centuries; its ability to link the church's past with its tumultuous present and uncertain future; and its ability to engender a sense of corporate identity among the faithful. Weighing strongly against this model, however, are its liabilities: its minimal connection to Scripture and the tradition of the early church; its encouragement of a passive laity and its weakness in promoting the Christian virtue of charity; its stifling of theological creativity; its creation of theological problems, especially its discouragement of ecumenism; and its failure to be adequately responsive to contemporary society's moves toward human rights and democratic forms of governance. In view of this assessment, Dulles warns against "exaggerated institutionalism," arguing that "the Church is not primarily institution; that it does not derive all of its reality and strength from its institutional features. The institutional elements in the Church must ultimately be justified by their capacity to express or strengthen the Church as a community of life, witness, and service, a community that reconciles and unites men in the grace of Christ" (45).

While developing a theory of community in the ethics of human development and community in chapter 3, I referred to the distinction between *Gesellschaft* and *Gemeinschaft*. I pointed out that *Gesellschaft* is mechanistic, viewing people as impersonal individuals, while *Gemeinschaft* is organic, viewing people as existing in community. Dulles also uses this distinction in elaborating the differences between the institutional/hierarchical and mystical communion (People of God) models. The characteristics of the church as institution (society) just outlined suggest *Gesellschaft*, while the characteristics of the mystical communion suggest *Gemeinschaft*—the People of God understood as a community.

Following Charles Cooley, Dulles suggests that, from the standpoint of human science, the church as a *Gemeinschaft* community entails relationships that are face-to-face, informal, unspecialized, nonbureaucratic, relatively permanent, and intimate—as in families, households, villages, and neighborhoods. Relative to church reform or renewal, the church would/should be more community-like, "a place in which one can establish rich and satisfying primary relationships—that is, person-to-person relationships founded on mutual understanding and love." Moreover, so conceived, the church would be seen as "a great community made up of many interlocking communities. Thanks to the unifying presence of the Holy Spirit, the many families of Christians are woven into a single large family" (57). Further, the church is "a community of persons each of whom is individually free" (53). "The Holy Spirit is the divine person who makes us one without our ceasing to be many. The Church is one Person (the Holy Spirit) in many persons (Christ and us)" (56).

Beyond human science, Dulles maintains that the People of God understanding has roots in both the Old and the New Testament and in Vatican II's Constitution of the Church. Moreover, the People of God and the closely related Body of Christ images are decidedly more democratic than the image of the church as institution/hierarchy, emphasizing the equality of all church members in their relationship to each other and the Holy Spirit and in their commitment to mutually serving each other in pursuit of the common good.

Dulles sees the People of God model as superior to the institutional/hierarchical model in most respects. It has a firmer foundation in scripture and the early Catholic tradition and is theologically better suited to ecumenism. It motivates prayer and spirituality and emphasizes "the warm vital interrelationships" at the heart of the New Testament message (59). Perhaps most importantly, "large institutions are accepted as at best a necessary evil. They are felt to be oppressive and depersonalizing. People find the meaning of their lives not in terms of such institutions but in terms of the informal, the personal, the communal." Noting the human quest for community (see Nisbet 1953/1990), Dulles says that people "long for a community which, in spite of all conflicts built into modern society, can open up loving communication" (59). The liabilities of this personally and socially satisfying model mostly concern the tensions between it and the institutional/hierarchical and other models. People may be so involved in the intense, sometimes healing and therapy-like, feelings generated by intimate face-to-face community relationships that they may become oblivious to the useful and necessary aspects of the church's institutional structure and the content of the Catholic belief system. This is the danger of overly emphasizing immediate and local interpersonal process to the detriment of more general and lawful content.

Dulles's comparative analysis of the institutional/hierarchical and People of God models of the church has obvious relevance to many facets of the clergy sexual abuse system that we have explored thus far. Simply put, the abuses of power entailed in the secret actions of clergy sexual abusers and church officials who have covered up for them and failed to show appropriate pastoral concern for victims and their families are, at least in part, manifestations of the church's hierarchical and clerical institutional structures. Had the church functioned more as the People of God, had the church been more open and transparent by virtue of the laity being more involved in the everyday life of the church and its governance, opportunities for abuse would have been greatly reduced, and the church's response would have been more charitable and pastoral and less obsessed with avoiding scandal. Further, if the hierarchy would share its power and meaningfully join with the laity in dealing with clergy sexual abuse and other matters of church governance, great strides would be made toward preventing future abuse and restoring trust and rebuilding the credibility of the church. Of course, as we have been seeing, ecclesiological matters are not the whole story, and either or both of the two models in question cannot do justice to the mystery of the church.

Pluralist third-position thinking requires a brief consideration of Dulles's other models of the church. Not only do I wish to avoid an institutional/community schism or dualism, but the inclusion of certain perspectives from these other models helps in mitigating the institutional/hierarchical model with the People of God model in addressing the clergy sexual abuse system.

If, in effect, the People of God are making their communal pilgrim journey on earth as a structured and organized group—as part of a church that is one, holy, catholic, and apostolic—then the model of church as sacrament emphasizes the symbolic integration of the communal and institutional aspects of the church. The church as sacrament has external (visible institutional) and internal (the expressions of faith, hope, and charity among persons-in-community) aspects, which together raise it from being merely a bare institution to being a true sacrament expressing in action the grace God freely gives human beings for their journey. Such a sacramental mentality would help avoid the "us versus them" approach that has characterized the hierarchy's handling of clergy sexual abuse. Rather, all Catholics would be in it together reaching out pastorally to victims/survivors and protecting children and other potential victims of the abuse of power.

A sacramentally integrated institutional and communal church has the duty to proclaim the truth of the world as illuminated by the word of God. A herald is one who learns the truth and proclaims it to the community. From the perspective of the model of the church as herald, the church is "constituted by the word being proclaimed and faithfully heard. The Church is the congregation that is gathered together by the word—a word that ceaselessly summons it to repentance and reform" (77)—thus, *ecclesia semper reformanda est* (the church must always be open to reform and development). This model would rule out the secret, backward-looking, scandal-avoiding defensiveness of

CHAPTER SIX

# Toward Reforms Addressing and Preventing Clergy Sexual Abuse

*Whenever groups of Catholics attempt to assert rights of popular decision making in the church, it is common for bishops to declare "the church is not a democracy." While this may be an accurate factual statement about the church today, the assumption that it is either a comprehensive historical statement or a biblically and theologically normative statement needs to be challenged.*

—Eugene C. Bianchi and Rosemary Radford Ruether, *A Democratic Catholic Church*

C LERGY SEXUAL ABUSE HAS SHOWN ITSELF to be like a system—part relates to part, and the whole is greater than the sum of the parts. Problematic system-like phenomena require systemic understanding followed by reform entailing system-wide intervention if we are to ameliorate and prevent them. As we have seen, a single act of abuse has many causes and consequences and must be understood historically and contextually. Multiple and interrelated past events and contexts affect the present context of a given act of abuse, and the moral/ethical consequences of a present action ripple through the future of the social world as when a stone thrown into a lake disturbs its calm surface, sending out ever-widening waves.

## RATIONALE FOR REFORMS ADDRESSING THE
## CLERGY SEXUAL ABUSE SYSTEM

In looking back at the analysis presented in earlier chapters, we have seen that complete understanding of a given priest's abuse of a child—yet to be achieved because of church officials' resistance to inquiring systematically into the nature of clergy sexual abuse—requires multiple levels of analysis, beginning with the priest's personal life-history. Here we encounter factors ranging from a priest's family and cultural background; to the development of his character and personality, especially as they relate to his psychosexual maturity; to his life experiences, or lack thereof, prior to entering the priesthood; to his seminary training; to the social support he receives from family, friends, parishioners, fellow priests, and the church hierarchy during his priesthood; to his experience in parishes and other church settings during his priesthood; to the kinds of experiences he had with children and their families, especially with his victims and their families. Reforms addressing clergy sexual abuse must take these factors into account.

This personal life-history context exists within broader contexts, starting with the history, traditions, culture, and ideology of the Catholic Church, especially its understandings of its own nature and the nature of its priesthood. Here we encounter the tension between the institutional/hierarchical and more communal People of God models of the church and the prevailing but controversial understanding of the priesthood as exclusively male and celibate. These considerations are basic in any reform efforts addressing clergy sexual abuse.

The reactions to and consequences of an abusing act are crucial aspects of the clergy sexual abuse system. A myriad of systemic influences come into play here, including church policies, insurance company pressures, the work and value systems of lawyers representing the church and the victims/survivors, the insatiable demands of the ever-present media, and the extent to which the laity participate in helping the church understand and address the clergy sexual abuse problem. At the outermost realms of the clergy sexual abuse system, and paradoxically, also at its center, we encounter the ways in which cardinals, bishops, and other church officials, including those in the Vatican, deal with the phenomenon and the other actors in the system. Reform at this level will be very difficult because many of the key reformers will have to take seriously the role they play in the clergy sexual abuse system and their need to reform themselves.

Further, as we have already seen, the aftermath of clergy sexual abuse entails not only the church's characteristic and systemic modes of dealing with the problem but also its moral/ethical effects in the social world. The harm caused by clergy sexual abuse and by church officials' reactions to it occurs at personal, relational, and social levels. At the personal level, victims typically experience physical, psychological, and spiritual pain and damage to their senses of trust and personal well-being. They also typically experience anxiety, depression, alienation, and fear of relationships and intimacy. They often manifest antisocial behavior, alcohol or drug abuse, and more general problems in living, sometimes even committing suicide or murder, and they are typically quite reluctant to report their abuse to either church or government officials. In many ways, this is the level most acutely in need of address through reforms. In recognizing the need for fundamental structural change, reformers must not lose sight of the need to ameliorate and prevent the harm and suffering experienced by the victims/survivors in the clergy sexual abuse system.

At the relational level, clergy sexual abuse weakens the church's ability to be pastoral and caring. It diminishes people's trust in the church and its ministers. It tends to weaken their sense of belonging to the church; their sense of shared values and emotional connection with others in the church, especially the clergy and the hierarchy; their experience of being with others in the church to help meet each others' needs; and their sense of influencing and being influenced by others in exercising their power in church governance. Nonabusing priests become alienated and overly cautious about relating to their parishioners, especially children. Clergy sexual abuse harms the church's spiritual life, threatening its very reason for existing, because it threatens its ability to foster spiritual growth and development and provide social support during many of life's crises. It weakens the church's ability to promote people's psychological sense of community. Reforms must enhance community in each parish and enable the church to function as a community of communities.

At the social level, clergy sexual abuse shocks and scandalizes. It fuels internal and external criticism of the church. It often causes decreased giving to

Catholic charitable endeavors. It erodes the people's trust in the church's teaching authority. It causes tension between the church and public and governmental agencies. Bishops', cardinals', and the Vatican's tendency to place the pastoral care of victims second to the values of protecting the church from scandal and preserving the power of the hierarchy has exacerbated the initial harm caused by clergy sexual abuse. The public's perception of the institutional church's secrecy, deceit, and seeming lack of concern for victims in responding to clergy sexual abuse has produced a chorus of calls for reform. Reform, then, must be fundamental and wide-ranging enough to move the church toward being a community that espouses total honesty, commitment to the truth, and free and uncoerced communication.

The ethical, human science, and ecclesiological analyses I have undertaken in previous chapters have identified a number of themes with relevance to reforms addressing clergy sexual abuse. Under the general rubric of the uses and abuses of power, which is at the heart of the clergy sexual abuse system, I have identified the need to reform the church by mitigating its use of directive or coercive power with caring and growth-enhancing power; its authoritarianism with natural authority; its masculine agency orientation with a more feminine communion orientation; and its Model I approach to ministerial practice and legalistic contract orientation with a Model II reflective-generative approach with a covenant orientation. In the spirit of Pope John XXIII, all this would be subsumed under a Vatican II–like commitment to reform by mitigating the church's institutional/hierarchical understanding of itself with an understanding emanating from seeing the church as the People of God.

Human science contributes insights to the reform process. Barbara Balboni's (1998) research showed that the bishops she interviewed used their power to maintain an organizational culture where preserving the church's prerogatives and power trumped any and all other concerns, even in the face of the obvious harms done to clergy sexual abuse victims and their need for caring pastoral ministry. Gene Burns (1992) showed that the church's ideology is founded on the Vatican's need to preserve its power and control over the most personal aspects of the lives of the faithful and the processes of church governance, despite the fact that this use of power erodes community and fails to respond to the needs of the victims of clergy sexual abuse. Eugene Kennedy and Sara

centralized, governmental, and other "top-down" command and control inter-
ventions to help rectify injustice. This form of societal intervention will continue to be necessary, at least to a certain degree, to achieve recognition of the
personhood of all. Democratic theory in the modern era has spawned attempts
to structure institutions so that the "top-down" consults with the "bottom-up"
when enacting decisions. This consultation, however, has often been inadequate, often merely procedural. Whatever the emerging postmodern world
holds in store for the church and other societal institutions, if we are to achieve
true community, we must foster participative decision-making, in the spirit of
the principle of subsidiarity, in which the emphasis shifts from deciding at the
upper levels of institutions to deciding based on validly assessed human-development needs in the immediacy of our everyday lives. Therefore, *community
requires participative decision making.*

The analyses in this book have shown clearly that clergy sexual abusers have
abused their power by molesting their victims, and many bishops and other
church officials have abused their power by covering up these criminal and sinful acts of abuse. For the church, or for that matter, any organization, to be truly
moral and ethical requires working toward a just distribution of power in which
all members, clergy and laity alike, participate in influencing what happens in
the life of the organization. As we have seen, participatory decision making is a
prerequisite for members' development of a meaningful psychological sense of
community. Here we enter the realm of democracy as a way of governing social
life. In that regard, James Carroll has argued: "Conversation is our hope. In that
simple statement lies the kernel of democracy, which is based not on *diktat* but
on interchange of mutuality" (Carroll 2002, 99). Relatedly, John XXIII's biographer Thomas Cahill has observed: "The ancient Church was the world's first
true democracy, and it can be so again—not a democracy of campaigns and
runoffs, of parties and platforms, but a democracy of the Spirit, in which every
human being, male and female, young and old, rich and poor, is accorded the
'equal human dignity' of which John wrote so movingly" (Cahill 2002, 236).
Carroll continues: "There is a special tragedy in the fact that, for contingent
historical reasons, the Catholic Church set itself so ferociously against the coming of democracy—tragic because Christianity began its life as a small gather-

ing of Jews who were devoted to conversation. . . . [A] democracy assumes that everyone must be protected from the unchecked, uncriticized, and unregulated power of every other, including the well-meaning leader. The universal experience of imperfection, finitude, and self-centeredness is the pessimistic ground of democratic hope. The Church's own experience—its grievous sin in relation to the Jews, and lately the inability of clerical leaders to dismantle an autocratic structure that enabled priestly child abuse—proves how desperately in need of democratic reform the Church is" (Carroll 2002, 99, 104).

In Nashville, Carroll's book *Constantine's Sword: The Church and the Jews* (2001) has been serving as the occasion for productive ongoing community-wide ecumenical discussions. One woman told me she was so moved by the book and the discussions that, for the first time in her life, she felt ashamed to wear the gold cross she ordinarily displayed with pride around her neck. The latest chapter of the church's clergy sexual abuse scandal was part of the rationale for Carroll's 2002 book *Toward a New Catholic Church*, in which he elaborates his earlier reform proposals and calls, in the spirit of John XXIII, for a Vatican III to address the church's need to be more democratic in structuring the governance of the People of God.

An important distinction must be made. Theologian John Coleman distinguishes between "democracy" and "democratization": "Democracy involves an interrelated set of principles, attitudes, patterns of behavior, and legal forms. Democratic principles espouse (1) equality before the law; (2) the freedom of individuals and corporate groups as a presumptive role against absolutism; (3) constitutionality; (4) open public opinion formation, a dialogue that is free, undistorted and open to all. The forms of democracy entail universal suffrage, representative organs for legislation, accountability structures for judges and executives, a division of powers, and a set of rights (such as the rights to free speech, freedom of the press and assembly) enshrined in law and enactable through a court system" (Coleman 1992, 228). Democratization shares much in common with democracy but is not the same thing: "Democratization, [which can exist] in forms of governance that are not democracies, envisions the formal enactment of consultation, accountability and due process, even in the absence of a mechanism for election" (229).

Democratization in the church, Coleman argues, would entail (1) collegiality in the relationships between the pope and the bishops, the bishops and priests, and all members of the hierarchy and the laity; (2) subsidiarity; and (3) justice as participation. Critics of the church's prevailing hierarchical form of governance can be arrayed along a continuum from advocates of democracy to advocates of democratization. For the purposes of this chapter, with an eye toward feasibility and practicality, I write more in the spirit of democratization than of democracy, and I subscribe to the principles that Eugene C. Bianchi and Rosemary Radford Ruether culled from the chapters in their edited book *A Democratic Catholic Church: The Reconstruction of Roman Catholicism* (1992)—namely, (1) participatory decision-making; (2) conciliarity, or the use of councils to structure church governance; (3) pluralism; (4) accountability; and (5) dialogue. And regarding the relationship between what Hans Küng calls the "shepherds" and the "congregation" (the laity), I subscribe to his third-position/synergic-power understanding that, if the shepherds and the congregation "stand all together under the one Father and Lord, who makes them all sisters and brothers, . . . the fullness of power of the church or congregation is not derived from the fullness of power of the shepherds, and the fullness of power of the shepherds is not derived from the fullness of power of church or congregation, but the fullness of power of *both* is directly derived from the fullness of power of the Lord of the church in his Spirit. The common origin of their fullness of power establishes the universal authorization of the congregation as well as the special fullness of power of the service of the shepherds. It is the support of the authority of the shepherds as well as of the participation of the 'laity' in decision making" (Küng 1992, 84).

Theologian Paul Lakeland captures nicely my feelings about democratizing the church:

> While the church is not quite like a secular democracy, many of the signs of health are common to both communities. To be specific, we should test the health of the ecclesial community in ways analogous to those we use to examine the health of the body politic. A healthy church will possess lively mediating structures, a strong public forum of ideas, and a clear conduit between those in positions of leadership and the members of the community.

This conduit must be a two-way street. The community needs to have confidence in the leadership's willingness to listen to its voice and incorporate that voice into decision making. Contrariwise, the leadership needs to be truly aware of its accountability to the people it serves. (Lakeland 2003, 215)

And accountability brings us to the relationship between people's trust in church officials and their willingness to grant these officials discretion in dealing with the clergy sexual abuse crisis.

## GRANTING DISCRETION TO CHURCH OFFICIALS

In the last chapter, I discussed the criticisms generated by the church's proposals for addressing the clergy sexual abuse system developed during 2002. It is important to note that many features of these reforms were based on earlier reforms known to, proposed by, or enacted by the U.S. bishops as long ago as the 1980s. As we saw in chapter 1, Carl M. Cannon has argued concerning the bishops' long-standing awareness of the problem that "there is simply no excuse for a bishop to not have figured that when he gets one of these cases, the only possible ethical response is to (a) remove the priest immediately; (b) call the cops; (c) make an honest effort to find all the victims; (d) deal with the problem publicly, even if that means opening your diocese to further lawsuits; (e) treat the kids and the parents—and all the other parishioners—humanely. That this wasn't being done 10 and 15 years after the 1985 Doyle/Mouton/Peterson report and half a dozen years after the bishops in the early 1990s adopted guidelines for dealing with this problem made the story more horrific, not less" (*American Journalism Review*, May 2002). Regarding those early 1990s guidelines, the document in question, dated June 1992 and titled "The Five Principles to Follow in Dealing with Accusations of Sexual Abuse," appears on the USCCB website (10 November 2002). The principles are: "1. Respond promptly to all allegations of abuse where there is reasonable belief that abuse has occurred. 2. If such an allegation is supported by sufficient evidence, relieve the alleged offender promptly of his ministerial duties and refer him for appropriate medical evaluation and intervention. 3. Comply with the obligations of civil law as regards reporting of the incident and cooperating with the investigation. 4. Reach out to the victims and their families and communicate sincere commitment to their spiritual and emotional well-being. 5. Within the confines of respect for privacy of the individuals involved, deal as openly as possible with the members of the community." A statement like Cannon's and the existence of a decade-old USCCB clergy sexual abuse policy suggest why victim/survivor advocates, lay groups, and many church observers have so bitterly criticized the bishops' 2002 policies. At the beginning of the Dallas USCCB meetings, Bishop Gregory had said: "As the victim/survivors told us, 'Listening is easy. Talk is cheap. Action is priceless.' That is our challenge. Ultimately, that is how we will be judged" (USCCB, 12 November 2002). The actions, and inactions, of Cardinal Law and many other bishops and church officials for almost twenty years were vividly in their memory as critics judged the church's 2002 policies. In government, business, and organizational practice, the processes of policy development, policy implementation, and policy evaluation are not the same things. Many policies are proposed and enacted but not implemented or evaluated for the sake of accountability, and when the discrepancy between words and actions becomes known, people get frustrated and angry, and they mistrust the policymakers.

A major issue, then, emerges in stark relief when we consider the church's characteristic approach to clergy sexual abuse—what we may call the *discretion-trust dynamic*: In order to do justice to the complexities and vast array of situational factors in the many cases of clergy sexual abuse throughout the United States and beyond, church policies must be flexible and grant discretion to bishops and other church officials if they are to address the problem sensitively and effectively; however, people must be able to trust those to whom discretion is granted, and many bishops and church officials have squandered the people's trust by covering up and mismanaging the problem in the first place. The problems inherent in this dynamic are greatly exacerbated when many of the key procedures the church proposes to use in dealing with alleged clergy sexual abusers will take place in secret using secret principles and decision-making criteria, as in the norms developed by the bishops in November and approved by the Vatican in December 2002. As Carroll has argued, "a power structure that is accountable only to itself will always end by abusing the powerless. Even then, it will paternalistically ask to be trusted to repair the damage" (2002, 15). An aspect of Carroll's argument, and my central thesis, is that the discretion-trust dynamic can only be overcome if the church enacts reforms that move toward democratization—reforms that, among other things, allow the laity to assume their proper and needed role in dealing with the clergy sexual abuse system, specifically, and in participating in church governance, more generally.

Arguments for the church being more open and democratic can be and have been made on many grounds other than clergy sexual abuse.[1] My intent here is to offer ideas relevant to democratization focusing on the discretion-trust dynamic in the clergy sexual abuse system.

## TOWARD THE RESTORATION OF TRUST IN THE CHURCH THROUGH DEMOCRATIC REFORMS

In this final section, my intent is to adopt Pope John XXIII's outlook in rethinking the church's understanding of itself, its ecclesiology, to provide the foundation for preliminary thoughts about systematic church reform at all levels of the church organization understood as a system—from the parish, to the diocese, to the national church, to the universal church. It is neither my place nor within my competence to offer specific and detailed recommendations, so I offer general programmatic suggestions. I begin by joining the issues of the discretion-trust dynamic and the need to reform the church in the direction of more democratic forms of governance with my discussion in chapter 5 of alternative models of the church that might help mitigate the institutional/hierarchical model's role in the clergy sexual abuse scandal.

The institutional/hierarchical church's unalloyed clericalism, juridicism, and triumphalism have served to create an organizational context that gave rise to the abuses of power that have characterized the secret actions of clergy sexual abusers and church officials who have covered up for them. A church operating less secretly, more transparently, more accountably, and more democratically by encouraging the involvement of the laity in all levels of church affairs would have greatly reduced the opportunities for priests to molest children. Less secrecy, more transparency, more accountability, and more democratization would also have increased the likelihood that church officials' responses to abuse victims and their families would have been more charitable and pastoral, by placing the avoidance of scandal and institutional defensiveness behind these more human and spiritual concerns in the church's scale of values. Looking to the future, if church officials share their power and join with the laity in dealing with the clergy sexual abuse system and other matters of church governance (following the People of God model rather than the institutional/hierarchical model), there will be movement on two fronts—first, in preventing future clergy sexual abuse and, second, in restoring the people's trust in the church and thereby its credibility and moral authority.

I turn now to the remaining alternative models of the church set forth by Avery Dulles (1974/1987): the church as sacrament, as herald, as servant, and as community of disciples. The model of church as sacrament further assists Catholics in meeting Pope John's Vatican II challenge to mitigate the prevailing institutional/hierarchical vision of church with the more community-like People of God vision. It symbolically integrates the visible institutional and the spiritual communal aspects of the church manifest in the caring actions of persons-in-community as they mutually live the virtues of faith, hope, and charity. The church thereby leaves behind the trappings of clericalism, juridicism, and triumphalism that have permeated many of its actions in the clergy sexual abuse system and beyond. It serves as a democratically ordered vehicle for the reception of God's freely given grace by all its people—hierarchy, clergy, religious, and laity alike. People relate to each other as persons who are fundamentally equal in God's eyes because they have been created in God's own image. Each person in her or his own way freely and openly performs a unique spiritual function in the democratically oriented and open community known as the mystical body of Christ. All Catholics mutually reach out to each other pastorally—especially to the vulnerable ones such as clergy sexual abuse victims/survivors—and have the collective responsibility for protecting children and other potential victims of the abuse of power, thereby preventing abuse to the extent possible and avoiding the hostile adversary relationships that have characterized the clergy sexual abuse system.

The model of church as herald also complements the other models in doing justice to the mystery of the church as it addresses the clergy sexual abuse system. Recalling Dulles's words, the church is "constituted by the word being proclaimed and faithfully heard. The Church is the congregation that is gathered together by the word—a word that ceaselessly summons it to repentance and reform" (Dulles 1974/1987, 77). Repentance and reform entail that the People of God must ongoingly interpret and rethink (repent) the nature of the word as it relates to the "signs of the times," and must apply and reapply their understanding by continually reforming and changing relative to experiences in their life world—*ecclesia semper reformanda est*. The People of God are not merely persons-in-community contentedly journeying together as pilgrims. The word of God inspires and guides them to work together as a democratically organized community—more precisely, a community of communities—to achieve their own and the common good. They are not slavish adherents to the kind of herald who insists on preserving the power and claimed truth of the hierarchy by admonishing them to pray, pay, and obey. Adding this vision of the church as herald to the other visions suggests that the church would foster open, honest, transparent, and democratically structured conversation in pursuit of reforms that would meaningfully address the clergy sexual abuse system, rather than encouraging the too typical secretive and scandal-avoiding defensiveness of the church's clerical and hierarchical culture.

The major beneficiaries of the service called for in the model of the church as servant are "all those brothers and sisters the world over, who hear from the Church a word of comfort or encouragement, or who obtain from the Church a respectful hearing, or who receive from it some material help in their hour of need" (Dulles 1974/1987, 97). This model reminds the church that it must transcend its tendency to look inward by seeing itself in relation to the world, not as an aspiring imperial triumphal leader but as a servant, one who serves all the people within a democratically ordered community. The metaphor inspiring servant leaders—hierarchy, clergy, religious, and laity alike—in this model is Christ washing the feet of his disciples, a ritual enacted each Holy Thursday by the pope and bishops throughout the world. As related to the clergy sexual abuse system, this model encourages pastoral outreach and caring for all those harmed by the abuses of church power and discourages the church's characteristically formal and legalistic approach to the problem.

Finally, in my attempt to provide the foundation for preliminary thoughts about systematic church reform addressing the clergy sexual abuse system, there is Dulles's own integrated construction of the church as a community of disciples. Here we see that the church is not like just any other community. It is comprised of people-in-community who join their personal narratives to the gospel narrative of Jesus Christ. From the standpoint of disciples as leaders, "the ordained leaders must collaborate closely with a larger body of lay ministers" (Dulles 1974/1987, 218). Again we sense a democratic sentiment in which hierarchy, clergy, religious, and laity alike are all in it together as they work toward achieving the mission of the church and, specifically, as they address the clergy sexual abuse system. Further, this model suggests directions for church renewal and reform, since disciples model themselves on the life of Jesus Christ.

In what follows, the basic rationale for ideas offered for reform at all levels of the church involves the needs to ameliorate the harm caused by clergy sexual abuse, to prevent future abuse, and to restore trust in the church. Throughout the book—in telling the story of McKeown in Nashville; in viewing clergy sexual abuse in a wider context and comparing the situations in Nashville and Boston; in viewing clergy sexual abuse through the lenses of the ethics of human development and community, the human sciences, and ecclesiology— I have identified many specific actions that might be taken regarding specific acts of clergy sexual abuse. I presented the pros and cons of many of these specifics in telling the story of the church's struggle to deal with the clergy sexual abuse scandal in 2002. I now conclude by presenting more general suggestions for reform at the structural and process levels, especially regarding the need for the church to function more like a democratic community than a hierarchical institution. In effect, these democratic structural and process reforms provide the stage on which the specifics of the clergy sexual abuse system might play out in the future.

## Reform at the Parish Level

A parish must be a community that enhances the spirituality and authentic human development of its members. Members should be growing spiritually and experiencing a meaningful psychological sense of community in the parish community—feeling a deep sense of belonging, being emotionally connected to each other and mutually sharing values, being able to count on each other in times of need, and feeling they have a say in what happens in their parish (Dokecki, Newbrough, and O'Gorman 2001). Parishes as communities promoting spirituality and authentic human development must treat the laity as mature adults capable of participating with their priests in democratically structured forums for parish decision making. Parish councils might fill this bill; however, they have had variable success over the years in providing a truly democratic forum for the laity. Nonetheless, some such structure is needed, one that operates fully in the open, avoiding characteristic Catholic secrecy. Such a parish community group, according to Lakeland,

> could certainly determine things like the ways in which the finances are managed and the causes to which it is ready to contribute. It should certainly feel free to set up its own system of religious education in the ways it sees fit. It should be empowered to determine who occupies its pulpit. It should definitely make decisions about the stands it will take in social-justice initiatives within the local community. But it does not belong to the community to ordain its own ministers or to determine how the doctrine of the real presence of Christ in the Eucharist will be understood within its own ranks. On the other hand, it may well have very pronounced views about ordination or real presence, and it certainly has the right to express those views. (Lakeland 2003, 218)

As suggested earlier, parish communities so understood would afford few opportunities for power-abusing priests intent on molesting children.

A sine qua non for a parish functioning as a community is that its pastor and priests must be leaders-for-community, who work with the laity as partners within democratic parish governance structures that encourage dialogue and free and uncoerced communication (Trout, Dokecki, Newbrough, and O'Gorman 2003). The priest as leader-for-community must be a person who has developed the moral character necessary to be such a servant leader and must be psychosexually mature. Seminaries must play a role in selecting people of high moral character—screening out persons with significant psychopathology, such as those with abusive tendencies—and helping priests-to-be develop their sexual identity and come to grips with the church's expectations around celibacy (see Cozzens 2000; Kennedy 2001). Seminaries should also impress on them the importance of avoiding clericalism and being sure their parishes do not become clerical cultures. Parenthetically, the laity must also be helped to avoid encouraging their priests' clericalism. Priests as leaders-for-community should also be socialized to be authoritative leaders who use their vocation and their ministerial knowledge and skill as Model II professionals, avoiding coercive and authoritarian use of power and dedicating themselves to enhancing community in the parish and promoting their parishioners' spiritual lives and human development.

## Reform at the Diocesan Level

A diocese must also be a community, more precisely, a community of communities. If a parish is to function as a community in the ways just described, a diocese should serve as an important means to that end. In an organization as large and complex as the Catholic Church, if the purpose of the church is to serve ordinary people in their quest to lead spiritual lives in their parish communities, the church must (a) discern what needs to happen to achieve this purpose at the lowest level of the organization as close as possible to the people, in this case the parish, and (b) structure each successive higher organizational level to help make sure it happens. Related to this is the principle of subsidiarity, which, in the context of this discussion, holds that decisions affecting the lives of ordinary people should be made as close as possible to them at the lowest feasible level of the church's organization. Bishops, then, should be sensitive to parish needs and should support parish leaders in their local, democratically made decisions. John Coleman observes that Johannes Messner "connects subsidiarity with the common good: 'The laws of subsidiary function and the law of the common good are in substance identical.' They are identical because in Catholic thought the common good envisions not only the good of the whole but the good of individuals who comprise that whole as well. . . . The law of the subsidiary function prescribes that authority act for the common good in accord with the dignity of the human person by allowing men and women and lesser societies through social action to freely pursue their own perfection, di-

versity, and creativity. The freedom and dignity of human persons sets constitutional limits on the power of authority, even within the church" (Coleman
1992, 233, quoting Messner).

Given what we have said about parish-leaders-for-community, bishops must
be diocesan-leaders-for-community. They should be selected after careful and
meaningful consultation with the people in their dioceses, clergy and religious
alike. They must be authoritative, Model II managers who garner people's trust
because they use their power as caring servants of the laity and the clergy. Dioceses as communities promoting spirituality and authentic human development in their constituent parishes must treat each parish, its priests and laity, as
being mature and capable of making competent decisions. But as Lakeland argues, "neither lay demands nor ecclesiastical fiat can be the last word in the decisions of the community" (2003, 218). He envisions complementary processes
for the bishop and for the laity in decision making. The bishop's process would
entail, in order, "listening/consultation, discernment, decision, listening for
consent" (218). The laity's ordering would be "discernment, voice, listening to
decisions, consent." Moreover, "this two-way street demands restraint and respect on both sides." Emphasizing the democratic leadership principles of consent and accountability, Lakeland maintains that "in our age, when all forms
of governance, even in the church, will be colored by the clear human preference for democratic forms of social organization, consent and accountability
will mark the life of the church" (219). Dioceses themselves should have representative and democratically structured diocesan decision-making forums
wherein priests and the laity work collegially with the bishop and the diocesan
staff, with all engaging in open dialogue and free and uncoerced communication. As with parish councils, diocesan pastoral councils have had varying degrees of success, but a democratic forum like this must be developed. Dioceses
so understood would afford few opportunities for clergy sexual abusers to be
hidden from public view or moved from place to place, and they would also
protect the rights of all actors in the clergy sexual abuse system, victims/sur-
vivors and priests alike, while restoring trust in the church.

## Reform at the National Church Level

The clergy sexual abuse scandal has significantly lowered trust in the church at all levels. What was suggested at the diocesan level about community, leadership-for-community, and democratically structured governance that entails a meaningful role for the laity applies as well to the national church. But there is an additional crucial issue involving enculturation and collegiality. In the aftermath of Vatican II, it seemed as if national church bodies, such as the United States Conference of Catholic Bishops (USCCB), would be returned to their earlier role in governance, manifest in more church council–oriented times, and would play a crucial role in the universal church by working collegially with each other and with the pope to achieve the mission of the church. This would have required significant decentralization of pre–Vatican II church governance; however, Pope John Paul II has been attempting to restore the church to those highly centralized and hierarchical ways.

The former Archbishop of San Francisco, John R. Quinn, in his *The Reform of the Papacy: The Costly Call to Christian Unity* (1999), developed a theologically sound and challenging rationale for achieving the Vatican II vision. Citing Robert Waterman, Quinn advanced the idea of "directed autonomy," a notion borrowed from international business: "In directed autonomy, people in every nook and cranny of the company are empowered — encouraged, in fact — to do things their way. . . . But all this takes place within a context of direction. People know what the boundaries are; they know where they should act on their own and where not" (Waterman 1987, quoted in Quinn 1999, 179). In a significant passage, Quinn argued:

> The Church, of course, is not an international corporation, nor, on the other hand, does it have a timeless, transcendent existence. The Church is both affected by and can learn from the world and in particular from the experience of international corporations. . . . Directed autonomy simply shows how secular corporations that are international, multicultural, and dealing with complex, diverse, and swiftly changing situations have learned an effective way of avoiding obsolescence, chaos, and fragmentation. Directed autonomy in international corporations can offer some suggestions to the Church

to help it to learn how, in the practical realm, it can decentralize, encourage diversity, elicit participation, and implement the principle of subsidiarity and the doctrine of effective collegiality without running the risk of chaos or of schismatic or national churches. (Quinn 1999, 179–80)

Quinn's argument, in the spirit of the rationale for diocesan democratic reform just presented, suggests that the Vatican should adopt a decentralizing mind-set committed to achieving the church's mission by empowering people at all the levels of the church so that culturally sensitive and relevant decisions are made at the lowest level of the organization, as close as possible to the people affected. If such had been the case, the USCCB could have addressed the clergy sexual abuse system as a historically and culturally contextualized phenomenon, as could each of the many national churches experiencing the problem, without the Vatican intervening with secret principles and curial legalisms.

## Reform at the Universal Church Level

Simply put, the reform needed at the level of the universal church is for the pope and Vatican officials to place at the top of their agenda the need to develop the church as a community of communities. They would be true leaders-for-community, coordinating democratically structured governance structures, with the laity playing a meaningful role, at all levels of the church. The major implication of my analysis throughout the book is as follows: The Catholic Church's exercise of authoritative power—geared to encouraging the participation of members at all levels of church—would promote Catholics' spirituality, enhance their authentic human development, and create the kind of community in which the abuse of power that has spawned clergy sexual abuse and its cover-up would be as rare as church defenders claim it to be.

As we saw earlier, John XXIII's biographer Thomas Cahill observed that "[t]he ancient Church was the world's first true democracy, and it can be so again—not a democracy of campaigns and runoffs, of parties and platforms, but a democracy of the Spirit, in which every human being, male and female, young and old, rich and poor, is accorded the 'equal human dignity' of which John wrote so movingly" (Cahill 2002, 236). He continued: "Only as the ombudsman for such a universal assembly—which has at least the potential to include the whole world—could the pope begin to fill the role discovered for him neither by theology nor by history but by the express yearning of the world's peoples during the pontificate of John XXIII: Father of the World" (236–37).

James Carroll based his call for Vatican III on the need for reform of the Catholic Church at all levels. He argued that "the twenty-first century desperately needs an intellectually vital, ecumenically open, and morally sound Catholicism, a Catholicism fully itself—that is, a Catholicism profoundly reformed. The world needs a new Catholic church" (Carroll 2002, 18). Throughout this book I have posed the question, What would Pope John XXIII do? I can find no better way to end the book than by citing the words of *il papa buono* that Carroll used to begin his book:

> It is not that the gospel has changed: it is that we have begun to understand it better . . . and know that the moment has come to discern the signs of the times, to seize the opportunity and to look far ahead.

# *Notes*

## CHAPTER ONE: ONE CLERGY SEXUAL ABUSER'S STORY

1. Clergy sexual abusers may have had sexual encounters with victims who are adult women or men, as well as victims who may be female or male minor children. In this book, I focus on male victims who are minor children. The term I prefer and typically use for the sexual abuse of minor children is *child sexual abuse* or, simply, *sexual abuse*. In recent years, it has become commonplace to divide such abuse into two categories: *pedophilia*, the sexual abuse of prepubescent children (age twelve and younger), and *ephebophilia*, the abuse of pubescent children (age thirteen and older). Certain experts claim that this distinction has differential implications for causation of abuse, choice of treatment, and prognosis, especially the likelihood of recidivism. Given the lack of research on the clergy sexual abuse phenomenon, however, such claims are in dispute, and I use one or the other alternative term only when the context dictates that such use helps clarify meaning or contributes to my analysis. Later in this chapter, I return to the issue of diagnostic terminology in trying to be specific about the nature of McKeown's abusive behavior.

2. Details of the McKeown story come from the *Tennessean* and other mostly local Nashville media and from court documents. The role of the media has been central to the clergy sexual abuse system in Nashville, Boston, and throughout the nation and the world. Especially in this chapter, I treat the media, particularly the *Tennessean*, not merely as sources of information but as *dramatis personae* as well. The McKeown story as we will come to know it in this chapter would have been a mere blip on the public's radar screen, rather than a long-standing and central matter of public concern in Nashville, had it not been for the activist role played by the *Tennessean*. The same was even more the case in Boston for the Pulitzer Prize–winning coverage of its clergy sexual abuse scandal by the *Boston Globe*.

I identify the sources for directly quoted material in the text and provide citations for all the material related to McKeown in the references that appear at the end of the book (specifically, in the section titled "III. Sources Related to the McKeown Case"). I remind the reader that the human science inquiry informing this chapter, as well as others throughout the book, entails social construction of the reality of McKeown's career as a child sexual abuser and is necessarily value-laden. I have attempted to tell a coherent, albeit it complicated, story with a beginning, middle, and end. The factual foundation of much of this story, in the case of newspaper sources, often comes from my *report* of what journalists, with their own personal and organizational agendas, have *reported* about what others have *reported* about events in their lives and the lives of others, often about what these *reported-on* persons have *reported* others to have *reported*. This inelegant and dizzying sentence shows that I (and my readers) face barriers to accurate interpretation. The seemingly straightforward act of reporting entails selective perception of whole phenomena, choosing among perceived elements those to be presented and interpreted, and, finally, making the result public orally or in writing. The use of court documents presents similar barriers, since the documents that lawyers for plaintiffs and defendants submit to the court contain selected material that constructs reality in ways most advantageous to their clients. Judges, for their part, are also selective in using the material submitted by litigants in making their interpretations and judgments and in crafting their rulings. A writer who uses court documents should keep in mind this selectivity and its motivations, as should the reader. In the face of these interpretive difficulties inherent in the use of newspaper and court sources, I have tried to be systematic, logical, consistent, accurate, and fair, attempting to find convergent sources and identifying irresolvable interpretive discrepancies where they exist. Research ethics considerations precluded my use of new interviews with the actors in the Nashville clergy sexual abuse situation.

3. In their June 2002 proposed clergy sexual abuse policy, the U.S. Catholic bishops cited their Canadian counterparts in defining child sexual abuse as including "contacts or interactions between a child and an adult when the child is being used as an object of sexual gratification for the adult. A child is abused whether or not this activity involves explicit force, whether or not it involves genital or physical contact, whether or not it is initiated by the child, and whether or not there is discernible harmful outcome" (Canadian Conference of Bishops 1992, 20). The Vatican, however, took exception to the broadness of this definition in its October 2002 response to the proposed American policy and defined clergy sexual abuse as violations of the sixth commandment.

Michel Dorais, in *Don't Tell: The Sexual Abuse of Boys*, defines sexual abuse of children "as removal of clothing, sexual touching, or sexual relations between people who are different in age and power, both physically and psychologically. These activities are not solicited by the younger children or adolescents, who are manipulated by abuse of trust, blackmail, coercion, threat, or violence" (Dorais 2002, 6). In addition to the increased likelihood that an abused child will become an abuser as an adult, Dorais's overview of specialists' estimations of the range of effects on the lives of sexually abused children includes: "fear, anxiety, negative self-image and low self-esteem, abuse of alcohol or drugs, violence directed against the self or others, and a tendency toward depression and suicide as well as toward a problematic sexuality" (4).

Although adult and female sexual abuse victims are not the focus of this book, it is important to keep in mind the words of Rev. Thomas Doyle, one of the pioneer analysts of sexual abuse by priests, who reminds us that "the majority of those actually sexually abused or harassed by Catholic clerics are women. Although society rightly considers child sexual abuse to be horrific beyond compare and rightfully so, [the sexual abuse of women] demands as much attention as the sexual abuse of children and young adolescents. Sexual abuse no matter what the age of the victim, is devastating with life-long consequences" (Doyle, 16 June 2002).

4. Dorais reports that approximately 16 percent of males report some form of sexual abuse before age eighteen, and that "the boy-girl ratio for abuse is generally held to be about 1:2," an estimate that fails to factor in boys' greater reluctance to report than girls. Regarding this reluctance, he continues:

> Because boys are more inclined to conceal their hurts, the physical and emotional trauma of abuse is less visible in boys. They are also aware of the sexist prejudice whereby adults are more reluctant to acknowledge that a boy can be sexually molested. Moreover . . . the masculine conception of virility is incompatible with the factual experience of having been a victim of sexual abuse, or of needing help following such a trauma: the assumption is that a "real man" would not allow himself to be dependent, vulnerable, weak, or passive; that a "real" man knows how to avoid problems or would at least be able to get himself out of a difficult situation. (Dorais 2002, 17)

It is likely that this reluctance would be greatly exacerbated where a trusted priest molests a young boy.

Regarding the controversy (see, e.g., Lyons, *Forbes*, 9 June 2003) over repressed and recovered memory—an adult's claimed reluctance or inability to acknowledge having been sexually abused as a child by a priest or other adult because of the inability to remember the event, only to come forward later claiming the traumatic memory has been recovered—consider this statement by Kenneth Pope (*Psychology, Public Policy, and Law*, 2000):

> Recovered memories of child sex abuse, whether accurate or false, are often termed repressed memories. The use of this term (often with ambiguity and confusion as to whether it simply means "forgotten" for a period of time or implies a specific mechanism of forgetting) has grown common in the popular media, legal cases, and some of the scientific literature. Interestingly, those at both ends of this controversy's extremely polarized spectrum have used the term to describe the relevant mechanism, for example, *Repressed Memories: A Journey to Recovery from Sexual Abuse* (Fredrickson, 1992) and *The Myth of Repressed Memory: False Memories and Allegations of Sexual Abuse* (Loftus & Ketcham, 1994).

In this article and others (Pope 1996, 1997), Pope reviews most of the issues in this controversy. He raises serious methodological questions about the validity of the claims that (1) false repressed memory of abuse occurs in large, even epidemic numbers; and (2) every recovered memory of childhood abuse by an adult is mistaken. He questions these claims on the grounds of their lack of basis in research, the use of unclear terms and fallacies of deductive logic, confirmatory bias and errors of inference, errors in following a chain of reasoning, unfair use of ad hominem attacks, and failure to consult original sources.

Finally, regarding reluctance to admit abuse by a priest, it is interesting to note the situation of adult women. Leslie Lothstein, director of psychology at the Institute of Living, says in the 9 August 2002 issue of *National Catholic Reporter*: "What hasn't come out yet is all the married women in the church who've had sex with priests. That's another huge scandal. The women have too much to lose. Since they're married, they would have to discuss it with their husbands, their families, so it's a secret. I had one priest from another state that was discovered only when someone noticed that some children going up for communion looked just like him. Then the whole thing came out."

5. I will have more to say about Richards in chapter 2.

6. *Appeal of the Plaintiffs to the Tennessee Court of Appeals, Middle Section from the Final Order of the Circuit Court of Davidson County Granting the Roman Catholic Diocese of Nashville's Motion for Summary Judgment. Court of Appeals for the State of Tennessee in the Middle Section of Nashville* (13 November 2001). The reader should keep in mind that the following quotations came from this document and not from the original clinical reports, which remain unavailable to the public.

7. The plaintiffs' appeal brief claimed that the bishop became aware of many of McKeown's earlier abusive acts on receipt of his Baltimore and Hartford medical records but failed to investigate beyond the one early-1970s case that initially brought McKeown's acts to the attention of diocesan officials in 1986.

8. Although the clinical records reported McKeown's preference for fourteen- to twenty-year-olds, there is no direct available evidence for his abuse of children older than high school age. We know for certain that he abused children between the ages of twelve and seventeen or eighteen. Further, with a fixated ephebophile man's attraction to fourteen- to seventeen-year-olds, according to Blanchette and Coleman (*America*, 22 April 2002), there is an issue whether "the adult male's attraction might be one of homosexuality rather than ephebophilia."

9. In a 7 June 2002 article in the *Boston Globe*, a number of the nation's leading legal, psychological, and medical experts concluded the following about child sexual abuse:

> Sexual contact by a person in authority represents *a severe abuse of power and manipulation of trust*, regardless of age or sexual orientation. Such violations, which often occur in the absence of threats or force, can have severe and long-term physical and emotional consequences for the victim.

Further, regarding homosexuality:

> There is no evidence that homosexuals abuse children, teens, or adults at a higher rate than heterosexuals. Studies in the *Journal of the American Medical Association* indicate that 90 percent of abusers of young children are male and 95 percent of those are het-

erosexual. Sexual assault is not an issue of uncontrolled sexual desire, but rather is rooted in *issues of power and control*. Focusing on homosexuality rather than on abuse serves only to perpetuate homophobia and the silencing of many victims.

Further, regarding blaming the victim:

> Abusers use trust, manipulation, threats, and fear to accomplish their abuse. Failure to see sexual assault in this light can have severe long-term consequences for victims of all ages. This may be made worse if the survivor's community disbelieves, minimizes, or excuses the abuse or attempts to "rank" victims' "worthiness." A coordinated community response, including offender and institutional accountability, is necessary to prevent sexual assault. The offending individual, and not the victim, should always take primary responsibility for the crime. (emphases added)

10. The material just reported, as well as certain other allegations made by the *Tennessean*, have been disputed by diocesan officials. As we will see, the presiding judge dismissed the suit brought by McKeown's victims and their families in the summer of 2001, and, predictably, their lawyers appealed. The appeals court sealed all documents and ordered all parties not to comment on the case publicly. The *Tennessean*, however, successfully petitioned that the appeal documents be opened to the public—puzzlingly, the gag order was left in force—and the *Tennessean* made available the complete appellate briefs from both sides on its website on 19 May 2002. The plaintiffs' brief, in addition to the medical information presented earlier, contained a time line of events in the case, constructed, as one might expect, so as to put the plaintiffs' appeal in the most favorable light. This time line was the basis for the newspaper story. The defendants' brief did not challenge the plaintiffs' construction of events in their brief, saying that the facts were irrelevant to the issues of law at stake in the appeal. Diocesan officials, for their part, claimed that the court's gag order prohibited them from replying when asked for comment by the *Tennessean* prior to the publication of its story. The diocese would only say that the plaintiffs had gotten many things wrong and that it was unfair and misleading for the paper to print only the plaintiffs' side of things. The combination of the still-standing gag order and not wanting to try the pending appeal in the press left diocesan officials in a publicly untenable position: They claimed the *Tennessean*'s presentation of the plaintiffs' facts was wrong or misleading without offering any specific reasons or counterarguments to back their claim.

11. See chapter 2 for a more detailed discussion of Voice of the Faithful and other laity involvement issues.

12. Gary Schoener is a nationally known clinical psychologist in Minneapolis who has worked extensively in the area of the sexual abuse of clients by professionals, including priests, and has been an advisor to bishops over the years. In addition to pointing out the comparative rarity of pedophilia among professionals, leading him to "have focused on abuse of adults and/or late adolescents," he asserted that "if you think this is a Catholic problem you have already lost. This is a community problem and needs community solutions. While each faith group and each profession has its piece of the problem, and its

responsibility for part of the solution, various tools, approaches, and solutions can be shared between groups to everyone's benefit." He emphasizes "doing something to aid victims and prevent future victimization" (Schoener 2002).

## CHAPTER TWO: CLERGY SEXUAL ABUSE IN THE WORLD

1. On 11 November 2002, *USA TODAY* published a survey of the nation's ten largest dioceses (Boston; Brooklyn; Chicago; Detroit; Los Angeles; Newark; New York; Orange County, California; Philadelphia; Rockville Centre), in which 31 percent of U.S. Catholics reside. The following findings were reported:

- Media coverage and public pressure galvanized bishops to action after years of ignoring or sheltering abusers. More priests have been removed or put on leave since the scandal erupted in January than in the previous 40 years combined. Still, even the dioceses *USA TODAY* surveyed have not released complete information about how many priests have been accused, and there could be hundreds more than the 234 cases since 1965 found by the *USA TODAY* study.

- Prosecutors also have been targeting priests accused of child abuse, even when the church has not. Of the accused priests 24% either face criminal charges or already have been convicted of crimes. Some have served their time and are back in the community.

- Very few accused priests remain in positions in which they can easily use their authority to abuse minors. About a tenth have been pulled from the priesthood and returned to lay status. Most of the others in the *USA TODAY* survey, while still under the authority of the church, have been removed from their positions and are forbidden to dress as priests or serve in public ministry. About a third have been placed on administrative leave pending investigation.

- Most abusive priests are not serial predators, despite the publicity about a few accused of abusing many children. One in 10 accused priests account for more than half the known allegations, while 40% have been accused of abuse by one person. Of the 25,616 priests who have served in the 10 dioceses since 1965, slightly fewer than 1% have been named publicly in allegations.

This 1 percent figure has often been cited; however, as we shall see, it is probably too low.

2. Bruni and Burkett have observed that "the records of criminal and civil cases filed against priests make it appear that females, for the most part, have been saved from victimization" (1993/2002, 68). They cite Minnesota clinical psychologist Gary Schoener, however, whose therapeutic experience leads him to believe that these public figures may mask an equal or greater number of actual female victims. Among the several factors cited by Schoener for the invisibility of girls as victims of clergy sexual abuse are the

fact that girls may not report their abuse for psychological reasons, such as their tendency to internalize damage rather than to call public attention to it, and that lawyers may not file civil suits on behalf of girls because they believe they are more difficult to win than cases involving boys. Bruni and Burkett have observed, moreover, that "some experts believe sexual abuse by nuns may be underreported—as is sexual abuse by women in secular society—and unrecognized even by those children who are its victims" (88).

3. Speaking to the U.S. Conference of Catholic Bishops in Dallas on 13 June 2002, clergy sexual abuse survivor Michael Bland told the bishops: "As a victim and thriving survivor I believe there should be a zero tolerance for the immoral, sinful and criminal act of sexually abusing a minor. Zero tolerance past, present, and future." This long-ignored victim sentiment weighed powerfully on the U.S. bishops during their June 2002 meeting held for the purpose of developing clergy sexual abuse policies responsive to victims, the media, the Catholic and non-Catholic public, canon law, and the Vatican.

4. It is difficult to generalize about the characteristics and experiences of abuse victims. Only limited data are available. The *Louisville Courier-Journal* (29 September 2002), however, analyzed the 185 clergy sexual abuse civil cases in the Archdiocese of Louisville, including interviews with 128 victims, looking for trends and commonalities. The findings included:

> It started, on average, when they were 11 years old, they say. Two claim they were first abused at age 5.
>
> Two-thirds say that it happened more than once—that they were molested two or three or 10 times or more.
>
> Eighty-five percent of them were boys.
>
> And many of them—men and women alike—say it destroyed their faith in people, in their religion, even in God. . . .
>
> One-fourth of those interviewed said that they or their parents reported their alleged abuse to church or school authorities, although many of those reports can't be confirmed because the officials are dead or plaintiffs say they can't remember their names.
>
> Well over half of those interviewed said they told nobody about the abuse when it allegedly happened—not their mother, father or best friend. And most of those say they kept it secret until they filed their lawsuits this year. Seven plaintiffs said they told a parent or other relative who didn't believe them.
>
> Most of the plaintiffs said they were fondled. One woman said she was raped and 16 others say they were victims of rape or attempted rape or oral sex or sodomy.
>
> Only eight said that someone other than themselves or the priest saw what happened, although lawyers who have prosecuted and defended such claims against the church say that is typical in this type of case. . . . Accused of misconduct are 25 priests and former priests—living and dead—as well as a deacon, a Franciscan brother, two parochial school teachers and a volunteer football coach. . . .

Many of the plaintiffs say they were exploited when they were emotionally vulnerable and desperately in need of comfort and consolation. . . .

Nearly five times as many plaintiffs claim to have been molested in the 1960s and 1970s as the 1980s or 1990s. Only 20 plaintiffs allege they were victimized since 1982. . . . Only one plaintiff said he was abused in the 1990s and 31 in the 1980s, compared with 86 in the 1960s and 58 in the 1970s. Fifteen allege they were abused in the 1950s. Some victims were counted more than once because their alleged abuse occurred in more than one decade.

5. I explore these matters in chapter 3.

6. The *National Catholic Reporter* (10 May 2002) identified

a Boston Globe report on April 29 that legal papers filed by Law's attorneys claim that "negligence" on the part of [abuse victim] Greg Ford and his parents in part contributed to the alleged abuse.

Legal observers here were quick to point out the cardinal's defense contained a common legal strategy. Boston attorney Carmen Durso, who represents other victims who have come forward with allegations of clerical sex abuse, told the Globe that the legal maneuver "is dumb beyond belief. . . . It is a stupid argument to make when you know that Catholics are already angry at you."

Rodney Ford, father of Greg Ford, expressed stronger sentiments. "To say that my son is legally responsible for his own abuse at the hands of this monster Shanley when my son was only 6 years old is horrific."

7. "The third position offers a normative ideal . . . that honors liberty, equality, and fraternity—balanced in a dynamic tension to develop a good society" (Dokecki 1996, 141; see Newbrough 1992 for the original development of this understanding). I develop the notion of the third position further in chapter 3.

8. VOTF is one of several Boston lay groups occasioned by the clergy sexual abuse crisis. Others include Parish Voice, the Parish Leadership Forum, Speak Truth To Power!, and the Coalition of Concerned Catholics. The Priests' Forum is a grassroots clergy reform-oriented group.

9. A 29 October 2002 address by VOTF president James E. Post, posted on the group's website (www.votf.org), presented the latest version of VOTF's rationale and agenda:

The case for reform could not be clearer. The clergy sexual abuse crisis has revealed a deep need for change in the governance and decision making processes of the Catholic Church. After months of discussion, American Catholics are developing a pretty clear vision of what must change.

*Morality.* Our Church lost its moral compass in dealing with these sexual abuse crimes. Our moral compass must be reclaimed. Children must be protected. There is no alternative.

*Accountability.* Those who have abused children must be punished. Sexual abuse is a crime and American civil law must hold predators accountable. John Geoghan will likely spend the rest of his life in prison. Paul Shanley may face the same fate. Their life of sexual abuse must come to an end. There is no alternative.

*Integrity.* The harms caused by abusive priests are incalculable. Lives have been ruined, and many survivors of clergy sexual abuse have been altered forever. Justice must be provided for survivors. The needs of each victim/survivor are likely to be different. The Church must commit to righting these terrible wrongs. There is no alternative.

*Power.* We know that power corrupts. And, as Lord Acton said so well, "absolute power corrupts absolutely." The structures, culture, and decision processes that contributed to this crisis must be changed. American bishops demonstrated an incredible willingness to hide the truth and cover up the crimes. Concentration of power must be tempered with the realization that a necessary check and balance is essential. There is no alternative.

10. A number of dissident groups have sprung up in Boston during the first months of 2002. In the midst of this turmoil, a proposal surfaced that called for enhancing the role of the laity in the workings of the Archdiocese of Boston by the establishment of an association of lay councils with representation from all of Boston's local parish councils. In that regard, the *National Catholic Reporter* (10 May 2002) described an emerging controversy over the proposal that shows the general approach Cardinal Law had adopted:

> The cause of protesters and lay organizers was fueled by a disclosure over the weekend that Law had instructed one of his top aides, Bishop Walter J. Edyvean, moderator of the archdiocesan curia, to send an archdiocesan-wide letter to parish pastors, instructing them not to "endorse" or "recognize" a proposal calling for an association of parish councils.
>
> Citing the 1983 Code of Canon Law, Edyvean wrote, "As a pastor or a vicar, you are not to join, foster or promote this endeavor among your parish pastoral council members or the community of the faithful." He said there already exist four "canonically recognized" bodies—Presbyteral Council, the College of Consultors, the Archdiocesan Finance Council, and the Archdiocesan Pastoral Council. "The latter represents the people of God of the archdiocese (Canon 512) and renders the proposed association superfluous and potentially divisive."
>
> "This is astonishingly stupid," said Mary Jo Bane, a Harvard University John F. Kennedy School of Government public policy professor. . . . Along with others, Bane helped draft the plan for the proposed association, which was the brainchild of attorney David W. Zizik, of Sherborn, Mass., where he serves on the parish council of St. Theresa Church.
>
> . . . The topic of Edyvean's letter surfaced at the Monday night meeting of Voice of the Faithful. Although he was unable to attend, Zizik sent a written statement that was read to the group. "I will continue to work toward the establishment of a mechanism— consistent with ecclesiastical tradition and archdiocesan synodal legislation—that will unite members of the laity, the hierarchy, parish priests, and women and men religious

throughout our archdiocese in a genuine and ongoing dialogue, with the goal of healing our local church and accomplishing the gospel mission that underlies everything we do as Catholic Christians," Zizik's statement read.

Edyvean's April 25 letter, he said, is having a chilling effect not only on the laity but also on archdiocesan parish priests.

11. Comments made by Father Tom Doyle at the VOTF meeting were even more challenging and confrontational:

What we have experienced in our lifetime is a disaster, the horror of which is perhaps equaled by the bloodshed of the Inquisition, but which certainly makes the indulgence scam of the Reformation pale by comparison. What we see before us are the beginning death throes of the medieval, monarchical model that was based on the belief that a small, select minority of the educated, privileged, and power-invested was called forth by God to manage the temporal and spiritual lives of the faceless masses. (*Boston Globe*, 21 June 2002)

12. In mid-November 2002, Robert Bullock, spokesperson for Boston's Priests' Forum, reported some of what priests had said to Cardinal Law during an October meeting with them: "By condemning the Voice of the Faithful, that makes things more difficult for us, because the Voice of the Faithful parishioners are our parish council members, lectors, religious education teachers, eucharistic ministers. To say that these people are somehow illegitimate or are somehow a threat to our catholicity is absurd. To say these parishioners cannot use their own buildings, which they pay for, is ridiculous" (*New York Times*, 13 November 2002). These remarks apparently contributed to Law's softening attitude toward Voice of the Faithful.

13. The Nashville chapter of VOTF sent the following message of solidarity, available on the VOTF website (www.votf.org):

We stand united with VOTF members in the Archdiocese of Boston in their condemnation of the new revelations of cover-ups and other unacceptable conduct by certain members of the Church hierarchy. We decry the criminal actions of certain bishops and priests in the Boston area, which have betrayed the confidence of Catholics in Boston and Catholics throughout the world. We believe that only prayer, openness, honesty and more lay participation in Church decision-making will protect our Church from future improper actions and promote healing between the Church and its victims. We understand that the road to meaningful reform of the Church is long, but we will persevere as long as it takes. Our mottos are and will remain: (1) Change the Church; Keep the Faith (2) Evil flourishes when good people do nothing.

14. Carroll added:

And even now, as the Boston archdiocese ducks and feints behind bankruptcy laws and lawyers, precisely to protect the wealth of its imperial sway, the Christ child comes as an infinite rebuke. Bishops and popes must stop living and acting like emperors.

Specifically, the Catholic estate on Lake Street should be cashed in and paid out to suing victims. Not a settlement—a penance.

Abused children can thus be an epiphany of all the sins committed by an imperial
church (ask the Jews), and the moral reckoning those now grown children demand can
be the occasion of a long overdue dismantling of an imperial structure that is itself a
blasphemy. The tradition demands sackcloth and ashes, but modesty and simplicity will
do. Until the church trades its silk robes and treasure for contemporary equivalents of
the way Jesus of Nazareth lived, his memory will continue to be dishonored. Imperial
decadence will reign. (*Boston Globe*, 17 December 2002)

15. Carroll described the church's situation as follows:

There are forces at work here that have already leveled the structures of denial and control. Those forces include the determination of victims to be heard, the energy of Catholic lay people expecting change, the demand of good priests to be respected, the actu-
arial reality that most of those good priests will be retired soon, the court's requirement
of full accounting for crimes, the duty of a free press to report news that matters, and the
still vital impulse of reform begun at Vatican II. All of this keeps the escalator moving
under the bishops, taking them where they do not want to go.

But there are even more irresistible forces in motion. World-wide impulses toward
democracy, the power of new female consciousness, pluralism's relativizing of triumphalist claims, religious self-criticism after 9/11—all of this has the ground moving
under Catholicism, too. (*Boston Globe*, 24 September 2002)

## CHAPTER THREE: PROFESSIONAL ETHICS AND
## THE CLERGY SEXUAL ABUSE SYSTEM

1. A November 2002 Gallup poll of practicing Catholics sponsored by the Founda-
tions and Donors Interested in Catholic Activities found that "fewer than half—45 percent—rate U.S. Catholic bishops high on financial accountability, while two-thirds
think 'the church should be more accountable on finances.' A like number say 'the revelations concerning the lack of financial accountability arising from the priestly sexual
abuse scandal are a cause for concern.'" Further:

Sixty-eight percent of churchgoing Catholics who responded to the poll say the church
should conduct and publish "an annual independent audit of finances at every church
level," while 79 percent agree "that each diocesan bishop should give a full accounting
of the financial costs of settlements arising from the priest sexual abuse scandal."

Fifty-five percent fear the cost of settlements from the priest sex abuse scandal will
negatively impact the church's ability to meet its mission, including programs that assist the disadvantaged members of society.

Nearly half would consider contributing to alternative non-diocesan charities as a
substitute for their current giving.

About a quarter said they would reduce their current giving if they learned their contributions were used to pay for lawsuits. And 18 percent have stopped contributing to national collections. (*National Catholic Reporter*, 20 December 2002)

Further, the *New York Times* (9 November 2002) reported the results of a Gallup poll of actively practicing Catholics (regular attendees at mass and participants in parish activities) concerning the impact of the clergy sexual abuse scandal on their giving to the church. "In the survey, about one in nine of the regular Mass-goers said they had been putting less money in their parish collection plate in the months since the abuse scandal began in January. About 3 percent of Catholics—mostly more affluent and conservative parishioners—reported increasing their parish giving. The nation's 194 dioceses have been harder hit: 19 percent of those surveyed said they stopped supporting their diocese, with some saying they were diverting those donations to other Catholic causes." Further: "Most of the questions in the Gallup survey focused on parishioners' attitudes about bishops' accountability, especially on financial matters, but one was very broad: 'Do you think the U.S. Catholic bishops have done a good job or a bad job in dealing with the problem of sexual abuse of young people by Catholic priests?' 'A bad job,' said 64 percent of those surveyed."

2. Earlier (Dokecki 1996) I wrote:

In this last decade of the twentieth century, we are busily fulfilling many of the prophecies Erich Fromm (1955) made in *The Sane Society*, a deeply ironic title for a book analyzing the *insane* society we have been creating in the modern world. We have been behaving like machines, like robots, dehumanizing each other in our selfish, narcissistic, egotistical, overly competitive, not sufficiently cooperative, and characteristically masculine (macho) pursuit of power. We are a society that not only tolerates but also invites the abuse of power.

Professionals are among those who, on behalf of their clients and the good of society, should be leading the effort against the abuse of power. But . . . they sometimes fall prey to the temptation to use the power inherent in their professional roles primarily for their own good and only incidentally or accidentally for the good of others, as their codes of ethics and professional traditions demand. A dramatic and disturbing instance of such professional abuse of power is that of professionals having sex with their clients. This behavior, the subject of endless movies and television scripts, is increasing in public awareness and all too common among a wide variety of professionals, including physicians, psychotherapists, teachers, ministers, lawyers, and the like.

3. I discuss the work of Kennedy and Charles in detail in chapter 4.

4. Leonard Swidler comments:

Surprising as it may be to many Catholics, the slogan of the French Revolution really encapsulates the essence of Catholicism and the fundamental Good News of Jesus: *Liberté, égalité, fraternité*. The essence of the love of neighbor is freely (*liberté*) to treat *all* men and women as brothers and sisters (*fraternité*—today we would eliminate the sexist language and probably use *solidarité*), especially the powerless of society (*égalité*). (Swidler 1996, 9)

## CHAPTER FOUR: HUMAN SCIENCE PERSPECTIVES
## ON THE CLERGY SEXUAL ABUSE SYSTEM

1. Richard Sipe, in *Sex, Priests, and Power: Anatomy of a Crisis* (1995), attempts to show that the interrelationship among the clerical role, celibacy, power, and doctrinal orthodoxy constitutes an important systemic feature of the Catholic Church. He focuses on the male qualities of power in writing that "the structure underlying the celibate/sexual system has seven interlocking and mutually reinforcing elements that influence its function and form both the contour and the character of its power. These elements are blame [of women], the superior group [men], [male] power, subjugation [of women by men], nature and God's will [that men subjugate women], sexual inconsistency [double standard for the faithful and the clergy], and necessary violence [to maintain the system and its power]" (163).

2. In his 2001 book *The Unhealed Wound: The Church and Human Sexuality*, Kennedy comments on the church's continuing failure to address sexual maturity issues in the priesthood:

> The National Conference of Catholic Bishops in the United States has resisted any efforts to understand the pedophilia crisis or the myriad associated concerns about the level of psychosexual maturity among candidates for the priesthood. The bishops, as a group, have not been able to overcome the institutional dynamics that they are pressed by Rome to honor even if they disagree with them. Their response is not spontaneous and healthy but calculated and officious, the same kind of denial employed by large corporations, such as tobacco companies when faced with the evidence that their product is a cause of cancer. Church officials, with few exceptions, have resolutely refused to consider that the complex sociopsychological factors in the celibate clerical culture may contribute to the problem of pedophilia or to other problematic conditions, including the homosexualization of the priesthood. (154)

3. Kennedy's analysis of the church's attempts to deal with clergy sexual abuse and other aspects of sexual morality leads him to conclude:

> [T]he sexual problematic for Catholicism is a function of acting as an institution does rather than as a church should, so that its bureaucratic intentions infect what its pastoral possibilities would otherwise heal. The bureaucracy is a shadow Church that reflects less the glory of God than the cunning of the world. . . . [T]he shadow Church keeps itself together as an Institution by investing its power in keeping its members in a frightened and dependent state. . . . [T]he institution knows that if it can control sexuality, it

can maintain its mastery over human beings. This emphasis on power diminishes its true authority to help ordinary men and women put away childish things and grow up even by small steps, the way we learn to walk and talk—the way, imperfect but tolerant of failings, we become human. (Kennedy 2001, 10)

4. The use of social phenomenology in this section on ideology appeared in slightly different form in Dokecki 1996.

5. Shupe also uses the criminal law concept of accessory after the fact, often said to apply to bishops in their response to clergy sexual abuse. Such bishops did not themselves perpetrate the crime of abuse, but "by way of remaining silent when they have knowledge of perpetration, facilitate its occurrence and invisibility" (Shupe 1995, 67). He continues:

Recidivism of clergy malfeasance clearly has been a beneficiary of such accessories. . . . For example, critics of the frequent response by Roman Catholic bishops to accusations and revelations of pedophiles and other sexual abuse have basically indicted dozens (if not many more) church elites for being accessories to the abuse, participating in an "old-boy network" pattern of stall-tactics and coverups. Andrew H. Greeley (1992) has remarked: "I am furious at my fellow priests who have denied and even to this moment are still denying the pedophilia-crisis which their indifference has created." (Shupe 1995, 67)

6. Some of the material in this section is adapted in slightly edited fashion from Dokecki, Newbrough, and O'Gorman 2001 and is used with permission of the *Journal of Community Psychology*.

7. See table 4.1 and chapter 3's discussion of Model I and Model II approaches to professional practice.

## CHAPTER FIVE: ECCLESIOLOGICAL PERSPECTIVES ON THE CLERGY SEXUAL ABUSE SYSTEM

1. I present Dulles's (1974/1987) analysis of various models of the church later in this chapter.

2. See chapter 3; Dokecki 1996; and Newbrough 1992.

3. Much of the material in this section came from papers and official documents found on the United States Conference of Catholic Bishops website (www.usccb.org) in an extensive section titled "Restoring Trust: Response to Clergy Sexual Abuse" (11 March 2002), retrieved from www.usccb.org/comm/restoretrust.htm.

4. Theologian Richard McBrien commented on Gregory's allegation:

The problem is that Bishop Gregory did not "name it clearly for what it is." He did not tell his fellow bishops who the "extremists" are, nor the content of their "agendas."

Was he warning the bishops against conservative Catholics who have been blaming the crisis on homosexuals and urging that gays not be admitted to seminaries nor ordained to the priesthood? If so, not a few of those extremists were sitting in the audience, right in front of him.

Are the "false prophets" those who favor optional celibacy for priests, a greater role for women in the church, and a change in the process by which bishops are appointed? Again, some of his fellow bishops favor these reforms. (*The Tidings*, 6 December 2002)

5. On 3 December 2002, the Zenit News Service reported Cardinal Ratzinger to have said about the clergy sexual abuse scandal:

> In the Church, priests also are sinners. But I am personally convinced that the constant presence in the press of the sins of Catholic priests, especially in the United States, is a planned campaign, as the percentage of these offenses among priests is not higher than in other categories, and perhaps it is even lower.
>
> In the United States, there is constant news on this topic, but less than 1% of priests are guilty of acts of this type. The constant presence of these news items does not correspond to the objectivity of the information nor to the statistical objectivity of the facts. Therefore, one comes to the conclusion that it is intentional, manipulated, that there is a desire to discredit the Church. It is a logical and well-founded conclusion.

Ratzinger's percentage claim was disputed. The *National Catholic Reporter* (10 January 2003) reported:

> Psychologist A. W. Richard Sipe told NCR he doubts the accuracy of Ratzinger's pronouncement that "less than 1 percent" of priests is guilty of abuse. Sipe said the bishops' office in Washington has in the past created such statistics by only including priests whose history of abuse has become public knowledge and withholding information about "a number of offenders who are not publicly known."
>
> Sipe, whose years of study of sexuality and the priesthood have led him to estimate that between 4 and 5 percent of U.S. priests have sexually abused minors, said that Ratzinger's comments miss "the core of the problem. The core is the revelation of systemic corruption. It isn't about bad priests. It is about a system that is hypocritical at its core. The faithful are up in arms because the system builds on and fosters a kind of hypocrisy."

Further, citing findings from what was called "the most complete compilation of data on the problem available," the *New York Times* (12 January 2003) reported:

> Every region [of the United States] was seriously affected, with 206 accused priests in the West, 246 in the South, 335 in the Midwest and 434 in the Northeast. The crisis reached not only big cities like Boston and Los Angeles but smaller ones like Louisville, with 27 priests accused, and St. Cloud, Minn., with 9. . . .
>
> The *Times* survey counted priests from dioceses and religious orders who had been accused by name of sexually abusing one or more children. It determined that 1.8 percent of all priests ordained from 1950 to 2001 had been accused of abuse.
>
> But the research also suggested that the extent of the problem remains hidden. In dioceses that have divulged what they say are complete lists of abusive priests—under court orders or voluntarily—the percentages are far higher. In Baltimore, an estimated 6.2

percent of priests ordained in the last half-century have been implicated in the abuse of minors. In Manchester, N.H., the percentage is 7.7, and in Boston it is 5.3.

The *Times* data include only cases in which priests were named, and many bishops have released only partial lists of accused priests, or refused to identify any.

6. The members of the Mixed Commission were:

Cardinal Dario Castrillón Hoyos, Colombian, prefect of the Congregation for Clergy; Archbishop Julian Herranz, a Spaniard, president of the Pontifical Council for the Interpretation of Legislative Texts; Archbishop Tarcisio Bertone, Italian, secretary of the Congregation for the Doctrine of the Faith; and Archbishop Francesco Monterisi, another Italian, secretary of the Congregation for Bishops. . . . For the Americans, members were Cardinal Francis George of Chicago; Archbishop William Levada of San Francisco; Bishop Thomas Doran of Rockford, Ill.; and Bishop William Lori of Bridgeport, Conn. (*National Catholic Reporter*, 7 November 2002)

7. An 11 November 2002 *National Catholic Reporter* editorial, titled "Now more than ever, bishops need laity," commented about the new norms:

It is laypeople—outsiders to the authority structure—who are left to judge the authenticity and integrity of episcopal efforts to make reparations and protect the young. The simple truth is: The bishops need the laity as never before. But do they understand this?

Consider this image: the U.S. bishops grouped together and sinking in quicksand. On solid ground are laymen and women waiting to throw ropes for the rescue. Curiously, in too many instances, we see bishops rejecting these ropes. Instead of embracing lay efforts within dioceses to watchdog bishops and work with them to bring local churches to greater health, we see bishops driving these lay groups out of their dioceses. We see lay boards being told they have no authority and, furthermore, that they must operate within the realm of secrecy that spawned the crisis in the first place. It is time this nonsense ends.

8. Responding to the newly adopted norms, victim advocate David Clohessy made these recommendations for what the bishops needed to do to help meet victim concerns:

Holding listening session[s] with survivors, as Archbishop Timothy Dolan has done in Milwaukee.

Releasing victims from unhealthy, church-imposed gag orders.

Allowing the Survivors Network of those Abused by Priests to publicize support group meetings in church bulletins.

Listing the names of abusive priests on diocesan Web sites.

Lobbying for longer statutes of limitations.

Allowing survivor-friendly independent lay-Catholic groups to meet in parishes without harassment.

In recent months, one or two bishops have adopted each of these suggestions, and their colleagues are being prodded to do likewise. These painless "baby steps" provide desperately needed hope to hurting victims and disillusioned Catholics, and prove that some church leaders can move beyond the flawed, bare-minimum measure approved in Washington. (*St. Louis Post-Dispatch*, 8 December 2002)

9. Allen also identified a number of issues the church would face in attempting to implement the newly approved norms:

What actually is meant by "sexual abuse?" The standard in the norms, "an external, objectively grave violation of the sixth commandment," leaves much room for interpretation, with the risk that the same act might have a priest restored to ministry in one diocese but barred for life in another.

How will the requirement of "pontifical secrecy" affect cooperation with civil and criminal authorities? Will both victims and accused priests be left in the dark for long periods of time as the legal machinery grinds on? Will a lack of transparency undermine public confidence in the process?

How will the American norms work with the new Vatican norms on sex abuse, proclaimed in secret 18 months ago and recently published for the first time on the NCR web site? How will church officials ensure that a uniform standard of justice is being applied at both levels?

Will the Vatican grant waivers from the statute of limitations, set at 10 years from the victim's 18th birthday, as a matter of course, as the U.S. bishops told the American press in Washington? Or will there be cases in which the evidence seems insufficiently compelling to Vatican officials, or the crime insufficiently grave, to justify reaching 30 or 40 years into the past? If so, how will victims and lay activist groups react when the accused priest is restored to ministry?

If a bishop removes a priest on the basis of norm nine, using administrative authority, when he can't secure a conviction in a canonical court but is convinced the priest is guilty, will the Vatican back him up on appeal? (Such an appeal from an administrative measure is technically called "recourse"). What happens if the bishop is overturned, since bishops have vowed that such men will never be returned to ministry?

Where do religious order priests and deacons fit in this process? They were written into the norms at the last minute in footnote #1, but almost everyone recognizes this is not a satisfactory solution. Will the orders be able to maintain their traditional autonomy while at the same time cooperating in the spirit of the new norms? (*National Catholic Reporter*, 20 December 2002)

10. During the summer of 2003, John Allen reported on the emerging pattern of experience regarding bishops' handling of priests accused of sexual abuse in light of the newly approved norms:

Under the norms, bishops are required to report all allegations found to be credible to the Congregation for the Doctrine of the Faith, which authorizes one of three procedures:

- Canonical trial.
- An extra-juridical procedure envisioned under canon 1720. This option allows the bishop, if he is morally certain the priest is guilty, to remove him from ministry without the time and expense of a trial. (The canon requires that the accused be notified of the charges and be given an opportunity for defense).
- Dismissal from the clerical state . . . [through] an involuntary laicization approved personally by the pope. This is a rare option. . . .

The news that may surprise Americans is that the inclination of the Congregation for the Doctrine of the Faith is today in many cases to authorize option two, the extra-judicial route. Last October, the Vatican rejected the norms approved by the U.S. bishops in Dallas on the basis of the need to protect due process rights. This led to concern about a proliferation of lengthy canonical trials that would delay closure. Sources say, however, that as American case files arrive in Rome, in many instances the accused priest's guilt is clear, and hence the Vatican is opting for the swifter solution.

Another reason for the extra-judicial route can be prescription, the statute of limitations in canon law (for the sexual abuse of a minor, the period is ten years from the victim's 18th birthday). When the American norms were debated, many victims' advocates worried that prescription would be used to shield accused priests. In fact, however, Vatican sources say such an outcome is far more likely in secular criminal law, where the statute of limitations is often an absolute barrier to action against the accused. . . . Canon law's bias . . . is that a rupture in the community has to be repaired even if penal action is barred.

To date, few if any canonical trials have actually been held in the United States, as dioceses await authorizations from the congregation. In the meantime, bishops have removed accused priests, placing them on administrative leave. Some priests have appealed that action in a process called recourse. Once canonical trials get underway, there will also be an automatic appeal to the Congregation for the Doctrine of the Faith.

To handle these appeals, the Vatican has considered creating a special tribunal of the Congregation for the Doctrine of the Faith in Washington. . . .

Finally, there remains the question of the "tough cases"—elderly priests with only one offense in the distant past, who have been faithful ever since. . . . A canonist I spoke with in Rome said he wonders if this isn't more myth than reality. "I ask myself if there really are one offense cases," he said, "because in every instance I've dealt with, sooner or later other offenses surface." (*National Catholic Reporter,* 11 July 2003)

11. Thomas Cahill has written of Pope John's view of the council and his influence on its thinking in these terms:

John's apostolic constitution convoking what would be known as the Second Vatican Council (Vatican II) was issued on Christmas day 1963. It contained a pointed ecumenical (in the Protestant sense) invitation to all Christians; and it stated that the work of the council was to "discern the signs of the times," as Jesus advises in Matthew's Gospel, and to be "at the service of the world"—new vocabulary within the Vatican, however ancient the concepts.

The coming council . . . began to stimulate innovative thinking at an accelerated speed. . . . No thinking was more innovative than that of a young Swiss theologian . . . whose name was Hans Küng. . . . The Catholic Church was in need of reform, said Küng, but then, in accordance with the Church's own ageless wisdom, *"ecclesia semper reformanda"* (the Church is always in need of reform). If the council carried out its reform properly by admitting that the Protestant reformers had made just demands — for vernacular liturgies, for the centrality of the Bible, for the recognition of the "priesthood of all the faithful," for the extrication of the papacy from politics — if the Church opened a dialogue with other cultures, reformed the Curia, and got rid of inanities like the Index of Forbidden Books, reunion could be achieved. Küng saw Pope John as the man to rouse Christendom from its slumbers, so that, wide awake, it might see as if for the first time the damaging scandal of its divisions, "an immeasurably crippling wound which absolutely must be healed." . . . Küng's trumpet call would become to a large extent the council's blueprint. (Cahill 2002, 188–89)

## CHAPTER SIX: TOWARD REFORMS ADDRESSING AND PREVENTING CLERGY SEXUAL ABUSE

1. See, for example, Bianchi and Ruether 1992; Cozzens 2002; D'Antonio et al. 1996; Fox 2002; Henn 2000; Kennedy and Charles 1997; Küng 2001; Lakeland 2003; Quinn 1999; Shaw 1994; Steinfels 2003; Swidler 1996; Whitehead and Whitehead 1988; and Wills 2000.

+ + + + + + + + + + + + + + + + + + + + + + + + + + + + + + + + + + + + + + + + + + + + + + + +

# References

The references have been divided into four sections: (I) books, chapters, and journal articles; (II) sources from newspapers, periodicals, and organizations (retrieved from the Internet); (III) sources related to the McKeown case; and (IV) court documents related to the McKeown case.

## I. BOOKS, CHAPTERS, AND JOURNAL ARTICLES

American Psychiatric Association. 1994. *Diagnostic and statistical manual of mental disorders*, 4th ed. Washington, DC: American Psychiatric Association.

Azevedo, M. 1987. *Basic ecclesial communities in Brazil*. Washington, DC: Georgetown University Press.

Bakan, D. 1966. *The duality of human existence: An essay on psychology and religion*. Chicago: Rand McNally.

Balboni, B. 1998. Through the "lens" of the organizational culture perspective: A descriptive study of American Catholic bishops' understanding of the sexual molestation and abuse of children and adolescents. Ph.D. dissertation, Northeastern University, Boston, MA.

Bandura, A. 1989. Human agency in social cognitive theory. *American Psychologist* 44: 1175–84.

Baum, G., and R. Ellsberg. 1990. *The logic of solidarity: Commentaries on Pope John Paul II's encyclical On Social Concern*. Maryknoll, NY: Orbis Books.

Baumrind, D. 1968. Authoritarianism vs. authoritative parental control. *Adolescence* 3, no. 11: 255–72.

Berger, P. L., and T. Luckmann. 1966. *The social construction of reality*. New York: Doubleday.

Bernstein, R. J. 1971. *Praxis and action: Contemporary philosophies of human activity*. Philadelphia: University of Pennsylvania Press.

———. 1976. *The restructuring of social and political theory*. Philadelphia: University of Pennsylvania Press.

———. 1983. *Beyond objectivism and relativism: Science, hermeneutics, and praxis*. Philadelphia: University of Pennsylvania Press.

———. 1986. *Philosophical profiles: Essays in a pragmatic mode*. Philadelphia: University of Pennsylvania Press.

———. 1992. *The new constellation: The ethical-political horizons of modernity/ postmodernity.* Cambridge, MA: MIT Press.

Berry, J. 1992/2000. *Lead us not into temptation: Catholic priests and the sexual abuse of children.* Urbana: University of Illinois Press.

Berry, T. 1988. *The dream of the earth.* San Francisco: Sierra Club.

Bianchi, E. C., and R. R. Ruether, eds. 1992. *A democratic Catholic Church: The reconstruction of Roman Catholicism.* New York: Crossroad.

Boff, L. 1986. *Ecclesiogenesis: The base communities reinvent the church.* Maryknoll, NY: Orbis Books.

Bok, S. 1978. *Lying: Moral choice in public and private life.* New York: Pantheon.

Browning, D. S. 1973. *Generative man: Psychoanalytic perspectives.* Philadelphia: Westminster Press.

Bruni, F., and E. Burkett. 1993/2002. *A gospel of shame: Children, sexual abuse, and the Catholic Church.* New York: HarperCollins.

Burns, G. 1992. *The frontiers of Catholicism: The politics of ideology in a liberal world.* Berkeley: University of California Press.

Cahill, T. 2002. *Pope John XXIII.* New York: Penguin Putnam Inc.

Canon Law Society of America. 2003. *Guide to the implementation of the U.S. Bishops' Essential Norms for Diocesan/Eparchial Policies Dealing with Allegations of Sexual Abuse of Minors by Priests and Deacons.* Washington, DC: Canon Law Society of America.

Carroll, J. 2001. *Constantine's sword: The church and the Jews: A history.* Boston: Houghton Mifflin.

———. 2002. *Toward a new Catholic Church: The promise of reform.* Boston: Houghton Mifflin.

Coleman, J. A. 1992. Not democracy but democratization. In *A democratic Catholic Church: The reconstruction of Roman Catholicism,* edited by E. C. Bianchi and R. R. Ruether, 226–47. New York: Crossroad.

Cowan, M. A., and B. J. Lee. 1997. *Conversation, risk, and conversion: The inner and public life of small Christian communities.* Maryknoll, NY: Orbis.

Cozzens, D. B. 2000. *The changing face of the priesthood: A reflection on the priest's crisis of soul.* Collegeville, MN: The Liturgical Press.

———. 2002. *Sacred silence: Denial and the crisis in the church.* Collegeville, MN: The Liturgical Press.

Craig, J. H., and M. Craig. 1973. *Synergic power: Beyond domination and submissiveness.* Berkeley, CA: Proactive Press.

D'Antonio, W. V., J. D. Davidson, D. R. Hoge, and R. A. Wallace. 1996. *Laity: American and Catholic: Transforming the church.* Kansas City, MO: Sheed and Ward.

Dewey, J., and A. Bentley. 1949. *Knowing and the known.* Boston: Beacon Press.

Dokecki, P. R. 1982. Liberation: Movement in theology, theme in community psychology. *Journal of Community Psychology* 10: 185–96.

———. 1986. Methodological futures of the caring professions. *Urban and Social Change Review* 191: 3–7.

———. 1987. Can knowledge contribute to the creation of community? *Journal of Community Psychology* 15: 90–96.

———. 1992. On knowing the community of caring persons: A methodological basis for the reflective-generative practice of community psychology. *Journal of Community Psychology* 20: 26–35.

———. 1996. *The tragicomic professional: Basic considerations for ethical reflective-generative practice.* Pittsburgh: Duquesne University Press.

Dokecki, P. R., J. R. Newbrough, and R. T. O'Gorman. 1993. Community and leadership in the postmodern church: III. Leadership for community. *PACE* (23 December): 36–40.

———. 2001. Toward a community-oriented action research framework for spirituality: Community psychological and theological perspectives. *Journal of Community Psychology* 29: 497–518.

Dorais, M. 2002. *Don't tell: The sexual abuse of boys.* Montreal: McGill-Queen's University Press.

Dulles, A. 1974/1987. *Models of the church: Expanded edition.* New York: Doubleday.

Dunst, C. J., C. M. Trivette, and A. G. Deal. 1988. *Enabling and empowering families.* Cambridge, MA: Brookline Books.

Erikson, E. H. 1950. *Childhood and society.* New York: Norton.

Flannery, A., ed. 1975/1984a. *Apostolicam actuositatem: The decree on the apostolate of the laity. Documents of Vatican II.* Grand Rapids, MI: Eerdmans.

———., ed. 1975/1984b. *Lumen gentium: The dogmatic constitution on the church. Documents of Vatican II.* Grand Rapids, MI: Eerdmans.

Fox, T. C. 2002. *Pentecost in Asia: A new way of being church.* Maryknoll, NY: Orbis.

Frankena, W. K. 1963/1973. *Ethics.* Englewood Cliffs, NJ: Prentice Hall.

Fromm, E. 1955. *The sane society.* New York: Rinehart.

———. 1976. *To have or to be?* New York: Bantam.

Greeley, A. M. 1993. *Fall from grace.* New York: Putnam.

Green, J. M. 1999. *Deep democracy: Community, diversity, and transformation.* Lanham, MD: Rowman and Littlefield.

Gula, R. M. 1996. *Ethics in pastoral ministry.* New York: Paulist Press.

Habermas, J. 1984. *The theory of communicative action.* Boston: Beacon Press.

Henn, W. 2000. *The honor of my brothers: A brief history of the relationship between the pope and the bishops.* New York: Crossroad.

Investigative Staff of the Boston Globe. 2002. *Betrayal: The crisis of the Catholic Church.* New York: Little, Brown.

Jenkins, P. 1996/2000. *Pedophiles and priests: Anatomy of a contemporary crisis.* New York: Oxford University Press.

———. 1998. *Moral panic: Changing concepts of the child molester in modern America.* New Haven, CT: Yale University Press.

———. 2003. *The new anti-Catholicism: The last acceptable prejudice.* New York: Oxford University Press.

Jordan, M. D. 2000. *The silence of Sodom: Homosexuality in modern Catholicism.* Chicago: University of Chicago Press.

Kelly, G. A. 1955. *The psychology of personal constructs.* New York: Norton.

Kennedy, E. 1971. *The Catholic priest in the United States: Psychological investigations.* Washington, DC: United States Catholic Conference.

———. 2001. *The unhealed wound: The church and human sexuality.* New York: St. Martin's Press.

Kennedy, E., and S. C. Charles. 1997. *Authority: The most misunderstood idea in America.* New York: Free Press.

Küng, H. 1992. Participation of the laity in church leadership and in church ejections. In *A democratic Catholic Church: The reconstruction of Roman Catholicism*, edited by E. C. Bianchi and R. R. Ruether, 80–93. New York: Crossroad.

———. 2001. *The Catholic Church: A short history.* New York: The Modern Library.

Lakeland, P. 2003. *The liberation of the laity: In search of an accountable church.* New York: Continuum.

Lebacqz, K. 1985. *Professional ethics: Power and paradox.* Nashville, TN: Abingdon Press.

Lyotard, J. F. 1984. *The postmodern condition.* Minneapolis: University of Minnesota Press.

Macmurray, J. 1957. *The self as agent.* London: Faber.

———. 1961. *Persons in relation.* New York: Harper and Bros.

Maritain, J. 1947. *The person and the common good.* New York: Scribners.

Marrow, A. 1969. *The practical theorist: The life and work of Kurt Lewin.* New York: Basic Books.

Mayeroff, M. 1971. *On caring.* New York: Harper and Row.

McMillan, D. W., and D. M. Chavis. 1986. Sense of community: A definition and theory. *Journal of Personality and Social Psychology* 14: 6–23.

Menand, L. 2001. *The Metaphysical Club: A story of ideas in America.* New York: Farrar, Straus, and Giroux.

Moroney, R. M. 1986. *Shared responsibility: Families and social policy.* New York: Aldine.

Newbrough, J. R. 1992. Community psychology in the post-modern world. *Journal of Community Psychology* 20: 10–25.

Newbrough, J. R., R. T. O'Gorman, and P. R. Dokecki. 1993. Community and leadership in the postmodern church: II. The St. Robert Consultation Project. *PACE* (23 November): 31–35.

Niebuhr, H. R. 1951. *Christ and culture.* New York: Harper & Row.

Nisbet, R. A. 1953/1990. *The quest for community: A study in the ethics of order and freedom*. San Francisco: ICS Press.

*Official Catholic Directory: Anno Domini 2002*. 2002. New York: P. J. Kennedy.

O'Gorman, R. T. 1990. Latin-American theology and education. In *Theological approaches to Christian education*, edited by J. L. Seymour and D. E. Miller, 192–215. Nashville, TN: Abingdon.

O'Gorman, R. T., P. R. Dokecki, and J. R. Newbrough. 1993. Community and leadership in the postmodern church: I. Lessons from Latin America—the Basic Ecclesial Communities. *PACE* (23 October): 29–33.

Pepper, S. 1942. *World hypotheses*. Berkeley: University of California Press.

Polkinghorne, D. E. 1983. *Methodology for the human sciences: Systems of inquiry*. Albany: State University of New York Press.

Pope, K. S. 1996. Memory, abuse, and science: Questioning claims about the false memory epidemic. *American Psychologist* 51: 957–74.

———. 1997. Science as careful questioning: Are claims of a false memory syndrome epidemic based on empirical evidence? *American Psychologist* 52: 997–1006.

Prilleltensky, I. 2001. Value-based praxis in community psychology: Moving towards social justice and social action. *American Journal of Community Psychology* 29: 747–78.

Quinn, J. R. 1999. *The reform of the papacy: The costly call to Christian unity*. New York: Crossroad.

Riger, S. 1993. What's wrong with empowerment. *American Journal of Community Psychology* 21: 279–92.

Rost, J. C. 1991. *Leadership for the twenty-first century*. New York: Praeger.

Ryan, W. 1971. *Blaming the victim*. New York: Pantheon.

Sarason, S. B. 1974. *The psychological sense of community*. San Francisco: Jossey-Bass.

Schneiders, S. M. 1989. Spirituality in the academy. *Theological Studies* 50: 676–97.

Schoener, G. R. 2002. *Some notes on solutions to the problem of sexual abuse and exploitation by clergy*. Minneapolis, MN: Walk-In Counseling Center.

Schön, D. 1983. *The reflective practitioner*. New York: Basic Books.

Shaw, R. 1994. *Understanding your rights: Your rights and responsibilities in the Catholic Church*. Ann Arbor, MI: Servant Publications.

Shupe, A. 1995. *In the name of all that's holy: A theory of clergy malfeasance*. Westport, CT: Praeger.

———. 1998. *Wolves within the fold: Religious leadership and abuses of power*. New Brunswick, NJ: Rutgers University Press.

Shupe, A., W. A. Stacey, and S. E. Darnell. 2000. *Bad pastors: Clergy misconduct in modern America*. New York: New York University Press.

Sipe, A. W. R. 1995. *Sex, priests, and power: Anatomy of a crisis*. New York: Brunner/Mazel.

Sonne, J. L., and K. S. Pope. 1993. Treating victims of therapist-patient sexual involvement. In *Sexual feelings in psychotherapy*, edited by K. S. Pope, J. L. Sonne, and J. Holroyd, 237–67. Washington, DC: American Psychological Association.

Steinfels, P. 2003. *A people adrift: The crisis of the Roman Catholic Church in America.* New York: Simon & Schuster.

Swidler, L. 1996. *Toward a Catholic constitution.* New York: Crossroad.

Toulmin, S. 1982. *The return to cosmology: Postmodern science and the theology of nature.* Berkeley: University of California Press.

———. 1990. *Cosmopolis: The hidden agenda of modernity.* New York: Free Press.

Trout, J., P. R. Dokecki, J. R. Newbrough, and R. T. O'Gorman. 2003. Action research on leadership for community development in West Africa and North America: A joining of liberation theology and community psychology. *Journal of Community Psychology* 31: 129–48.

Waterman, R. H., Jr. 1987. *The renewal factor.* New York: Bantam Books.

Weigel, G. 2002. *The courage to be Catholic: Crisis, reform, and the future of the church.* New York: Basic Books.

White, S. W. 1991. *Privileged information.* New York: Viking.

Whitehead, J. D., and E. E. Whitehead. 1988. *The emerging laity: Returning leadership to the community of faith.* New York: Doubleday.

Wilkes, P. 2002. The reformer: A priest battles for a more open church. *New Yorker* (2 September).

Wills, G. 2000. *Papal sin: Structures of deceit.* New York: Doubleday.

———. 2002. *Why I am a Catholic.* Boston: Houghton Mifflin.

## II. SOURCES FROM NEWSPAPERS, PERIODICALS, AND ORGANIZATIONS

Against abuse. 8 October 2002. *Boston Globe.* Retrieved from www.boston.com/globe/.

Allen, J. L. 7 November 2002. Bishops forcefully deliver ambiguous message. *National Catholic Reporter.* Retrieved from www.natcath.com.

———. 11 November 2002. Secret Vatican norms on abuse show conflicts with U.S. policy. *National Catholic Reporter.* Retrieved from www.natcath.com.

———. 20 December 2002. The word from Rome. *National Catholic Reporter.* Retrieved from www.natcath.com.

———. 11 July 2003. The word from Rome. *National Catholic Reporter.* Retrieved from www.natcath.com.

Appleby, R. S. July 14, 2002. 'Betrayal': Covering the church crisis. *New York Times.* Retrieved from www.nytimes.com.

At meeting, leader of bishops urges healing. 12 November 2002. Associated Press. Retrieved from www.nytimes.com.

Belluck, P. 17 April 2002. Cardinal Law met with pope on scandal. *New York Times.* Retrieved from www.nytimes.com.

———. 31 May 2002. Angry at scandal, lay group seeks quiet uprising. *New York Times.* Retrieved from www.nytimes.com.

———. 13 November 2002. Cardinal Law's new approach to abuse cases. *New York Times.* Retrieved from www.nytimes.com.

———. 5 December 2002. Boston church panel will allow archdiocese to weigh bankruptcy. *New York Times.* Retrieved from www.nytimes.com.

———. 19 December 2002. New Boston church leader is to push for settlement of suits. *New York Times.* Retrieved from www.nytimes.com.

Belluck, P., and F. Bruni. 14 December 2002. Law, citing abuse scandal, quits as Boston archbishop and asks for forgiveness. *New York Times.* Retrieved from www.nytimes.com.

Blanchette, M. C., and G. D. Coleman. 22 April 2002. Priest pedophiles: Pedophiles and ephebophiles have no capacity for authentic sexual relationships. *America.* Retrieved from www.americamagazine.org.

Canadian Conference of Bishops. 1992. From pain to hope. Retrieved from www.usccb.org.

Cannon, C. M. May 2002. The priest scandal: How old news at last became a dominant national story . . . And why it took so long. *American Journalism Review.* Retrieved from www.ajr.org.

Cardinal Ratzinger sees a media campaign against church. 3 December 2002. Zenit News Service. Retrieved from www.zenit.org.

Cardinal's rebuff. 24 July 2002. *Boston Globe.* Retrieved from www.boston.com/globe/.

Carroll, J. P. 24 September 2002. The escalator of change. *Boston Globe.* Retrieved from www.boston.com/globe/.

———. 17 December 2002. The sadness of a Catholic. *Boston Globe.* Retrieved from www.boston.com/globe/.

Catholic bishops and sex abuse. June 2002. *Dallas Morning News.* Retrieved from www.DallasNews.com.

Catholics vow to break bishops' grip on finances. 20 July 2002. Reuters. Retrieved from www.nytimes.com.

Church won't take group's donations. 23 July 2002. Associated Press. Retrieved from www.nytimes.com.

Clohessy, D. 8 December 2002. People, not policies, protect our children. *St. Louis Post-Dispatch.* Retrieved from www.stltoday.com.

Colbert, C. 26 April 2002. New groups push for change. *National Catholic Reporter.* Retrieved from www.natcath.com.

———. 10 May 2002. Fueling Boston's fires of outrage. *National Catholic Reporter.* Retrieved from www.natcath.com.

———. 7 June 2002. Boston reform group meets with bishop. *National Catholic Reporter.* Retrieved from www.natcath.com.

Day, S. 24 April 2002. Cardinals to recommend removal of serial abusers. *New York Times.* Retrieved from www.nytimes.com.

DiGiulio, K. 9 August 2002. Church in crisis: Interview of Dr. Leslie Lothstein. *National Catholic Reporter.* Retrieved from www.natcath.com.

Dillon, S. 9 November 2002. Poll finds Catholics decry bishops' handling of scandal. *New York Times.* Retrieved from www.nytimes.com.

———. 12 November 2002. No welcome mat for victims' groups. *New York Times.* Retrieved from www.nytimes.com.

———. 8 December 2002. Church's accounting of abuse is criticized. *New York Times.* Retrieved from www.nytimes.com.

Donovan, G. 10 January 2003. Church in crisis. *National Catholic Reporter.* Retrieved from www.natcath.com.

Doyle, T. 16 June 2002. Reaction to the Charter for the Protection of Children and Young People. Retrieved from www.thelinkup.com.

Editorial with a life of its own. 22 March 2002. *The Pilot.* Retrieved from www.rcab.org.

Enrique, A. 26 July 2002. Boston reform movement inspired by dissident international group. *The Pilot.* Retrieved from www.rcab.org.

Farragher, T. 20 September 2002. Settlement doesn't heal victims' hearts: After Geoghan case, plaintiffs feel defeat. *Boston Globe.* Retrieved from www.boston.com/globe/.

Ferder, F., and J. Heagle. 10 May 2002. Clerical sexual abuse: Exploring deeper issues. *National Catholic Reporter.* Retrieved from www.natcath.com.

Feuerherd, J. 20 December 2002. Lay leaders urge financial transparency *National Catholic Reporter.* Retrieved from www.natcath.com.

Gallicho, G. 16 August 2002. Voices of the faithful: Some louder than others. *Commonweal.* Retrieved from www.commonwealmagazine.org.

Goodstein, L. 16 April 2002. "Got to do something," a U.S. leader says. *New York Times.* Retrieved from www.nytimes.com.

———. 25 April 2002. One-strike plan splits group. *New York Times.* Retrieved from www.nytimes.com.

———. 12 November 2002. Bishops seek to reclaim authority. *New York Times.* Retrieved from www.nytimes.com.

———. 14 November 2002. Bishops pass plan to form tribunals in sex abuse cases. *New York Times.* Retrieved from www.nytimes.com.

———. 12 January 2003. Trail of pain in church crisis leads to nearly every diocese. *New York Times.* Retrieved from www.nytimes.com.

———. 10 September 2003. As the Boston Archdiocese moves, others may follow. *New York Times.* Retrieved from www.nytimes.com.

Grossman, C. L., and A. DeBarros. 11 November 2002. Facts of priest sex abuse at odds with perception: As U.S. bishops meet today to finalize their abuse policy, an analysis by *USA TODAY* brings crisis into sharper focus. *USA TODAY.* Retrieved from www.usatoday.com.

Group draws support amidst scandal. 12 June 2002. Associated Press. Retrieved from www.nytimes.com.

Hamilton, M. 10 April 2003. The Catholic Church and the clergy abuse scandal: Act three. *FindLaw's Writ—Legal Commentary*. Retrieved from http://writ.findlaw.com/hamilton/20030410.html.

Hayes, D. L. 31 May 2002. Not the time to hide behind legal advice. *National Catholic Reporter*. Retrieved from www.natcath.com.

Jenkins, P. 24 March 2002. The proper view on "pedophile priests." *Our Sunday Visitor*. Retrieved from www.catholicmatters.com.

Kennedy, E. 2 August 2002. Dallas: The latest remake of Frankenstein. *National Catholic Reporter*. Retrieved from www.natcath.com.

Kurkjian, S., and M. Rezendes. 24 July 2002. In rift with Law, agency to accept lay group's funds. *Boston Globe*. Retrieved from www.boston.com/news/globe/.

Lampman, J. 4 April 2002. Calls for change come from Catholics in the U.S. and around the world. *Christian Science Monitor*. Retrieved from www.csmonitor.com.

Letter from Bishop Wilton D. Gregory to Cardinal Giovanni Battista Re regarding the Essential Norms for Diocesan/Eparchial Policies Dealing with Allegations of Sexual Abuse of Minors by Clergy or Other Church Personnel. 18 October 2002. *National Catholic Reporter*. Retrieved from www.natcath.com.

Lyons, D. 9 June 2003. Battle of the shrinks. *Forbes*. Retrieved from www.forbes.com.

Major settlements in Catholic sex abuse cases. 10 September 2003. Associated Press. Retrieved from www.boston.com.

McBrien, R. P. 15 November 2002. Spiritual renewal or structural reform? *Tidings*. Retrieved from www.the-tidings.com.

———. 6 December 2002. What's wrong with an agenda? *Tidings*. Retrieved from www.the-tidings.com.

McNamara, E. 14 April 2002. Reclaiming their church. *Boston Globe*. Retrieved from www.boston.com/globe/.

Mehren, E. 2 February 2002. Reports of priests' abuse enrage Boston Catholics. *Los Angeles Times*. Retrieved from www.latimes.com.

Murphy, C. 13 November 2002. Access to bishops limited: Survivors of abuse note contrast with meeting in Dallas. *Washington Post*. Retrieved from www.washingtonpost.com.

Now more than ever, bishops need laity. 11 November 2002. *National Catholic Reporter*. Retrieved from www.natcath.com.

O'Brien, D. 20 November 2002. To reform the church, laity must take action. *Boston Globe*. Retrieved from www.boston.com/globe/.

Olin, D. 25 May 2002. Pay the victims, protect the church. *New York Times*. Retrieved from www.nytimes.com.

Pagnozzi, A. 10 September 2002. Voice of the Faithful needs a dose of bravery. *Hartford Courant*. Retrieved from www.ctnow.com.

Paulson, M. 18 April 2002. Cardinals may face obstacles at summit. *Boston Globe*. Retrieved from www.boston.com/globe/.

——. 1 May 2002. Catholics drawn to lay group in Wellesley. *Boston Globe*. Retrieved from www.boston.com/globe/.

——. 21 June 2002. Lay Catholics issue call to transform their church. *Boston Globe*. Retrieved from www.boston.com/globe/.

——. 16 September 2002. Church meets dissenting voices with silence. *Boston Globe*. Retrieved from www.boston.com/globe/.

——. 1 October 2002. Bishop bans group from meetings at parish. *Boston Globe*. Retrieved from www.boston.com/globe/.

——. 10 October 2002. Catholic group fights bishop over banning from church. *Boston Globe*. Retrieved from www.boston.com/globe/.

——. 18 October 2002. National Review Board issues statement on Mixed Commission. Retrieved from www.vermontcatholic.org.

——. 5 December 2002. Curb imposed on Newton parish. *Boston Globe*. Retrieved from www.boston.com/globe/.

——. 10 December 2002. Fifty-eight priests send a letter urging cardinal to resign. *Boston Globe*. Retrieved from www.boston.com/globe/.

Paulson, M., and M. Rezendes. 17 April 2002. Law saw pope, discussed quitting: Made secret Rome trip; says he'll address crisis. *Boston Globe*. Retrieved from www.boston.com/globe/.

——. 12 November 2002. Bishop raps critics of abuse policy: Calls for unity, warns against "false prophets." *Boston Globe*. Retrieved from www.boston.com/globe/.

Paulson, M., and W. V. Robinson. 19 December 2002. Lennon promises effort to settle abuse claims: Seeks a break from litigation. *Boston Globe*. Retrieved from www.boston.com/globe/.

Pfeiffer, S., and M. Carroll. 23 July 2002. Law to reject donations from Voice of the Faithful. *Boston Globe*. Retrieved from www.boston.com/globe/.

——. 14 December 2002. Legal ramifications: Despite departure, archdiocese faces "a real mess" in court. *Boston Globe*. Retrieved from www.boston.com/globe/.

Pope, K. S. 2000. Pseudoscience, cross-examination, and scientific evidence in the recovered memory controversy. *Psychology, Public Policy, and Law*. Retrieved from www.kspope.com.

Pope John Paul's address on pedophilia. 23 April 2002. Reuters. Retrieved from www.nytimes.com.

Pope laments sexual abuse by priests. 28 July 2002. Associated Press. Retrieved from www.nytimes.com.

Powers, W. 23 April 2002. Sex, lies, and journalists. *The Atlantic*. Retrieved from www.theatlantic.com.

Q and A: Clerical sex abuse policy. 13 November 2002. Associated Press. Retrieved from www.nytimes.com.

Questions that must be faced. 15 March 2002. *The Pilot*. Retrieved from www.rcab.org.

Sennott, C. M. 24 April 2002. Pontiff says cases mishandled, voices solidarity with victims. *Boston Globe*. Retrieved from www.boston.com/globe/.

———. 29 November 2002. Some in U.S. question Vatican's strong hand. *Boston Globe*. Retrieved from www.boston.com/globe/.

Shaw, K. A. 4 December 2002. Lawyers leery of secret tribunal. *Worcester Telegram and Gazette*. Retrieved from www.telegram.com.

———. 6 December 2002. Canon lawyer explains tribunals. *Worcester Telegram and Gazette*. Retrieved from www.telegram.com.

Steinfels, M. O. 13 June 2002. The present crisis through the lens of the laity. Retrieved from www.usccb.org.

Steinfels, P. 4 May 2002. Extent of abuse in church not understood. *New York Times*. Retrieved from www.nytimes.com.

———. 14 September 2002. Abused by the media. *The Tablet*. Retrieved from www.thetablet.co.uk.

Text of statement released by U.S. church leaders. 24 April 2002. Reuters. Retrieved from www.nytimes.com.

United States Conference of Catholic Bishops. 12 June 2002. News conference: Opening remarks by Bishop Wilton Gregory. Retrieved from www.atrio.org.

———. 18 October 2002. National Review Board issues Statement on mixed commission. Retrieved from www.nccbuscc.org.

———. 6 November 2002. A Catholic response to sexual abuse: Confession, contrition, resolve. Presidential address—Bishop Wilton D. Gregory, Dallas, Texas—June 13, 2002. Retrieved from www.usccb.org.

———. 10 November 2002. Bishop Gregory remarks on Mixed Commission on Sex Abuse Norms. Retrieved from www.usccb.org.

———. 10 November 2002. The five principles to follow in dealing with accusations of sexual abuse: U.S. Conference of Catholic Bishops—June 1992. Retrieved from www.usccb.org.

———. 10 November 2002. Revised "Essential Norms" build on actions taken in Dallas. Retrieved from www.nccbuscc.org.

———. 11 November 2002. The bishop as God's agent of genuine comfort: "Comfort, give comfort to my people, says your God." Retrieved from www.usccb.org.

———. 12 November 2002. News conference statement by Bishop Wilton Gregory, Friday, June 14, 2002. Retrieved from www.usccb.org.

———. 14 November 2002. Bishops reconcile procedural issues and assert strength of the Charter for the Protection of Children and Young People. Retrieved from www.usccb.org.

———. 18 November 2002. Comparative texts for November 2002 meeting: Essential norms for diocesan/eparchial policies dealing with allegations of sexual abuse of minors by priests or deacons: June 14, 2002–October 29, 2002. Retrieved from www.usccb.org.

——. 11 March 2002. Restoring trust: Response to clergy sexual abuse. Retrieved from www.usccb.org.

Unraveling the old myths that foster sexual violence. 7 June 2002. *Boston Globe*. Retrieved from www.boston.com/globe/.

U.S. Church leaders express regret. 25 April 2002. Associated Press. Retrieved from www.nytimes.com.

Vatican. 14 October 2002. Letter of Cardinal Prefect Giovanni Battista Re of the Congregation for Bishops: Answer to the "Essential Norms for Diocesan/Eparchial Policies Dealing with Allegations of Sexual Abuse of Minors by Priests, Deacons or Other Church Personnel" ("Norms"). Retrieved from www.vatican.va.

Voice of the Faithful. Website at www.votf.org.

Washington, R. 9 September 2003. Reactions of abuse victims mixed. *Boston Herald*. Retrieved from www.bostonherald.com.

When pettiness rules. 24 July 2002. *Boston Herald*. Retrieved from www.bostonherald.com.

Whistle-blower priest in trouble with diocese. 2 December 2002. Associated Press. Retrieved from www.abc-7.com.

Wolfson, A. 29 September 2002. Church in crisis: Alleged victims say incidents altered lives: Comprehensive look at lawsuits against archdiocese shows many similarities. *Courier-Journal*. Retrieved from www.courier-journal.com.

You are known by the company you keep. 6 September 2002. *The Pilot*. Retrieved from www.rcab.org.

### III. SOURCES RELATED TO THE MCKEOWN CASE

These sources are listed in chronological order. Unless otherwise noted, they have been retrieved from the *Tennessean* website (www.Tennessean.com).

Pinkston, W., and A. Paine. 31 January 1999. Former priest charged with molesting teen-aged boy.

Warren, B. 2 February 1999. Police expand probe of former priest.

Loggins, K. 5 February 1999. Boy's past put him in custody of rape suspect.

——. 28 February 1999. Police fumbled sex probe of ex-priest, mother says.

——. 7 March 1999. D.A. investigating second ex-priest in sex abuse case.

——. 18 March 1999. Former priest's not guilty plea beginning of negotiations.

——. 18 June 1999. Ex-priest sentenced to 25 years for abuse.

——. 19 June 1999. Mother awaits explanation for dropping investigation.

Alligood, L. 19 June 1999. Church aims for healing, prompt response.

——. 19 June 1999. Parishioners see ex-priest's fall as rare breach of trust.

——. 27 June 1999. Diocese remained silent as reports of molestation grew.

Frank, L. 4 July 1999. Diocese to speak on pedophile priests at Mass today.

Bishop's statement. 4 July 1999.

Shiffman, J. 5 July 1999. Father F condemns abuse by ex-priests.

Bishop's statement. 7 July 1999.

Frank, L. 8 July 1999. Bishop's letter left out third complaint against priest.

——. 25 July 1999. Court let ex-priest keep boy despite pedophilia report.

——. 27 July 1999. Clerk insists judge neglected to warn him of ex-priest's past.

Child abuse case: Text of Norman's statement. 27 July 1999.

Judge orders review of ex-priest's case. 28 July 1999.

Frank, L. 29 July 1999. Child abuse case: 1995 claim against priest lacked evidence, police.

Child abuse case: The Nashville Police Department statement. 29 July 1999.

Frank, L. 30 July 1999. Attorney Norman leads inquiry.

——. 30 July 1999. Lawyer: Police ignored law by not telling state of McKeown.

Priest's alleged molestation crimes may be too old to prosecute. 30 July 1999. Associated Press.

Frank, L. 31 July 1999. Committee appointed to look into ex-priest rape case.

——. 17 August 1999. Custody mistake could happen again.

——. 14 September 1999. Clerk: No warning priest was pedophile.

——. 19 October 1999. Juvenile Court finds 2nd pedophile employee.

——. 29 December 1999. Special commission targets child sex abuse.

——. 20 January 2000. Lawsuit seeks $35 million for molestations by priest.

——. 21 January 2000. Lawyers want to know what church, Metro knew.

Zechman, B. 16 June 2000. Hearing today for former youth pastor.

Loggins, K. 16 August 2000. Diocese: Victims should share blame.

Waddle, R., and K. Loggins. 17 August 2000. Catholics debate church responsibility.

Loggins, K. 19 August 2000. Two more defendants added to lawsuit.

——. 19 August 2000. Diocese's defense is a legal first.

——. 28 August 2000. Metro resists giving up McKeown files.

East, J. 28 August 2000. Bishop disputes accounts of sex-abuse cases.

Text of Bishop K's letter. 29 August 2000.

Loggins, K. 29 August 2000. Response by church lawyers to lawsuits.

——. 29 August 2000. Boys' lawyer takes issue with bishop's letter.

Carlson, K. 28 October 2000. Court to reveal diocese response in abuse case.

Church: Blame for sex victims' trauma should be shared. 4 November 2000.

Loggins, K. 14 November 2000. Doctors who treated pedophile priest deny liability.

——. 16 November 2000. Church argues against use of title "Father" for molester.

——. 17 November 2000. Ex-priest McKeown no "Father," judge rules.

——. 18 November 2000. Diocese lawyers say abuse laws don't apply in case.

——. 29 November 2000. Diocese wins round in sex case.

——. 6 December 2000. Two boys' lawyers drop some claims against diocese.

——. 16 December 2000. Revised suits claim diocese silent on risk.

——. 3 June 2001. Diocese says it tried to protect the public from ex-priest.

———. 7 June 2001. Diocese denied deposition in priest case.

———. 16 June 2001. Lawyers say church failed duty.

———. 21 June 2001. Sex abuse suit dismissed against Nashville Diocese.

Epright, D. 22 June 2001. Court dismisses lawsuits against Nashville Diocese. *Tennessee Register*.

Kimbro, P. L. 29 June 2001. Hearing today for pastor accused of molesting boy.

Loggins, K. 2 August 2001. Diocese wants legal costs repaid.

Letter to the editor: This legal strategy leads church astray. 8 August 2001.

Letter to the editor: Diocese trying to recoup its expenses. 14 August 2001.

Loggins, K. 25 August 2001. Teens told to pay part of diocese defense bill.

Letter to the editor: Organized religion being tested lately. 8 March 2002.

Eaststate dealing with priest's admission. 11 March 2002. Associated Press.

Sweat, J. 14–20 March 2002. A Bishop's bygone days: Former Tennessee bishop Anthony O'Connell resigns as part of a widespread sex scandal. *Nashville Scene*.

Wadhwani, A. 16 March 2002. Dioceses reacting to priests' sex crimes.

Chavez, T. 30 March 2002. Time for Catholic Church to drop celibacy as condition for the priesthood.

Letter to the editor: Catholic Church must screen its candidates. 2 April 2002.

Zralek, J. 2 April 2002. Zralek: Remember the priests who've served Nashville.

Chavez, T. 24 April 2002. Dioceses need group of laity as watchdogs.

A timid step in Rome offers scant comfort. 26 April 2002.

Hill, L. 26 April 2002. Cardinals have Catholics turning red.

Musacchio, R. 26 April 2002. Rick Musacchio: Adequate watchdogs already in place to pursue abuse charges.

Letter to the editor: Where is the outrage by Catholic hierarchy? 27 April 2002.

Frank, L. 28 April 2002. U.S. priests abuse cases find some local parallels.

Letter to the editor: Don't throw stones at abusive priests. 28 April 2002.

Letter to the editor: The moral thing to do is to remove priests. 28 April 2002.

Wadhwani, A. 29 April 2002. Priest recruiter not discouraged by scandal.

Letter to the editor: Catholic Church is more like a monarchy. 30 April 2002.

Letter to the editor: Cardinal Law has tested church faithful. 5 May 2002.

A growing church scandal. 11 May 2002.

Letter to the editor: Many Catholic priests have blessed our lives. 11 May 2002.

Parsons, E., L. Alligood, and E. Heffter. 11 May 2002. Abuse charges put witness at risk of shunning.

Letter to the editor: Columnist seems to delight in Catholic mess. 12 May 2002.

Chavez, T. 18 May 2002. Catholic leaders must resign to let healing start.

Frank, L. 19 May 2002. Unsealed file on pedophile priest contradicts church statements.

Stories based on summaries of legal testimony. 19 May 2002.

The Catholic Diocese responds. 19 May 2002.

Problems 30 years in the making. 19 May 2002.

Letter to the editor: Closeness to God doesn't require church. 19 May 2002.

Catholic Church's stance appalls members. 21 May 2002.

Chavez, T. 21 May 2002. Church acts, charter bill's Senate delay hurt children.

McNeese, L., D. Klausnitzer, and B. Lewis. 22 May 2002. Minister has record as sex offender.

All Catholics should work to heal hurt of scandals. 25 May 2002.

Letter to the editor: Loyal attendance is what church needs. 25 May 2002.

Lewis, B. 26 May 2002. Bishop calls newspaper report false, misleading.

——. 26 May 2002. Parishioners dispute way report portrayed pastor.

Text of K's letter of May 24, 2002. 26 May 2002.

Chavez, T. 6 June 2002. Catholics responding to a chance for change.

Walker, H. 6–12 June 2002. Frankly speaking The Diocese of Nashville says *The Tennessean* is unfair. *Nashville Scene*.

Editorial: Catholic bishops hold key to healing process. 8 June 2002.

Lewis, B. 9 June 2002. Nashville Catholics hoping for changes.

——. 15 June 2002. Nashville diocese's abuse policy mirrors bishops' document.

Catholics must focus their efforts on change. 16 June 2002.

Priests who molest should be behind bars. 16 June 2002.

Bishops' sin of omission. 18 June 2002.

Letter to the editor: Catholic laity has failed abused children. 18 June 2002.

Walker, H. 20 June 2002. Desperately seeking the news: Columnist or Catholic? *Tennessean* columnist Tim Chavez walks tightrope. *Nashville Scene*.

Chavez, T. 22 June 2002. Catholics still hearing voice of bureaucracy.

Letter to the editor: Child abuse occurs in different churches. 22 June 2002.

Sweat, J., and L. Murray Garrigan. 27 June–3 July 2002. M. C. was the victim of sexual abuse by a Catholic priest. Decades later, his tragic tale surfaces. *Nashville Scene*.

DeFeo, T. 5 July 2002. Abuse investigation continues.

Chavez, T. 6 July 2002. Catholics must keep up pressure for reforms.

——. 13 July 2002. A call to action.

Laurence, T. 19 July 2002. Victim of McKeown tells story. *Tennessee Register*.

Lewis, B. 20 July 2002. Catholic group hopes to bring positive change.

Meeting today will be historic for church. 20 July 2002.

Lewis, B. 21 July 2002. Catholic laity group seeks positive change for church.

Frank, L. 23 July 2002. Church could have done more to stop abuse, victim.

——. 23 July 2002. Priests bound to obey church law if crimes confessed.

McKeown time line. 23 July 2002.

Lewis, B. 24 July 2002. Area Catholics weigh options to fight abuse.

Letter to the editor: No organized religion is above the law. 25 July 2002.

Frank, L. 6 August 2002. Sides debate diocese's handling of abuse reports.

Lewis, B. 15 August 2002. Nashville bishop to discuss church sex scandal at open meeting.

Abuse policy undergoes full review. 16 August 2002. *Tennessee Register.*

Filteau, J. 16 August 2002. Religious order heads tackle clergy charter. *Tennessee Register.*

Lawsuit update. 16 August 2002. *Tennessee Register.*

Lewis, B. 17 August 2002. Local meeting set today as diocese reviews procedures.

——. 18 August 2002. Local group's reaction mixed as bishop talks about abuse.

Letter to the editor: Accusations against priests must be valid. 20 August 2002.

A list of accused priests. 23 August 2002.

Bishop discusses abuse prevention at meeting. 30 August 2002. *Tennessee Register.*

Diocese conducts abuse prevention class. 30 August 2002. *Tennessee Register.*

Lewis, B. 5 September 2002. Possible priest list raises dilemma among Catholics.

de la Cruz, B., and R. Johnson. 13 September 2002. Bredesen urges more time to try child sex abuse cases.

Lay review board named. 13 September 2002. *Tennesse Register.*

Lewis, B. 14 September 2002. Board will guide diocese in sex cases.

A fine panel for diocese. 17 September 2002.

Chavez, T. 19 September 2002. Local priest an example of clergy's good deeds.

Lewis, B. 24 September 2002. Sexual abuse of kids to be forum's focus.

——. 1 October 2002. Diocese updates sex abuse policies.

Letter from the editor. 4 October 2002. *Tennessee Register.*

Bishop asks forgiveness for sex scandal's harm. 5 October 2002.

Frank, L. 6 October 2002. Details on polygraphs of K, D.

——. 6 October 2002. Dying man told his brother of sex with D as a teen.

——. 6 October 2002. Ex-R principal accused of molesting students.

——. 6 October 2002. K's account of sexual abuse.

Letter to the editor: Alleged abuse a source of pain and betrayal. 8 October 2002.

Chavez, T. 10 October 2002. Catholics defined by service, not by scandal.

Local paper's abuse claims challenged. 11 October 2002. *Tennessee Register.*

A message from Rome. 25 October 2002.

Revisions leave bishops' charter intact. 8 November 2002. *Tennessee Register.*

Lewis, B. 12 November 2002. Catholic lay group to change leadership.

Bishops approve compromise sex abuse policy. 14 November 2002.

Pimental, R. 22 November 2002. An enemy within damaging church.

Lewis, B. 10 December 2002. Catholic Church still getting new faces.

——. 17 December 2002. Catholic group urges bishop to start council.

A belated resignation. 18 December 2002.

Smith, D. 19 December 2002. Some at St. Mary's seek removal of Bishop O'Connell's name.

Corino, K. 26 December 2002. Believers stand strong.

Loggins, K. 9 September 2003. Dismissal of lawsuit against diocese upheld.

## IV. COURT DOCUMENTS RELATED TO THE MCKEOWN CASE

These documents are listed in chronological order.

*Answer of the Defendant, Roman Catholic Diocese of Nashville, to the Plaintiffs' Second Amended Complaint.* 9 June 2000. No. 00C-164.

*Memorandum and Order. Fifth Circuit Court for Davidson County, Tennessee.* 28 November 2000. No. 00C-164 and 00C-172 Consolidated.

*Memorandum and Order. Fifth Circuit Court for Davidson County, Tennessee.* 20 June 2001. No. 00C-164 and 00C-172 Consolidated.

*Appeal of the Plaintiffs to the Tennessee Court of Appeals, Middle Section from the Final Order of the Circuit Court of Davidson County Granting the Roman Catholic Diocese of Nashville's Motion for Summary Judgment. Court of Appeals for the State of Tennessee in the Middle Section of Nashville.* 13 November 2001. No. 00C-164 and 00C-172 Consolidated; No. M2001-01782-COA-R3-CV Consolidated under No. M2001-01780-COA-R3-CV.

*Defendant's brief in response to the Appeal of the Plaintiffs to the Tennessee Court of Appeals, Middle Section from the Final Order of the Circuit Court of Davidson County Granting the Roman Catholic Diocese of Nashville's Motion for Summary Judgment. Court of Appeals for the State of Tennessee in the Middle Section of Nashville.* 13 December 2001. No. 00C-164 and 00C-172 Consolidated; No. M2001-01782-COA-R3-CV Consolidated under No. M2001-01780-COA-R3-CV.

*Appeal from the Circuit Court for Davidson County, John Doe 1, a Minor Child, by Next friend, Jane Doe 1, Individually; and John Doe 2 v. Roman Catholic Diocese of Nashville, et al.* No. M2001-01780-COA-R3-CV. Filed 22 September 2003.

# Index